CLUES FROM KILLERS

CLUES FROM KILLERS

Serial Murder and Crime Scene Messages

DIRK C. GIBSON

PRAEGER

Westport, Connecticut
London

Library of Congress Cataloging-in-Publication Data

Gibson, Dirk Cameron, 1953–
  Clues from killers : serial murder and crime scene messages / Dirk C. Gibson.
    p. cm.
  Includes bibliographical references and index.
  ISBN 0–275–98360–9 (alk. paper)
    1. Serial murderers—United States—Case studies. 2. Serial murders—United
States—Case studies. 3. Crime scenes—United States—Case
studies. 4. Criminal psychology. I. Title.
  HV6529.G53   2004
  363.25/9523—dc22   2004050967

British Library Cataloguing in Publication Data is available.

Library of Congress Catalog Card Number: 2004050967
ISBN: 0–275–98360–9

First published in 2004

Praeger Publishers, 88 Post Road West, Westport, CT 06881
An imprint of Greenwood Publishing Group, Inc.
www.praeger.com

Printed in the United States of America

The paper used in the book complies with the
Permanent Paper Standard issued by the National
Information Standards Organization (Z39.48–1984).

10 9 8 7 6 5 4 3 2 1

Every reasonable effort has been made to trace the owners of copyright materials in
this book, but in some instances this has proven impossible. The author and
publisher will be glad to receive information leading to more complete
acknowledgments in subsequent printings of the book and in the meantime extend
their apologies for any omissions.

This book is respectfully dedicated to my loved ones, who sacrificed and allowed me to complete this work.

To Mitchell and Erica, thanks for being such exceptional children.

To my brother Dean, for his keen insight and uncommon strength.

To my mother, Betty Gibson, whose love and wisdom have been unconditional gifts of inestimable value for fifty years.

Most of all, to my wife Angela, the best blessing among thousands in my life.

Contents

Acknowledgments

Many sources need to be acknowledged. James A. Fox and Jack Levin have made substantial contributions by their respective 1985 and 1994 books; *Mass Murder: America's Growing Menace* (New York: Plenum Press), and *Overkill: Mass Murder & Serial Killing Exposed* (New York: Plenum Press). Elliott Leyton produced an important work, *Hunting Humans: Inside the Minds of Mass Murderers* (New York: Simon & Schuster, 1986).

Brian King's 1996 work, *Lustmord: The Writings & Artifacts of Murderers* (Berkeley, Calif.: Bloat Publishing) must be mentioned, as a source of serial killer communication artifacts. Two other books, Brian Lane and Wilfred Gregg's 1992 work, *The Encyclopedia of Serial Killers* (New York: Berkeley Books), and Michael Newton's *Hunting Humans: The Encyclopedia of Serial Killers* (Port Townsend, Wash.: Loompanics Unlimited, 1990) should be acknowledged.

Important contributions by former FBI agents should be acknowledged. John C. Douglas and Mark Olshaker have written three noteworthy books; *Obsession* (New York: Scribners, 1998), *The Anatomy of Motive* (New York: Simon & Schuster, 1999), and *The Cases that Haunt Us* (New York: Scribners, 2000). Robert K. Ressler and Tim Schactman's 1992 book, *Whoever Fights Monsters* (New York: St. Martin's Press) was quite useful.

In addition to these general works on serial murder, I am deeply indebted to authors of books on the killers discussed here. These works include two important items on the Mad Butcher, John J. Badal's *In the Wake of the Butcher: Cleveland's Torso Murders* (Kent, Ohio: Kent State University Press, 2001), and *Torso: The Story of Eliot Ness and the Search for a Psychopathic Killer,* by Steven Nickel (Winston-Salem, N.C.: John F. Blair Publisher, 1989).

The Son of Sam analysis was significantly enhanced by Lawrence Klausner's *Son of Sam: Based on the Authorized Transcription of the Tapes, Official Documents and Diaries of David Berkowitz* (New York: McGraw Hill Book Company, 1981).

Much of my Black Dahlia information came from John Gilmore's 1994 work *Severed: The True Story of the Black Dahlia Murder* (Los Angeles: Zanja Press). I also extensively used a book by Janice Knowlton and noted serial murder expert Michael Newton, *Daddy Was the Black Dahlia Killer* (New York: Simon & Schuster, 1995). Another valuable Black Dahlia resource was Pamela Hazelton's Web site, Bethshort.com (http://bethshort.com, 1999).

The BTK Strangler chapter did not rely on a book, but David Lohr's series in The Crime Library (http://www.crimelibrary.com) should be acknowledged. The Heirens chapter also benefited from Tomas Guillen's "Crime Scene Communiqués: Helpful or Hurtful?" *Journal of Criminal Justice & Popular Culture* 9 (2002). This valuable piece was also used in the chapters on the Zodiac and The BTK Strangler.

The Zodiac chapter was informed significantly by Robert Graysmith's 1986 book, *Zodiac* (New York: Berkeley Books). I also relied on Zodiac Killer.com (http://www.zodiackiller.com).

John Robinson's crimes were documented by John Glatt, in his valuable book, *Internet Slavemaster* (New York: St. Martin's Press, 2001).

I am grateful to the Public Records Office, U.K., for access to the Ripper correspondence. Another important research resource is the Ripper casebook, at http://www.rippercasebook.org.

Finally, my sincere gratitude is due to four; Sha-Shana N. L. Crichton, Esq. of CRICHTON & ASSOCIATES, Suzanne I. Staszak-Silva, Senior Editor at Greenwood Publishing Group, Ida Walker of Bytheway Publishing Services, and my friend and this book's illustrator, John Weisgerber.

CLUES FROM KILLERS

Introduction

Son of Sam. Jack the Ripper. The Unabomber. These serial killers, separated in time and nationality, had one major thing in common: besides killing many people over the years, they all engaged in repeated acts of crime-related communication.

It is clear that communication is an integral part of many, if not most, serial murder cases. My research into more than two hundred such cases has convinced me that most serial murderers communicate about their murders during or after the murders. Most serial killers, in fact, communicate more than once. They communicate in a variety of ways, to a variety of audiences, on a variety of subjects.

The motives behind their communications similarly vary. Some seem to relish taunting the police, while others leave clues. Although a few offer explanations for their murders, others try to justify their homicidal acts.

Six main topics are considered in this introduction: (1) the concept, (2) the significance of serial killer communication, (3) the purpose of this book, (4) the method used in this book, (5) the rhetorical perspective on serial murder, and (6) a preview of this book.

THE CONCEPT

Communication by serial killers is the basic concept behind this book. That communication takes many forms. At the crime scene (or dump site), some serial killers may leave messages scrawled on walls and other surfaces. Occasionally, they use the human body as a communication medium. Other serial killers leave notes at the crime scene.

Subsequent to the discovery of serial victims by law enforcement, another set of communication acts by serial murderers has been noted over the years. Numerous serial murderers write letters and make telephone calls. A few send body parts through the mail. More recently, crime-related e-mail has been sent. These messages from the murders are directed to law enforcement, the media, and, perhaps as a sign of ultimate cruelty, to the victims' families.

Quite frequently, crime-related notes have been discovered on the person of or in the possession of serial murderers. In addition, serial murderers often keep records of their homicidal acts in the form of diaries, journals, logs, notes, and, more recently, computer records.

This book discusses my research into serial killer communication. I consider the communication behavior of ten serial murderers: Jack the Ripper, the Mad Butcher, the Black Dahlia Avenger, William Heirens, the Unabomber, the Son of Sam, the Zodiac, the BTK Strangler, John Robinson Sr., and the DC Sniper. Despite the variety represented by these ten cases, certain recurrent communication tendencies will be noted.

This serial killer communication is not spontaneous or frivolous. Rather, it seems to be a standard part of many serial murder cases, serving a variety of psychological and rhetorical functions for the killers. Some killers appear to be leaving clues for the police. To ignore or overlook these rhetorical motives is tantamount to conducting an incomplete investigation.

THE PURPOSE

What is the role of communication in serial murder? Is communication important to serial killers? Do some serial killers deliberately leave clues to aid in their apprehension? These are important questions, and while I cannot promise to answer them to every person's satisfaction, it is possible to address serial killers' rhetorical behavior.

The primary purpose of this book is simple. I want to enhance our understanding of the communication of serial killers. This book describes the crime scene communicative behavior of serial killers, as well as other subsequent crime-related serial killer communication.

THE SIGNIFICANCE OF SERIAL KILLER COMMUNICATION

Serial killer communication is a significant phenomenon. In fact, both serial murder and serial murder communication can be described as extraordinarily important law enforcement concerns. Serial murder authorities Jack Levin and James Alan Fox reported in 1994, "It has been estimated that 3% of all males in our society could be considered sociopathic." They concluded, "There may be tens of thousands of people who are motivated in such a way that they could find serial murder to be psychologically rewarding."[1] Numerous studies and opinions echo Levin and Fox's conclusions.

The exact number of serial murderers in the United States is un-known. In 1991, one source counted approximately 170 serial killers at work in this country.[2] Donald Sears stated, "There are anywhere from 35 to 500 serial murderers at large in the United States...and it is believed that of all homicides since 1983 one in four has been com-mitted by a multiple murderer."[3] According to Ronald M. Holmes and Steven T. Holmes, "Ted Bundy...stated that it was his feeling that there were at least 100 serial murderers at large in the United States. Even this number may be too small. From our contacts with law en-forcement officials all over the United States, we believe that a more accurate estimate may be as high as 200."[4] For the purposes of this study, serial murder is defined as repetitive homicide with a separation of time.

Regardless of the total number of active serial killers, they ac-count for a substantial death total. Joel Norris states, "In 1983 alone, according to the FBI, approximately five thousand Americans of both sexes and all ages—fifteen people a day and fully twenty-five percent of all murder victims—were struck down by murderers who did not know them and killed them for the sheer 'high' of the experience."[5] Robert Ressler et al. reported on the "118 known victims of 36 se-rial murderers. The consequent impact of this small but very violent subset of offenders is indeed large." And serial murder might be increasing.[6]

It is common practice for serial murderers to engage in a variety of communication acts. Interactions between murderers and the media have formed part of the characteristic profile of serial murder, sociol-ogist Mark Seltzer has commented. He concluded, "There is by now nothing extraordinary about such communications to the mass media, from the Ripper letters to the letter bomber called Unabom."[7] ABC-News.com agreed in 2002. It reported that messages from serial killers, whether written in lipstick or encoded in cryptic symbols, have fre-quently caused police interest.[8] This book discusses William Heirens's lipstick writing and the Zodiac's cryptograms.

RESEARCH METHODS

In this book I organize, analyze, and integrate the findings of numerous previous studies into a cohesive narrative. This research method was once known as historical/critical research, but Ernest Boyer of the Carnegie Foundation on Education has renamed it integrative research. I also used rhetorical criticism methods extensively.

The Carnegie Foundation on Higher Education report, edited by Boyer, described the dimensions of the scholarship of integration: "What we mean is serious, disciplined work that seeks to interpret, draw together, and bring new insight to bear on original research.... Such work is, in fact, increasingly important as traditional disciplinary categories prove confining, forcing new typologies of knowledge." Boyer also recognized that "The scholarship of integration also means interpretation, fitting one's own research—or the research of others—into larger intellectual patterns." Boyer asserted this conclusion:

> These examples illustrate a variety of scholarly trends—*interdisciplinary, interpretive, integrative.* But we present them here as evidence that an intellectual sea change may be occurring. Today, interdisciplinary and integrative studies, long on the edges of academic life, are moving to the center.... As the boundaries of knowledge are being dramatically reshaped, the academy surely must give greater attention to the *scholarship of integration.*[9]

My analysis of serial killer communication is essentially rhetorical criticism, a traditional method of understanding and evaluating communication. The basic purpose of rhetorical criticism is systematic description of discourse, followed by analysis. Generally, rhetorical criticism process is to quote the message directly, describe it completely for content and appearance, then analyze its content and form. The rhetorical critic seeks to describe clearly and accurately the rhetoric in question as the foundation for the criticism and judgment to follow.

A RHETORICAL PERSPECTIVE ON SERIAL MURDER

My background is primarily in speech communication and mass communication, with doctoral training in historiography (the science of history). Because of this, I am able to approach serial murder from a fresh vantage point. Rhetorical and mass communication methods are not generally used in studies of serial murder. My systemic study of the types of serial killer communication examines aspects of this rhetoric not found elsewhere.

A PREVIEW

This book follows a simple organizational structure. There are ten chapters devoted to careful and complete consideration of the serial killer communication produced by the killers examined in this book. It concludes with a final chapter offering a synthesis and analysis of the diverse and frequent communication acts described for each killer. The significance of serial killer communication is reaffirmed, and general conclusions are advanced. I try to integrate what each of these ten cases tells us about serial killer communication into a meaningful set of conclusions.

Five of the killers were caught—David Berkowitz (Son of Sam), the DC Sniper, Ted Kaczynski (the Unabomber), John Robinson Sr., and William Heirens. In two of these cases, the serial killer's communication provided the decisive clues: Kaczynski was apprehended in large part because of his writings, and communication was also considered very incriminating in the DC Sniper case, as well. In the Heirens and Robinson cases, these killers' communication also played a substantial role in their eventual apprehension and conviction.

It is difficult to generalize about the motives behind serial killer communication. Some serial murderers have stated explicitly their agenda and/or objectives, while the others' messages elude our understanding. Similarly, communication played different roles in these cases, from deliberately left clues for the police to enigmatic warnings and self-impressed bragging.

The Son of Sam

He didn't kill that many people, and he engaged in no acts of pre- or postdeath torture or mutilation. Nevertheless, the Son of Sam is one of the best-remembered and most infamous of serial killers. During his crime spree, he terrorized New York City as few others have done.

He wrote one famous note, which he left at a crime scene. He wrote a famous letter to *New York Daily News* columnist Jimmy Breslin. His criminal persona, the Son of Sam, is recognized widely as standing for David Berkowitz, a former postal worker and the arsonist behind an estimated 1,500 fires in New York. Active between 1976 and 1977, his shootings were magnified, explored, and exaggerated according to critics of the intense media coverage afforded these crimes. Despite a massive investigation, Berkowitz was caught almost by accident when a parking ticket he received at what would be his last shooting led to his identification.

The Son of Sam was not merely one of the best-known serial killers, he was also a committed communicator. He left notes at crime scenes and mailed letters to journalists and others. He even drew pictures and wrote bizarre messages on the walls of his apartment. He also kept a diary and wrote out crime plans.

One thing is evident. This communication meant a great deal to Berkowitz. His frequent use of so many communication methods proves this. The theme of many of his messages was fantasy, a common serial killer concern. A few letters and notes were a bit more rational.

THE ATTACKS BEGIN

Berkowitz had attempted to kill before his first fatal shooting. On Christmas Eve 1975, a little more than six months before his first killing, he had his initial experience with attempted murder. "I didn't want to hurt them, I only wanted to kill them," Berkowitz reportedly explained of the attack.[1] Berkowitz later told police that he left his apartment and drove to Co-Op City intent on committing a murder.[2] He saw a victim, parked his car, walked toward her, and stabbed her in the back. "I stabbed her, and she didn't do anything. She just turned and looked at me. It was terrible. She was screaming pitifully and I didn't know what the hell to do. It wasn't like the movies. In the movies you sneak up on someone and they fall down quietly. Dead. It wasn't like that. She was staring at my knife and screaming. She wasn't dying," Berkowitz recalled.[3] It is believed that this lucky woman's heavy winter coat saved her life.[4]

Panicked by his intended victim's loud screaming and her refusal to die, Berkowitz ran. Within a block, he encountered Michelle Foreman, a fifteen-year-old girl. He stabbed her several times; she was hospitalized with six stab wounds in her head and body, and a collapsed lung. According to Berkowitz, "I stabbed her, she looked at me. I stabbed her again. It was terrible. I never heard anyone scream like that. The way she screamed constantly, I kept stabbing and nothing would happen. She kept fighting harder and screaming more."[5]

There would be one more unsuccessful Son of Sam foray before his attacks became lethal. On July 6, 1976, a little more than two weeks before his first murder, Berkowitz left home carrying a handgun planning on shooting and killing someone, anyone. Two girls in a car appealed to him as targets, and he followed them to their driveway. By the time he parked his car and approached their house, they were gone.[6]

Then, on July 29, 1976, Donna Lauria and Jody Valenti were shot. They were assaulted as they sat in a parked car on Buhre Avenue in the Queens, New York, just after one A.M. The first shot struck Lauria in the neck, and the second hit Valenti in her thigh. As Lauria lay dying, Valenti, who would survive, screamed and honked the horn to summon assistance.[7]

Lauria was eighteen years of age and a medical technician; Valenti was a nineteen-year-old student nurse. They were shot by a man who seemed to come out of nowhere, took a gun from a bag, and began shooting for no reason and without saying a word.[8] A total of five shots were fired through the car's windshield. Berkowitz said, "I knew I had to get them. Those were my orders. I never saw them until moments before the shooting."[9] Berkowitz later decided that he was in love with Lauria and that a demon had arranged for him to marry her spirit.[10]

THE BEGINNING OF COMMUNICATION

A little-known note was left at the scene of that first fatal shooting. "He slipped a note into the seat of a car in which his first victims lay dying," claimed former FBI profiler Robert Ressler. According to Ressler, "a note in crude letters" declared, in part, "Bang-bang, I'll be back." The note was signed "Mr. Monster."[11]

Three aspects of this note merit attention: the gunshot simulation would be repeated in the second note, the promise (or threat) to return is mentioned, and a name—Mr. Monster—is provided for the killer. The last two points are particularly important. The note's threat of future murder demonstrated a theme of rhetorical intimidation, and self-publicity. The last point is important as the press would give the killer several other nicknames, like the .44 Caliber Killer and the Son of Sam.

There were six noteworthy dimensions of the style of this note, or at least the fragmentary parts with which I am familiar. It was brief and reportedly crudely written. It was both implicitly threatening ("I'll be back") and explicitly threatening ("Bang Bang"). It was relatively simple in word choice and syntax. Perhaps the dominant stylistic impression was a mildly unsettling, weird sensation felt by readers.

MORE KILLINGS

Three months and a week later, on October 23, 1976, Berkowitz shot and wounded Carl Denaro and Rosemary Keenan as they sat in a parked car outside a Flushing, Queens, bar. The shooter crouched behind the car and fired a bullet through the rear window, missing Keenan (daughter of a New York Police detective) and wounding Denaro. Police found the shell casing on the back floorboard of the vehicle. Denaro, twenty, and Keenan, eighteen, apparently were caught completely off-guard by their assailant. Friends rushed Denaro to the Flushing Hospital and Medical Center.[12]

Berkowitz left his apartment that evening at 1:45 A.M. with the specific purpose of ending a human life. When he spotted the couple caressing in their car, he pulled up directly behind their Volkswagen.

"I was more frightened than they were.... Boy, did I mess up. But really, I was very nervous," Berkowitz claimed.[13]

On November 27, Donna DeMasi and Joanne Lomino were wounded as they stood in front of the Lomino residence, also in the Queens. The sixteen-year-old DeMasi and her eighteen-year-old friend Lomino were walking home from the movies when they noticed Berkowitz hiding behind a lamppost. DeMasi said, "Joanne, there's a guy watching us over there. He's kind of scary. Let's walk faster."[14] According to Berkowitz, "By the time I was able to get back and hide behind the lamppost, they started to walk. I followed. They saw me and walked faster.... I didn't want to get them frightened, so I began to ask them for directions," Berkowitz recalled. He added this chilling conclusion, "I had the gun out and pointed it in their direction. Then I shot twice. They both were hit and they fell on either side of the stoop. It was just like it should be. You shot them, and they fell. It was as simple as that."[15]

The initial 1977 shooting occurred on January 30, when Christine Freund was killed and John Diel unhurt as they sat in a parked car in the Queens. They were kissing in the car when bullets shattered their windshield, and Freund was killed immediately. Freund was twenty-six, and Diel was thirty, making them the oldest victims. Freund and Diel were planning on announcing their engagement on St. Valentine's Day, two weeks away.[16] The two had just entered the car, and as they began to kiss, the windshield exploded, and Diel heard Freund scream as two bullets struck her. Diel fell out of the car after the shooting and tried to stop a passing motorist for assistance, to no avail.[17] Berkowitz recalled, "We just passed each other. We almost touched shoulders."[18]

On March 8, Virginia Voskerichian was shot and killed. Voskerichian and her family were from Armenia. She was an honors student in her sophomore year at Columbia University's Barnard College. Voskerichian was attacked while walking down the sidewalk toward her home in Forest Hills. She raised a book she was carrying to fend off the attack, but the bullet penetrated the book and struck her in the face, killing her instantly.[19] Voskerichian was nineteen when she was killed.[20] This crime scene was within three hundred yards of where Berkowitz shot Freund and Diel.

Valentina Suriani and Alexander Esau were both murdered in their parked car in the Bronx on April 17. The crime scene was a few blocks from the site of the Lauria/Valenti shootings. The two were killed by a "fusillade of shots that killed them both instantly, fired from point-blank range."[21] Suriani was an eighteen-year-old student at Lehman College, and Esau was a twenty-year-old tow truck assistant. "It was my best job because it resulted in two deaths. Plus, I left my first carefully concocted note on the scene. My shooting pattern improved greatly due to my fearlessness, which slowly developed, and my two-handed shooting method. Four shots were fired. Three hit the victims out of four fired," Berkowitz later bragged.[22]

THE BORRELLI NOTE

Their killer left "a childishly scribbled note" in the street at the Suriani/Esau murder scene.[23] Although the note is rather lengthy, it is worth including in its entirety. As in all of Berkowitz's correspondence quoted in this chapter, words will be spelled as in the note, and the original stanza structure will be preserved.

> I am deeply hurt by your calling
> me a wemon hater. I am not.
> But I am a monster
> I am the "Son of Sam." I am a little
> "brat."/
>   When Father Sam gets drunk
> he gets mean. He beats his
> family. Sometimes he ties me
> up to the back of the house.
> Other times he locks me
> in the garage. Sam loves to
> drink blood./
> "Go out and kill," commands
> Father Sam./
> Behind our house some
> rest. Mostly young—raped
> and slaughtered—their
> blood drained—just bones
> now./
>   Papa Sam keeps me locked
> in the attic, too. I can't
> get out but I look out the
> attic window and watch
> the world go by./
>   I feel like an outsider.
> I am on a different wave

length then everybody
else—programmed too
kill./
    However, to stop me you
must kill me. Attention
all police: shoot me first-
shoot to kill or else
keep out of my way or
you will die!/
    Papa Sam is old now.
He needs some blood to
preserve his youth.
He has had too many
heart attacks. Too many
heart attacks. "Ugh me
hoot it urts Sonny Boy."/
    I miss my pretty
princess most of all.
She's resting in
our ladies house
But I'll she her soon./
    I am the "monster"
"Beelzebub"—The
"Chubby Behemouth."/
    I love to hunt. Prowling
the streets looking for
fair game—tasty meat. The
wemon of Queens are Z
prettyist of all. I must
be the water they drink.
I live for the hunt—my life.
Blood for papa./
    Mr. Borelli, Sir,
I don't want to kill anymore
No sir, no more but I
must, "honour thy father."/
I want to make love to the
world. I love people.
I don't belong on Earth.
Return me to yahoos./
To the people of Queens,

I love you. And I
want to wish all of
you a Happy Easter.
May God bless you
in this life and in
the next and for now
I say goodbye and
goodnight./
Police—let me
haunt you with these
words;
I'll be back!
I'll be back!
To be interprreted
as—bang, bang, bang
bank, bang—Ugh!!

Yours in
murder
Mr. Monster.

Berkowitz began writing the note on April Fool's Day. He told an interviewer that it took him two days to write. Berkowitz told police after his arrest that he wrote the note in the hope that police would investigate and arrest Sam Carr.[24] Police were able to lift three clear fingerprints from the letter and envelope.

This very important note, intentionally left by the killer at the crime scene to be discovered by the police, revealed much about the psyche and agenda of the Son of Sam. Seven content dimensions deserve individual consideration. Initially, it must be recalled that while this note referred to the serial killer as "the Son of Sam," he also called himself "Beelzebub," and the "Chubby Behemouth," and the letter was signed, "Mr. Monster." Previously, he had been called the .44 Caliber Killer, because of his weapon of choice. This changed with the note. A second salient fact worth noting is that this note referred to a controlling figure in the killer's life. That was "Father Sam," of whom the killer wrote, "'Go out and kill,' commands Father Sam." Father Sam was also called "Papa Sam" twice in this note.

The note admitted the writer's responsibility for murders: "I feel like I am on a different wave length than everybody else—programmed too kill." A fourth fact about the note is that future murders were predicted, or promised. The note revealed the importance of killing to the Son of Sam: "I live for the hunt—tasty meat." The New York City borough of Queens was singled out twice in this note. "The wemon of Queens are Z prettyist [sic] of all," the Son of Sam wrote. He added later in the note that "To the people of Queens, I love you. And I want to wish you a Happy Easter. May God bless you in this life and in the next."

A New York City Police Department officer, Joseph Borrelli, was mentioned in the note. Borrelli had been publicized as a leader in the serial killings probe in media coverage of the investigation. According to the note, "Mr. Borrelli, Sir, I don't want to kill anymore."

We now consider another important aspect of the content of this note: the Son of Sam repeatedly taunted the police. The note bragged, "However, to stop me you must kill me. Attention all police: shoot me first—shoot to kill or else keep out of my way or you will die." The note ended, "Police—let me haunt you with these words;/ I'll be back,/I'll be back."

A final content item to consider is signature. Like the first note, it was signed, "Mr. Monster," not Son of Sam. Did police and the media misunderstand the killer's chosen name and inadvertently rechristen him? All we know is the initial two notes were not signed "Sam" but "Mr. Monster."

Five stylistic dimensions of this note might be examined. This was prose, although of a decidedly disorganized and rambling nature. It was not tightly structured like the note found on Berkowitz at his arrest, but rather loose and seemingly haphazard in structure. It was also unbalanced, with a mixture of long and short paragraphs. Unlike other messages to come, this one was not all capital letters.

THE BRESLIN LETTER

Berkowitz wrote to *Daily News* columnist Jimmy Breslin, on May 30, 1977:

> HELLO FROM THE GUTTERS OF N.Y.C.
> WHICH ARE FILLED WITH DOG MANURE,
> VOMIT, STALE WINE, URINE AND BLOOD.
> HELLO FROM THE SEWERS OF N.Y.C. WHICH
> SWALLOW UP THESE DELICACIES WHEN
> THEY ARE WASHED AWAY BY THE SWEEPER
> TRUCKS. HELLO FROM THE CRACKS IN THE

SIDEWALKS OF N.Y.C. AND FROM THE
ANTS THAT DWELL IN THESE CRACKS
AND FEED ON THE DRIED BLOOD OF THE
DEAD THAT HAS SEEPED INTO THESE CRACKS.
JB, I'M JUST DROPPING YOU A LINE
TO LET YOU KNOW THAT I APPRECIATE
YOUR INTEREST IN THOSE RECENT AND
HORRENDOUS .44 KILLINGS. I ALSO
WANT TO TELL YOU THAT I READ YOUR
COLUMN DAILY AND I FIND IT QUITE
INFORMATIVE.
    TELL ME JIM, WHAT WILL YOU
HAVE FOR JULY TWENTY-NINTH?
YOU CAN FORGET ABOUT ME IF YOU
LIKE BECAUSE I DON'T CARE FOR
PUBLICITY. HOWEVER, YOU MUST
NOT FORGET DONNA LAURIA AND
YOU CANNOT LET THE PEOPLE FORGET
HER EITHER. SHE WAS A VERY
VERY SWEET GIRL BUT SAM'S A
THIRSTY LAD AND HE WONT LET ME
STOP KILLING UNTIL HE GETS HIS
FILL OF BLOOD./
MR BRESLIN, SIR, DON'T THINK
THAT BECAUSE YOU HAVEN'T HEARD FROM
ME FOR A WHILE THAT I WENT TO SLEEP.
NO, RATHER, I AM STILL HERE. LIKE
A SPIRIT ROAMING THE NIGHT.
THIRSTY, HUNGRY, SELDOM STOPPING
TO REST; ANXIOUS TO PLEASE SAM.
I LOVE MY WORK. NOW, THE VOID
HAS BEEN FILLED./
PERHAPS WE SHALL MEET FACE TO
FACE SOMEDAY OR PERHAPS I WILL
BE BLOWN AWAY BY COPS WITH
SMOKING .38'S. WHATEVER, IF I
SHALL BE FORTUNATE ENOUGH TO
MEET YOU I WILL TELL YOU ALL ABOUT
SAM IF YOU LIKE AND I WILL
INTRODUCE YOU TO HIM. HIS NAME
IS "SAM THE TERRIBLE."/

NOT KNOWING WHAT THE FUTURE
HOLDS I SHALL SAY FAREWELL AND
I WILL SEE YOU AT THE NEXT JOB.
OR SHOULD I SAY YOU WILL SEE
MY HANDIWORK AT THE NEXT JOB?
REMEMBER MS. LAURIA. THANK YOU.
           IN THEIR BLOOD
           AND
           FROM THE GUTTER
           "SAM'S CREATION" .44
HERE ARE SOME NAMES TO HELP YOU ALONG
FORWARD THEM TO THE INSPECTOR FOR
USE BY N.C.I.C:
"THE DUKE OF DEATH"
"THE WICKED KING WICKER"
"THE TWENTY-TWO DISCIPLES OF HELL"
"JOHN WHEATIES—RAPIST AND SUFF-
OCATOR OF YOUNG GIRLS."
PS; JB, PLEASE INFORM ALL THE
DETECTIVES WORKING THE SLAYING TO REMAIN.
PS; JB, PLEASE INFORM ALL THE
DETECTIVES WORKING THE
CASE THAT I WISH THEM THE BEST
OF LUCK. "KEEP 'EM,
DIGGING, DRIVE ON, THINK
POSITIVE, GET OFF YOUR
BUTTS, KNOCK ON COFFINS, ETC."
UPON MY CAPTURE I PROMISE TO
BUY ALL THE GUYS WORKING
ON THE CASE A NEW PAIR OF
SHOES IF I CAN GET UP THE
MONEY.
           SON OF SAM.

The back of the envelope bore an inscription: "BLOOD AND FAMILY, DARKNESS AND DEATH, ABSOLUTE DEPRAVITY. 44."

This letter was received at the *Daily News* on the afternoon of June 1, 1977. Berkowitz claimed that he used block lettering to achieve a "ghoulish effect."[25] Although *most* of the letter was released, one page was withheld, or "embargoed," at police request. Berkowitz explained why he wrote Breslin, "I wrote Mr. Breslin because he had an obsession with the shootings. That was evidenced in his columns and how he wrote them. I also wanted him to write about Donna Lauria because the newspapers did not cover her properly. They just had Donna down as a name."[26] Fingerprints were found on the letter.

This lengthy letter contained a great deal of information, and we might underscore several of these message dimensions. First, there were repeated references to New York City, abbreviated as N.Y.C. in the first paragraph. In fact, the letter began, "HELLO FROM THE GUTTERS OF N.Y.C." There were also repeated references to Jimmy Breslin, the newspaper columnist who had received this Son of Sam letter. Breslin was referred to as "JB," "JIM," and "MR. BRESLIN."

Donna Lauria, who was slain by the killer in July 1976, prompted several specific references in the letter. "YOU MUST NOT FORGET DONNA LAURIA AND YOU CANNOT LET THE PEOPLE FORGET HER EITHER," the Son of Sam declared. His letter concluded, "REMEMBER MS. LAURIA. THANK YOU." The anniversary of Lauria's death was noted in the letter.

The letter taunted the police. Taken as a whole, the document implicitly teased the police for their inability to apprehend him. It went so far as to offer a series of names for investigators to run through the National Crime Information Center (NCIC) computerized arrest records. There was a thematic ambiguity about this letter, with its chilling yet casual idiom.

This Son of Sam letter promised future murders. "I WILL SEE YOU AT THE NEXT JOB OR SHOULD I SAY YOU WILL SEE MY HANDI-WORK AT THE NEXT JOB?" the literary serial killer smugly declared. Some prominent names were mentioned in this letter. It referred to "SAM THE TERRIBLE," and was signed "SAM'S CREATION." Reference was made to "JOHN WHEATIES—RAPIST AND SUFFOCATOR OF YOUNG GIRLS," an alleged Satanic cult member who died a violent and suspicious death. In fact, "John Wheaties" was a composite of two real people—Berkowitz's perceived enemy Sam Carr's children, John Carr and Wheat Carr.

The style of this important letter deserves some attention. It was entirely capitalized, and there were seven main sections, including a lengthy postscript. There was a lack of balance between the main units. Two sections had eleven and twelve lines, respectively, while others had seven, eight, and nine lines. The postscript was a twenty-two-line extravaganza.

Perhaps the most notable stylistic dimension of this letter was the language. Berkowitz employed very vivid language to convey his message of fear and death. He wrote "FROM THE GUTTERS OF N.Y.C.," which were full of "DOG MANURE, VOMIT, STALE WINE, URINE AND BLOOD."

A man named Craig Glassman, one of Berkowitz's neighbors, received five letters from Berkowitz. All five were relatively similar; long, disjointed, and full of nonsequiturs. The first Glassman letter, sent June 7, 1977, typified all five:

Craig Glassman,
   You have been chosen. You have been chosen
to die.
   Craig I curse your mothers grave. I curse
your mothers grave, I am pissing on her
Craig, urinating on her head.
   Your mouth is filled with cum. You
blood is sour.
You, Craig Glassman, are truly Satan's
child, and now, he wants you by his side.
Come join him in death little ones.
Master Glassman, you are a man with
power (the power of darkness). You are hereby
ordered to unleash your terror upon the
people. "Destroy all good and ruin peoples'
lives. Begin immediately."

Mighty Craig, where is your weapon
If you don't obey thes commands, the
commands of your father then you will
be punished. I swear, Glassman, your life will
be pure Hell.
We will kill you. We will murder you.
Remember, Craig that your mother the harlot
the lesbian whore wants to love you
so make her happy—kill some your child.
Remember if you dont do as we say you
will surely die a premature death.
        Your brothers & sisters
        Craig darling
  Craig Glassman the cruelest sickest man
on earth.

cruel Glassman, cruel Glassman,
mean, terrible, cruel, hateful Craig Glassman.
Die Craig Die.

The return address on the envelope was, "Mother, the Cemetery/ 174 Coligni Avenue/ New Rochelle, NY 10801.[27]

Six content dimensions of this letter might be noted. Craig Glassman dominated this message, as he was referred to fourteen times. Glassman's mother was mentioned four times. Killing received three mentions, as did the notion of death. There were two threats issued against Glassman, and he was ordered to kill by the letter-writer. The theme conveyed a clear threat.

This letter's style was characterized by the use of upper- and lowercases. There were six main paragraphs and a postscript. The letter was unbalanced, as the paragraphs consisted of sentences of varying length. There were two two-word sentences, one had three words, and other sentences had five, six, and eight words each.

Two words were spelled incorrectly. "This" was written as "Thes," and the writer used "You" instead of "Your." The letter was rambling and repetitive; for instance, it began, "You have been chosen. You have been chosen to die." Later, the letter ended by declaring "Craig Glassman the cruelest sickest man/ on earth/ cruel Glassman, cruel Glassman,/ mean, terrible, cruel, hateful Craig Glassman."

A final noteworthy aspect of this letter's style is the vivid language choices made by the author. "Your mouth is filled with cum. You blood is sour," the letter suggested of Glassman. It also declared that "Craig I curse your mothers grave. I curse your mothers grave, I am pissing on her Craig, urinating on her head."

In addition to the five letters to Glassman, another neighbor provoked Berkowitz's literary efforts and may have inspired Berkowitz's self-selected nickname. The name "Sam's Creation," was inspired by Berkowitz's neighbor Sam Carr, whose Labrador Retriever's barking kept Berkowitz awake late at night. Irritated by the incessant barking, he mailed Carr a series of hate letters, and in April 1977, he shot and injured the dog.[28]

THE KILLINGS RESUME

Berkowitz left his apartment on his deadly self-assignment about ten o'clock the evening of June 26. He parked in the Bayside section of

Queens and walked in search of victims.[29] Salvatore Lupo and Judith Placido sat in a car borrowed from a friend. "All of a sudden," Placido recalled, "I heard echoing in my car. There wasn't any pain, just ringing in my ears."[30] Four shots were fired through the windshield at the couple. Lupo was struck in the right forearm; Placido was hit in her head, neck, and shoulder. Berkowitz was irritated by the outcome of the attack on Placido and Lupo; he didn't understand how they survived.[31]

The final murder victim, Stacy Moskowitz, was killed and her companion Robert Violante blinded by Berkowitz on July 31. The couple sat in their car near the Brooklyn shore when they were shot four times in the head. This crime took place in the Gravesend Bay section of Brooklyn, a generally quiet middle-class neighborhood. Moskowitz, twenty, was a telex machine operator, and her twenty-year-old companion, Violante, was a clothing salesman. Violante was shot twice in the face and suffered permanent blindness, while his date was killed. Although there was conflicting information about whether Moscowitz survived for any time after the shooting, it was officially established that the time of death was 5:22 P.M. on August 1.[32]

"They kissed and embraced. I had an erection. I had my gun out, aimed at the middle of Stacy's head, and fired," Berkowitz recalled.[33]

A MASS MURDER PLAN?

Berkowitz was arrested on August 10, 1977, as he walked to his car. While investigators do not know his destination with certainty, there is a chilling possibility that a mass murder was barely averted. When Berkowitz was taken into custody, police discovered "a .44 Bulldog revolver inside his car, along with a semiautomatic rifle and a note outlining Son of Sam's plans to cut loose with a rifle in a chic Hamptons disco."[34] Berkowitz had originally planned an attack in the Hamptons, Leyton recalled, but he changed plans and intended to assault a nightclub in Riverdale, New York, instead.[35] Police found a semi-automatic rifle with four additional cartridges full of bullets, an Ithica 12-gauge shotgun, and a pair of .22 caliber rifles in Berkowitz' car. According to a History Channel documentary, when police searched Berkowitz' car prior to his capture, they found a note addressed to the New York City Commissioner of Police. It threatened an attack on a Long Island, New York, nightclub.[36]

On August 6, 1977, Berkowitz drove to the Hamptons, to carry out his plan. But that was an inclement evening, and the rampage had to be postponed. Berkowitz blamed the bad weather on demons: "They had enough force to call these clouds to stop me."[37]

A NOTE FOUND ON BERKOWITZ

When the police arrested Berkowitz, they found a poem addressed to his apartment building co-tenant Craig Glassman in his wallet. The text of the note appeared in ten lines in capital letters:

> BECAUSE CRAIG IS CRAIG
> SO MUST THE STREETS
> BE FILLED WITH CRAIG (DEATH)/
> AND HUGE DROPS OF LEAD
> POURED DOWN UPON HER HEAD
> UNTIL SHE WAS DEAD
> YET, THE CATS STILL COME OUT
> AT NIGHT TO MATE
> AND THE SPARROWS STILL
> SING IN THE MORNING.

At first, Berkowitz's note was discounted by the police and case investigators as nothing more than the meaningless verbalization of a deeply demented individual. But that might have been a serious mistake on their part. Careful analysis of this message reveals at least three things about the content of the note found on the Son of Sam.

It must be conceded that while Berkowitz was sufficiently unbalanced to kill several innocent people and wound even more, he was nevertheless relatively rational and in touch with reality. The note was actually part prose and part verse, as Berkowitz wrote it in ten lines, or five pairs, one of which rhymed; "POURED DOWN UPON HER HEAD/ UNTIL SHE WAS DEAD." A second noteworthy fact about this note is that Berkowitz's obsession with death was clearly and unmistakably manifested. "CRAIG" was equated with "DEATH," and an unidentified female was killed, according to the two rhyming lines. Vague threats against Craig Glassman were the theme of this rhetoric. Glassman was associated with death, as in other "Sam" rhetoric.

One stylistic comment should be considered. The note was tightly structured, in ten relatively even lines. There was a deliberate balance in the five pairs of lines.

THE SECRET SON OF SAM DIARY

Besides the crime plans discovered in his car and the poem to Craig Glassman found on his person, there was yet another Berkowitz communication act—he kept a secret diary. To date, little has been revealed publicly about this document. Newton referred to "a secret journal" that "lists the details of 300 fires for which he was allegedly responsible around New York."[38] Berkowitz's crime diary began when he was about twenty-one, when he started recording the location of fires he set.[39] According to the Web site A 2 Z of Serial Killers, Berkowitz admitted to setting 1,488 fires in New York City between September 1974 and December 1975, keeping a diary entry on each blaze.[40] The diary was actually three stenographer's notebooks. Two were completely filled, and the third was about half-full of fire entries.[41]

WALL WRITING

Berkowitz also engaged in wall writing. Although these messages were in his apartment, unlike most such writings found at crime scenes, some of it seemed salient to the serial murders. After his arrest, police found a large hole in the wall of Berkowitz's apartment. Next to the hole was written, "Hi. My name is Mr. Williams and I live in this hole. I have several children who I'm turning into killers. WAIT Til they grow up."[42]

Three aspects of the content of this specific wall writing should be noticed. First, it explicitly referred to killing. The wall writer exclaimed, "I have several children who I'm turning into killers." The note added a second factor, the threat posed by these children. According to the wall writing, "WAIT Til they grow up." A final noteworthy dimension of the content of this wall writing is the reference to Mr. Williams. The style of this wall writing was unimpressive and somewhat nondescript. There were four sentences, of varying length; one was one word, another had five words, while two others contained nine and eleven words, respectively.

Police also found the walls covered with handwritten messages like "Kill for My Master."[43] There were three meaningful content aspects of this relatively brief wall message. It referred to killing and to the killer's acting on behalf of another, unseen controlling figure. It also explicitly referred to another as his "Master."

Berkowitz inscribed several other bizarre messages on the walls. One message referred prominently to Craig Glassman, with a mention of another Berkowitz foil, Sam Carr:

> God Save
> Us From
> Craig Glassman/
> My name is
> Craig Glassman
> And I Shall Never
> let a soul rest/
> CRAIG
> GLASSMAN
> WORSHIPS
> THE
> DEVIL AND
> HAS POWER
> OVER ME
> KILL
> FOR
> SAM
> CARR/
> SAM
> CARR
> MY MASTER.

We can examine the message conveyed through this wall writing in six ways. First, there were three references to Craig Glassman, a favorite subject of the Son of Sam rhetoric. There were also two references to Sam Carr; in fact, the writing concluded by referring to "SAM CARR MY MASTER." A third message factor was the reference to killing, again with regard to Mr. Carr: "KILL FOR SAM CARR." There was another explicit reference to someone being the Son of Sam's "MASTER." Another noteworthy aspect of this message is the specific references to God and the Devil.

The style of this wall writing was similar to others in some ways, but distinctive in others. This message began in upper- and lowercase, and then switched to all capital letters. There were four unbalanced sections to the message. The sentences were very short, as there were ten one-word lines, and eight lines of two words.

"In this hole lives the wicker king," proclaimed another Berkowitz apartment graffiti.[44] This message referred to the hole occupied by Mr. Williams, according to another of the graffiti.

These wall writings, taken collectively, revealed Berkowitz's pathological personality, as well as his serial murder tendencies. His threat to raise a new generation of serial killers was literally untrue, but it was entirely consistent with his homicidal preoccupation and communicative tendencies. These enigmatic messages, scrawled in black Magic Marker, gave Berkowitz another platform in his informal, ongoing communication campaign.[45]

THE CRIMINAL

As with many serial killers, Berkowitz felt the desire to attend the funerals of his victims. He did not, however, because he knew that police routinely videotaped such gatherings to search for suspects. He did, "hang around diners near police stations to try and overhear cops talking about his crimes."[46] He also reportedly searched for the graves of his victims, without success. We can best understand the phenomenon of the Son of Sam shootings, in conclusion, by considering four factors; Berkowitz's family life, his sanity, his sexuality and relationships, and his motivation.

Berkowitz was abandoned by his birth mother and raised in an orphanage until his adoption by the Berkowitz family. He was especially close to his adoptive mother, Pearl, and her death when he was sixteen greatly affected him.[47] Shortly after Pearl Berkowitz's death, her grieving husband, Nathan, and son, David, moved into Co-Op City, a self-contained residential area in the Bronx's northeast corner, consisting of more than thirty high-rise apartment buildings. David Berkowitz finished high school and immediately entered the U.S. Army.

Like many adoptive children, Berkowitz wanted to meet his biological parents. After years of searching he located his birth mother, Betty Falco. But, to his dismay he discovered that Tony Falco, Betty's former husband, was not his real father; Betty's married lover, a man named Joseph Kleinman, was his biological father.[48] "I was an accident, unwanted," Berkowitz complained. "My birth was either out of spite or by accident."[49]

After his arrest, Berkowitz's uncertain mental state was questioned. His motivation behind the killings revealed both paranoid and schizophrenic tendencies. Although he was deemed fit to stand trial, he was definitely mentally unwell.[50] Lane described Berkowitz as "an obvious paranoid schizophrenic."[51] A panel of psychiatrists diagnosed Berkowitz as a severely delusional paranoid schizophrenic who was incompetent to stand trial. Dr. Daniel W. Schwartz, Director of Forensic Psychiatry at the Downstate Medical Center in Brooklyn, wrote, "It is the opinion of each of us that the defendant is an incapacitated person, as a result of mental defect or disease, who lacks capacity to understand the proceedings against him or to assist in his own defense."[52] Their unanimous diagnosis? Severely paranoid. However, another psychiatrist, Dr. David Abrahamson, decided Berkowitz was sane and that he understood his actions were wrong and, in fact, criminal.

Perhaps the reason he left Co-Op City as soon as he could was his loneliness, caused by his seeming inability to make friends or to develop meaningful interpersonal relationships with others. Some claim he never had an intimate relationship with a woman and was a virgin. However, according to A 2 Z of Serial Killers, he contracted a venereal disease from a prostitute while serving in the military in Korea.[53] Out of embarrassment, he lied about his sexual inexperience when necessary and invented sexual exploits for conversational purposes. "Berkowitz was prone to fabricate elaborate lies about his bedroom prowess, all the while intent upon revenge against the women who habitually rejected him," according to Newton.[54] Berkowitz reportedly masturbated frequently; at the time he entered the army, he was masturbating several times daily.[55]

What motivated Berkowitz? It was demonic dog messages, some say. It was commonly believed that he killed because of perceived demonic messages conveyed by the barking of dogs. Abrahamson, the psychiatrist who found Berkowitz fit to stand trial, later interviewed the killer in prison and wrote a book about the case. Abrahamson theorized that during Berkowitz's childhood, he must have seen his adoptive parents making love and had repressed the memory. There may be an additional motive to consider; interpersonal loneliness. The timing of the crimes may support this motive theory. Berkowitz did not start killing until after he left the army, settled into an unfulfilling but stable career at the post office, and his adoptive father's marriage to a woman who did not get along with David and their subsequent move to Florida. Then, when he discovered the complex reality of his paternity, he came unglued, Abrahamson suggested.[56]

In many respects, Berkowitz differed little from the rest of us. He was very intelligent; in fact, "He was an exceptional student," according to one study.[57] In 1960, he scored 118 on an IQ test, a score considered to be a superior performance.[58] Like many schoolchildren, he was teased for being different; mean-spirited schoolmates teased Berkowitz for being Jewish. One of his most basic difficulties may have been the fact that he was an introvert. Serial murder expert Eric Hickey suggested, "His main character trait seemed to be that he was introverted and liked to roam the streets alone at night."[59]

CONCLUSION

Although we know a good deal about Berkowitz, and we understand the facts of the case, somehow something seems missing. The Son of Sam shootings of course caused great sorrow for the loved ones of victims, but why the widespread public fear? I suggest that the Son of Sam communication was responsible, as Foreman noted, "He'd killed six people, blinded or paralyzed another two and wounded an additional seven. But it was not the numbers so much as the mystery surrounding Son of Sam that inspired terror. It was the demented, illiterate letters that he wrote to the newspapers."[60]

Berkowitz was a complex and enigmatic person, due to his mental illness or because he chose to be that way. His arson and murder career was impressive in that he offended repeatedly and escaped each time. But his communication eclipsed his crimes. His rhetorical themes varied, from specific taunts and threats to flights of fantasy.

He was a diverse communicator. He wrote numerous letters to newspapers and individuals against whom he held a grudge. He wrote notes left at crime scenes and was apprehended with a note on his person. Police found plans for a mass murder in his car, and his apartment walls were embellished with numerous writings. He even kept a diary. There can be little doubt that communication played a central role in the Son of Sam murders.

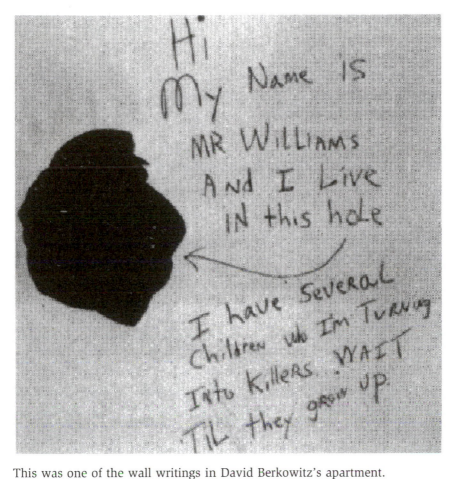

This was one of the wall writings in David Berkowitz's apartment.
Mr. Williams was a common topic. (Courtesy of the New York City Police
Department.)

I AM DEEPLY HURT BY YOUR CALLING
ME A WEMON HATER. I AM NOT.
BUT I AM A MONSTER.
I AM THE "SON OF SAM." I AM A LITTLE
"BRAT"
  WHEN FATHER SAM GETS DRUNK
HE GETS MEAN. HE BEATS HIS
FAMILY. SOMETIMES HE TIES ME
UP TO THE BACK OF THE HOUSE.
OTHER TIMES HE LOCKS ME
IN THE GARAGE. SAM LOVES TO
DRINK BLOOD.
  "GO OUT AND KILL" COMMANDS
FATHER SAM
  BEHIND OUR HOUSE SOME
REST. MOSTLY YOUNG — RAPED
AND SLAUGHTERED - THEIR
BLOOD DRAINED — JUST BONES
NOW
  PAPA SAM KEEPS ME LOCKED
IN THE ATTIC, TOO. I CAN'T
GET OUT BUT I LOOK OUT THE
ATTIC WINDOW AND WATCH
THE WORLD GO BY.
  I FEEL LIKE AN OUTSIDER.
I AM ON A DIFFERENT WAVE
LENGTH THEN EVERYBODY

ELSE - PROGRAMMED TOO
KILL.
  HOWEVER, TO STOP ME YOU
MUST KILL ME. ATTENTION
ALL POLICE: SHOOT ME FIRST-
SHOOT TO KILL OR ELSE.
KEEP OUT OF MY WAY OR
YOU WILL DIE!

  PAPA SAM IS OLD NOW.
HE NEEDS SOME BLOOD TO
PRESERVE HIS YOUTH.
HE HAS HAD TOO MANY
HEART ATTACKS. TOO MANY
HEART ATTACKS. "UGH, ME
HOOT IT URTS SONNY BOY."

  I MISS MY PRETTY
PRINCESS MOST OF ALL.
SHE'S RESTING IN
OUR LADIES HOUSE
BUT I'LL SEE HER SOON.

  I AM THE "MONSTER" -
"BEELZEBUB" — THE
"CHUBBY BEHEMOTH".

I LOVE TO HUNT. PROWLING
THE STREETS LOOKING FOR
FAIR GAME — TASTY MEAT. THE
WEMON OF QUEENS ARE Z
PRETTYIST OF ALL. I MUST
BE THE WATER THEY DRINK.
I LIVE FOR THE HUNT - MY LIFE.
BLOOD FOR PAPA.

  MR. BORRELLI, SIR,
I DONT WANT TO KILL ANYMORE
NO SIR, NO MORE BUT I
MUST, "HONOUR THY FATHER."

I WANT TO MAKE LOVE TO THE
WORLD. I LOVE PEOPLE.
I DONT BELONG ON EARTH.
RETURN ME TO YAHOOS.

TO THE PEOPLE OF QUEENS,
I LOVE YOU. AND I
WANT TO WISH ALL OF
YOU A HAPPY EASTER.
MAY GOD BLESS YOU
IN THIS LIFE AND IN
THE NEXT AND FOR NOW

I SAY GOODBYE AND
GOODNIGHT.

POLICE: LET ME
HAUNT YOU WITH THESE
WORDS:

I'LL BE BACK!

I'LL BE BACK!

TO BE INTERRPRETED
AS — BANG BANG BANG
BANG, BANG — UGH!!

          YOURS IN
          MURDER
    MR. MONSTER

This note was addressed to NYPD Captain Joseph Borrelli and
left in the street at a shooting site. (Courtesy of the New York City
Police Department.)

The DC Sniper

2

The DC Sniper was a relatively recent entrant into the list of serial murderers. Active in the fall of 2002, John Allen Muhammad and Lee (John) Boyd Malvo were convicted in 2004 of the sniper shootings that terrorized the Washington, D.C. area. This case shocked the entire nation.

The DC Sniper practiced several types of communication. Notes left at crime scenes, telephone calls, and crime records in the form of a laptop computer diary signify the value of communication to the DC Sniper. These were communication-based crimes, because each note and telephone call was instrumental in accomplishing the extortion scheme.

Relatively few serial murderers demand ransom. This makes the DC Sniper's communication-based extortion attempt another unique aspect of this case. They planned on using a stolen credit card to access a $10 million line of credit, accessible anywhere in the world.

Although there were two individuals acting in concert, I will use the singular term DC Sniper. Prior to the arrest of Malvo and Muhammad, the term DC Sniper, or Beltway Sniper, became commonplace, so I will therefore refer to the offenders as one sniper.

The DC Sniper communication led to the identification of the suspects. There were two sets of clues—telephonic and cyber—for the police to follow. The telephone clues identified the suspects; the cybercommunication incriminated them.

THE TERROR BEGINS

The DC Sniper killings began on October 2, 2002, when James D. Martin was killed in the parking lot of a grocery store as he loaded groceries into his vehicle. Fifty-five-year-old Martin had been shopping at a Shoppers' Food Warehouse, purchasing items for his son Ben's church youth group. He had worked his way through Southeast Missouri State University. He was involved in many charitable and civic activities: he helped his son's Boy Scout troop, served on the board of his Methodist church, and participated in the adopt-a-school program by assisting Washington D.C.'s Shepard Elementary School.[1]

The next day the DC Sniper claimed four lives. The initial October 3 victim was James L. Buchanan, shot while mowing a lawn, followed shortly by taxi driver Premkumar A. Walekar, who was killed at a gas station. Later that day, both Sarah Ramos and Laurie Ann Lewis-Rivera had fatal encounters with the DC Sniper.

Buchanan, known as "Sonny" to his friends and family, was thirty-nine when he was killed. Buchanan had operated a successful landscaping business, but was retired. Like Martin, Buchanan was known to spend his time working on behalf of others, having served on the board of the Boys & Girls Clubs of Greater Washington for a decade. Although he was retired, Buchanan had responded to a long-time former client's pleas for assistance mowing the lawn of his auto dealership, a response resulting in his death.[2]

Premkumar A. Walekar died at the age of fifty-four. He came to the United States from his native India in 1968. He attended Montgomery College after his arrival in this country, and he had gotten a job driving a taxi. He and his wife, Margaret, planned to return to their native India someday, and they had already purchased a house toward that end. The couple had two children, Andrea and Andrew. Walekar was shot as he gassed up and purchased a lottery ticket. Reportedly, after he was shot, his last words were, "call an ambulance."[3]

Sarah Ramos was thirty-four years old with one year of law school behind her when she encountered the DC Sniper. She, her husband, Carlos, and their son, Carlos Jr., had emigrated from El Salvador, where he was a professor of economics, finance, and calculus, so that he might pursue employment opportunities. She was a deeply religious woman and did not speak much English. Ramos was shot while sitting on a bench waiting for her ride to work.[4]

Laurie Ann Lewis-Rivera was a nanny by trade, and twenty-five years old when murdered. She had moved to Washington, D.C. from her hometown of Mountain Home, Idaho, population approximately ten thousand. To prepare herself for her vocation, she had attended the Northeast Nannies Institute, near Portland, Oregon. She attended a Spanish-language Mormon church with her husband, Nelson, and their daughter, Jocelyn. She had taken the family mini-van to the local Shell gas station and was vacuuming the interior when she was shot.[5]

The DC Sniper allegedly killed Pascal Charlot on October 3, at Georgia Avenue and Kalmia Road, NW, at 9:15 P.M. The seventy-two-year-old man had come to the United States from his homeland, Haiti. The skilled carpenter cared for his five children and his wife, who suffered from dementia. Charlot enjoyed tending to his flower and vegetable gardens and playing Lotto.[6]

A woman was wounded by a DC Sniper attack on October 4, but she survived her wounds. The forty-three-year-old woman has two children. She was loading packages into her van at a Michael's store in Spotsylvania County, Virginia, when a bullet entered her lower back. She has requested to remain anonymous, and to date, the media and public have respected her wishes.[7]

Iran Brown, a thirteen-year-old schoolboy, was seriously hurt three days later, October 7. The freckle-faced youth was shot at 8:09 A.M. as he was about to enter school. His aunt, Tanya Brown, a nurse at Washington's Children's Hospital, had just dropped him off at Benjamin Tasker Middle School when he was shot. She sped him to the local Bowie Medical Center, where he was stabilized before being rushed to Children's Hospital with a shattered lung and severely damaged spleen, stomach, diaphragm, pancreas, and liver.[8]

THE FIRST DC SNIPER MESSAGE

The sniper left three written crime scene messages. The first, a tarot card, the death card in particular, was left next to a shell cartridge at the Brown crime scene. Police sources disclosed that the items were found on matted grass 150 yards from the school, suggesting that the gunman had lain in wait. Written on the card was a message that included the key phrase, "Dear policeman, I am God."[9]

Another report about this first communication referred to a message left by the sniper on a tarot card with simply "I am God" written on it.[10] Although the exact wording has not been revealed, there was another message in this initial communication. Angie Cannon reported, "The card had contained a warning not to divulge its existence to the press."[11]

There are specific dimensions of the content of this note that are noteworthy. The message seemed to be a bit grandiose. Self-declarations of personal divinity tend to strike most others as a bit much. It is also important to note that this message was addressed specifically to the police. It was part of the sniper's overall plan for law enforcement to find the card. Perhaps the most important content aspect of the note, however, was its intended use. The sniper wrote, "I am God," which is how he identified himself in subsequent notes and telephone calls. Thus, the phrase was used in this initial communication as a way of authenticating subsequent messages.

The style of this note deserves comment, as well. The fact that it was written on a tarot fortune-telling card, the death card in particular, was an obviously intentional choice. They wanted to frighten and unnerve the public, and possibly the investigators as well. This was a terse note, and the brevity was similarly intentional.

THE KILLINGS RESUME

Dean Harold Meyers was killed on October 9. He was fifty-three. Meyers grew up with three brothers in farm country outside of Philadelphia, Pennsylvania. He had served and was seriously wounded in the Vietnam War, and he had to have surgery on his badly damaged arm on his return to the States. Meyers attended Pennsylvania State University. He worked as a project manager for Dewberry & Davis, a civil engineering firm. He had lived alone in Gaithersburg, Maryland, for twenty-five years prior to his death.[12]

The DC Sniper murdered again two days later. Keith Bridges, a fifty-three-year-old businessman and father of six children, was shot in the back and killed at a gas station in Virginia on October 11. He had stopped to gas up the rental vehicle he was driving. After graduating from Hillsdale College, Bridges went on to earn a Master's of Business Administration degree from the prestigious Wharton School of Economics at the University of Pennsylvania. A self-help organizational entrepreneur, he cofounded the MATAH Network, a distribution firm catering to African American clients, and P.O.W.E.R, or People Organizing and Working for Economic Rebirth.[13]

An off-duty FBI agent named Linda Franklin was killed on October 14. The forty-seven-year-old was helping her husband, Ted, load shelves into their car when she was shot and killed. She had earned an honor's degree in education from the University of Florida and was a terrorism expert at the FBI at the time of her death. She was also a cancer survivor.[14]

THE DC SNIPER TELEPHONES

The Rockville Police Department received a call from the DC Sniper at 4:45 P.M. on October 15. The caller spoke from a pay phone in Woodbridge, Virginia. He said, "Don't say anything—just listen. We're the people causing the killing in your area. Look on the tarot card. It says 'Call me God. Do not release to the press.' We have called you three times to set up negotiations. We've gotten no response. People have died." The dispatcher tried to stall the caller, telling him "I need to refer you to the Montgomery County Hotline. We're not investigating the crime. Would you like the number?"[15] The caller hung up.

The content of this call included four important facts. First, the caller identified himself as the DC Sniper. A second important item mentioned was the authenticating phrase, "Call me God." This was included so that police would know that they were talking to the note-writer, and the killer. A third important content dimension of this call was the claim that the DC Sniper had tried unsuccessfully on several occasions to contact the authorities. This theme of course was continued in the lengthy Ponderosa note. A final noteworthy aspect of the content of this call is the claim that victims were shot because of the previous unsuccessful communication attempts.

The DC Sniper made at least three calls to the Rockville Police Department on October 17. The first was placed at 4:35 P.M., and little is known about this call. About an hour later, at 5:40 P.M., another call was made to the police department, where public information officer Derek Baliles took it. The caller said, "I am God! Don't you know who you're dealing with? Just check out the murder-robbery in Montgomery if you don't believe me!"[16] This later call included two important content items. First, the legitimizing "I am God" phrase was included. And, the caller provided investigators with their first inkling of a link between the D.C.-area shootings and previous shootings in other states. This link led to the eventual apprehension of the DC Sniper suspects. The theme of all of these calls—the caller's authenticity and the seriousness of the sniper's resolve.

The style of this brief call can be characterized as arrogant and abusive. The caller wanted to show his superiority to the police by giving them previously unknown information to establish his "street cred" (or credibility) as a criminal. The call was smug and patronizing.

Later that evening, frustrated by the two unsuccessful calls to the police, the DC Sniper called a priest at St. Ann's Roman Catholic Church in Ashland, Virginia. Monsignor William Sullivan received a call from an older man who said, "Here, someone wants to talk to you." A younger man then came on the line, "ranting," and incomprehensible because of an accent. This person repeatedly said, "I am God," and told the priest to write it down and tell the police. He also told Sullivan that he had shot a man near St. Ann Street in Montgomery, Alabama.[17]

It is difficult to evaluate meaningfully and accurately so brief a call. However, we can note the caller used the "I am God" identification line, and again, he mentioned a shooting in Montgomery, Alabama. The theme of this and previous calls centered on criticism of police incompetence and self-recognition of the killer's skills.

THE EXTORTION NOTE

A man survived a shooting at a Ponderosa Steakhouse in Ashland, Virginia, on October 19. This attack is best remembered for the letter found tacked to a tree. Jeffery Hopper of Melbourne, Florida, a thirty-seven-year-old man, described as being deeply religious and who performed country music, was shot at 7:59 P.M. He was with his wife, Stephanie, a Boeing engineer on loan to NASA. "I've been shot," he said after the bullet ripped through his abdomen, stomach, pancreas, kidney, and chest. He lost sixty pounds and the normal use of his spleen, pancreas, and stomach.[18]

Hopper was shot to draw attention to the second note, the extortion document. This second message was the longest, a three-page missive with a cover sheet. According to Cannon, "The note was four pages long and had been placed in a bag tacked to a tree."[19] It was found outside the Ponderosa restaurant.

Two *Washington Post* writers analyzed the appearance and writing quality of this second note. It was printed in a neat hand, using a pen, and written on lined notepaper. There were mistakes in grammar, syntax, and spelling—including omitted letters, words, and punctuation—and inconsistent capitalization.[20] The *Washington Post* later suggested that the letter was not written by Malvo, a high school dropout. It conceded, however, "The stars bordering the handwriting on the cover page are more common among teenagers."[21] The stars resembled asterisks. Carole E. Cheski, a linguist in Georgetown, Delaware, has testified on syntactic variations in state and federal criminal trials. She declared, "These are not illiterate ramblings. Not given the letter's use of Roman numerals, gerunds, complex sentences, hyphenations at syllable breaks and parentheses and quotation marks."[22]

An interesting aspect of this note was the connection to rap music.

The note concluded with, "Word Is Bond." Songs by several recording artists, including Busta Rhymes and House of Pain, include that phrase. A song by House of Pain begins, "Word is bond. Pop pop pop pop. Grab your chest. Now ya bleedin' (punk)."[23]

Montgomery County Police Chief Charles Moose responded to the note, calling a last minute news conference to address the sniper directly: "To the person who left us a message at the Ponderosa last night: You gave us a phone number. We do want to talk with you. Call us at the number you provided."[24]

The U.S. Secret Service Crime Laboratory's Questioned Documents Branch determined that the note was in the same handwriting as the tarot card message. Because an incorrect telephone number was given in the note, the FBI set up teams at both numbers, in case either number was called.

The second note had a cover page. It read:

> "For you Mr Police"
>> "Call me God"
>> Do not release to the
>> press.

There were two stars over the message and three stars beneath. The letter itself reads as follows (with errors intact):

> For you Mr Police
> "Call me God"
> Do not release to the press
> We have tried to contact you
> to start negotiations, But the
> incompetence of your forces in
> (i) Montgomery Police Dept. "Officer Derick"
> at 240 772 9000 Friday
> (ii) Rockville Police dept. "female officer"
> at 301 309 3100
> (iii) Task Force "FBI" "Female"
> at 1 888 32_ 8800 (four times)
> (iv) priest at ashland
> (v) ___ Washington DC at {Redacted}
> These people took of calls
> for a hoax or a joke, so your
> failure to respond has cost
> you five lives

If stopping the killing is
more important than catching us
now, the you will accept our
demand which are nonnego-
tiable
(i) You will place ten million
dollar in Bank of america
Account no. {Redacted}
{Redacted}
Pin no. {Redacted}
Activation date {Redacted}
Exp. date {Redacted}
name: {Redacted}
member since {Redacted}
Platinum Visa account
we will have unlimited ["withdra" is crossed out]
withdrawl at any atm world-
wide
You will activate the bank
account, credit card, and Pin
number/
we will contact you at
(ashland, VA)
Ponderosa Buffet tel # {Redacted}
6:00 Sunday Morning
You have until 9:00 A.M.
Monday morning to complete
transaction
Try to catch us withdrawing
at least you will have less
body bags
(BUT)
(ii) If trying to catch us now
more important, then prepare
your body bags
If we give you our word
that is what takes place
"Word is Bond"
P.S. Your children are not
safe anywhere at any time.

This second written communication from the DC Sniper was the longest, and it probably was the focus of the crimes, from the criminal's perspective. The murders were committed as leverage to extort ten million dollars. Numerous aspects of the content of this note are worthy of consideration. The extortion message began with a reference to the legitimacy-establishing phrase, "For you Mr. Police 'Call me God.'" The snipers wanted the authorities to know that this message was from the killers, not imposters. As in the initial tarot card–borne message, there was a request to keep the message away from the media. The extortion demand, and the killer's terms and instructions, comprised the theme of this note. There was considerable criticism of the police, too.

Frustration was evident in the note's lengthy criticism of law enforcement personnel staffing the telephone tip lines at a number of locations. It complained that "We have tried to contact you to start negotiations," but that contact was prevented by "the incompetence of your forces." The note listed five different phone calls; four were to the police, and one to a priest. The note criticized "Officer Derick," a "Rockville Police dept. 'female officer'," a "Task Force 'FBI' 'Female'," and someone at an unidentified institution in Washington, D.C.

The consequences of the delayed "negotiations" were fatal. The note declared, "your failure to respond has cost you five lives." The note demanded a specified amount of money ($10 million) to stop killing, and it also specified the manner in which the funds were to be made available. A stolen VISA card was to be set up with worldwide, unrestricted access. The note specified the mode and timing of future communication from the killers. The note told authorities to await a call at a specified phone number at 6:00 A.M. on Sunday, October 20. In addition, the authorities were given a deadline of 9:00 A.M. Monday, October 21. The consequences of failure to comply with the note's threatening demands were made clear "Try to catch us withdrawing at least you will have less body bags."

The note's chilling postscript was initially withheld by the police, but was eventually released in the public interest. "Your children are not safe anywhere at any time" was an effective conclusion. It clearly conveyed the killer's seriousness of purpose.

The style of this note might best be characterized as calculated and lengthy. It is noteworthy that the note named or otherwise identified four law enforcement personnel whose telephone behavior irritated the killers, resulting in five more murders. A lot of thought went into the planning and writing of the note. There were spacing and textual organizational devices, like enumeration, and it was embellished with art, as two stars preceded the message and three ended it. Despite the careful preparation, there were several mistakes. "Of" was used instead of "our," and the "n" was deleted from the word "then," resulting in the unintended word "the." The notewriter also incorrectly listed the telephone number to be called to initiate contact at the Ponderosa in Ashland, Virginia, writing it as (804) 798-9205, when in fact the last four digits should have been 8205.

THE SNIPER CALLS AGAIN

Three days later the DC Sniper was back on the telephone, making killing-related calls. The FBI Tip Line received a call on Sunday, October 20, at 9:40 A.M. from the DC Sniper. Police were instructed to search the woods near the Ponderosa restaurant to find the lengthy note wrapped in plastic and tacked to a tree. The DC Sniper placed a final call to the designated Ponderosa number on October 21. "Call me God," the caller repeatedly stated, in a call that reminded the police that the sniper's demands were not negotiable. The call was described as "jumbled, the words hard to decipher."[25] The call ended with a repetition of the threat to children. It is worth noting that again, the caller established his authenticity with the "Call me God" signal. Other repeated content themes were the nonnegotiable demands and the threats to the safety of children.

FINAL MURDER AND COMMUNICATION

Conrad Johnson was the final DC Sniper slaying victim. Johnson, called "Ceejay" or "Rad" by family, friends, and acquaintances, was born in Kingston, Jamaica, and moved to Maryland with his family when he was ten years old. The six-foot-tall, 235-pound man and his wife, Denise, had two sons. Johnson drove a bus on the Montgomery County Ride-On bus route. As his bus was parked that morning on Grand Pre Road, near Connecticut Avenue, Johnson stepped out onto the top step of the vehicle. He was shot in the upper stomach.[26]

According to two law enforcement sources, the last written

communication from the DC Sniper was a note found near where Johnson was killed. The note reportedly demanded $10 million, the same request that was made in a note found at a previous DC Sniper shooting site.[27] "Your incompetence has cost you another life," this third note reportedly declared. Cannon added that this last note "again repeated the demand for money, and the threat to harm children."[28]

It is difficult to analyze the content and style of this final note without knowing the precise text. Nevertheless, certain conclusions can be advanced. The DC Sniper claimed that another person was shot solely because of the communication difficulties between them and the police. This third note also mentioned both the $10 million extortion demand and the threat to children. The style can be characterized as abusive, taunting, and controlling. It was reportedly relatively brief. The note author can be fairly described as arrogant and manipulative.

INCRIMINATING COMMUNICATION CLUES

Computer communication figured prominently in the DC Sniper case. The suspects in the case were linked to a stolen laptop, which in turn was linked to the shootings. Again, the killer's communication proved to be potentially incriminating when phone calls revealed too much. The suspects were identified and arrested when their Montgomery, Alabama, shooting was linked to the DC Sniper murders because of the phone calls to the police and the FBI Tip Line. ABC News reported that a stolen laptop found in Muhammad and Malvo's vehicle contained dated journal entries on the shooting attacks in Maryland, Virginia, and Washington, D.C., that killed ten people and injured several others. Other contemporary reports concurred. Subsequent to the arrests on October 24, police linked the sniper attacks to Muhammad and Malvo through a stolen Sony Viao laptop found in their car. Malvo and Muhammad reportedly stole the Sony laptop from Paul LaRuffa, a Clinton, Maryland, restaurant owner. LaRuffa was "shot six times at close range" on September 6, 2002.[29] LaRuffa's assailants took $3,000 in cash and the computer from the Margellina Restaurant.

Muhammad used the computer often. The *New York Times* reported that residents of the Washington area who believed they saw Muhammad and Malvo, said Muhammad was frequently observed working on the laptop in his car or at Y.M.C.A centers. One witness described "blue light glowing from the passenger side of the car" where Muhammad and

Malvo were residing. She thought it was from a television, but "another look revealed that the blue light was coming from a laptop computer, not a TV."[30]

The computer thieves tried to remove the evidence of their crime. An attempt was made to erase the highly visible product serial number on the bottom of the laptop. But police confirmed that it was the stolen laptop thanks to a camouflaged identification number and a hidden computer file created by the original owner.[31]

A November 8 report hinted at the significance of the laptop. The police, it claimed, had found the most incriminating evidence yet. A Sony laptop computer discovered in the suspects' possession on their arrest suggested that they had cataloged their crimes.[32] "You could basically press the print button on that laptop and close a pretty strong case. At the very least, it puts them at the scene of places where they have been accused of shootings," said an investigation source. Another official described the material as a daily criminal diary.[33]

Phone calls made by Malvo were the clue leading to his identification as a suspect. According to a media report, "It came down to three calls....One, police say, came from the sniper himself. Those led police to a killing in Montgomery, Ala. A fingerprint in Alabama gave them a name. That name gave them another name and a local connection."[34]

THE DC SNIPERS

Malvo and Muhammad were convicted in the initial DC Sniper trials, as this book went to press. Malvo, a seventeen-year-old Jamaican national, and the forty-one-year-old Muhammad were arrested on October 24, 2002, and charged with six counts of first-degree murder in Montgomery County, Maryland. Both were also indicted on similar charges in Washington, D.C., Baton Rouge, Louisiana, and Montgomery, Alabama. Muhammad was also charged on October 29 with violation of a federal extortion law, in a death penalty case. A Virginia jury convicted Muhammad on November 24, 2003, and recommended the death penalty. In a March 9, 2004, decision, Circuit Court judge Leroy F. Millette Jr. accepted the jury's recommendation, and set Muhammad's punishment as death. The next day, Malvo was sentenced to life in prison without the possibility of parole.

The two reportedly lived in a 1990 Chevrolet Caprice during the murder spree that terrorized the District of Columbia and captivated the nation. The vehicle was modified with a concealed rifle port to facilitate clandestine sniping. The Caprice was noted repeatedly at crime scene roadblocks, but excited no alarm because authorities were searching for a white van.

They lived a spartan lifestyle, staying when they could in homeless shelters and Y.M.C.A. facilities. Nathaniel Osbourne befriended them when they came to his diner looking for his brother Walford, whom they had met in Antigua. He said that he "felt pity for the two, who appeared disheveled and seemed to have little money." Muhammad and Malvo wore "the same rumpled clothes, day after day," according to Osbourne.[35] In Bellingham, Washington, the two lived for a time at the Lighthouse Mission.[36]

The two shared a passion for the same nutritional and lifestyle orientation. Osbourne said they always had their copy of Donald P. Reid's *The Tao of Health, Sex and Longevity* with them.[37] This book, according to a brief self-description, introduces Westerners to Taoist philosophy, including information on nutrition, breathing, diet, "sex therapy," and aphrodisiacs. One final common characteristic of Malvo and Muhammad was mentioned. They seemed to enjoy playing basketball together.[38]

John Lee Malvo Jr.

Also known as Lee Boyd Malvo and Lee Malvo, John Lee Malvo Jr. was born in Kingston (Jamaica) Hospital, on February 18, 1985. The birth certificate does not list a father's name. Malvo was an illegal alien in the United States, having emigrated with his mother, Una James. They reportedly left their former home of St. Elizabeth, Jamaica, for Haiti. After a time they continued on to Miami in a tugboat.

The family traveled on to Bellingham where Malvo enrolled in Bellingham High School. School officials were repeatedly assured that his transcripts were en route. When his promised transcripts still had not arrived more than a month into the school year, school officials called the police.

Malvo's mother and Muhammad, who met in Bellingham, did not always coexist peacefully. A U.S. Border Patrol report documented that the Bellingham Police Department responded to a domestic disturbance call involving the two on December 19, 2001.[39] She had Muhammad arrested.

Malvo and his mother were subsequently arrested and detained for the Immigration and Naturalization Service (INS) by a Border Patrol agent. They were transferred to INS custody in Seattle, Washington, but were released pending deportation hearings.

After Malvo's arrest, his defense attorney requested a psychiatric evaluation for his client. "We're not certain what makes Mr. Malvo tick," declared Michael Arif.[40] The judge declined the request at that time, saying it might be in order later in the process.

Malvo reportedly confessed to being the primary shooter in the DC Sniper shootings. But Malvo's attorneys indicated that they would try to suppress the confession, because he should not have been interrogated without a lawyer being present. One Malvo attorney, Mark Petrovich, contended, "Knowing circumvention of the right to have counsel present is a violation of the Sixth Amendment right to counsel." Robert F. Horan Jr., Fairfax County, Virginia's, chief prosecutor, countered that, "He understood the warnings given to him, the nature of his rights, and he voluntarily waived them."[41] The court sided with the state. The Associated Press reported that, "Sniper suspect Lee Boyd Malvo's laughing confession to two of the deadly attacks can be used against him at trial this fall, a judge ruled Tuesday."[42]

Malvo's demeanor was described and criticized as inappropriate. Raymond Morrogh, a Fairfax County, Virginia, Deputy Commonwealth's Attorney, observed Malvo's behavior during the interrogation sessions and as he confessed as, "calm and rather boastful."[43] Malvo reportedly told investigators, "You can't build a jail strong enough to hold me," and "Kill me. I don't care. Torture me. . . . Nothing bothers me."[44] The Associated Press reported, "Washington-area sniper suspect Lee Boyd Malvo bragged about his shooting prowess, taunted investigators and said he shot some victims in the head for horrific effect."[45] "Evidently, Malvo found it amusing that as the errant bullet flew past the boy's head he swatted at the air as if a bee had buzzed too close," recalled Morrogh.[46] June Boyle, a homicide investigator who interviewed Malvo, said, "I asked where he shot her [Linda Franklin]. He laughed and pointed at his head."[47]

In custody, Malvo has experienced some difficulties. He complained that his jail-issue mattress was too thin and that he was not allowed to have reading material. In addition, he said that his cell was illuminated twenty-four hours a day and that he was being denied vegetarian meals. Juvenile Court Judge Charles Maxfield denied a request by Michael Arif, Malvo's attorney, for better treatment. "You're going to have to present a lot more evidence" of maltreatment to justify any changes in Malvo's custodial conditions, Maxfield told Arif when he denied the defense counsel's motion.[48]

John Allen Muhammad

He was born John Lee Allen in rural Louisiana. He graduated from Scotlandville High School in 1978. The warrant for his arrest issued on October 23, 2002, described him as a six-foot, one-inch tall, 180-pound black man, who should be considered armed and dangerous. He married Carol A. Williams in Baton Rouge, Louisiana, in 1981. He and his high school sweetheart separated four years later; they were divorced in 1987.

Former neighbors had a high impression of him. Kay Whitlock lived in the block behind the Allen's former residence in Tacoma, Washington. She recalled him as being "a tough disciplinarian," but she never saw him being violent with the children or his wife.[49]

He joined the Army National Guard of Louisiana directly after his graduation from high school. In the service, he qualified as a sharpshooter during U.S. Army rifle training. His second wife, Mildred Muhammad, recalled that he wanted to be a career soldier.[50] Muhammad's military career, however, encountered problems. He was convicted at two courts-martial. One involved his striking a superior officer, and the other resulted from his failure to report for duty and disobeying a command.

What changed Muhammad? He told Mildred Muhammad that in the 1991 Persian Gulf War, black soldiers were victimized by discrimination. He was accused of dropping an incendiary grenade into a tent, so he was hog-tied and handcuffed. Then, when sirens sounded later to warn soldiers to don their gas masks, no one came to help him. It had only been a drill, a fact he was unaware of, and the experience embittered him.[51]

Muhammad met Mildred in 1985, while still married to his first wife. He concealed his marital status from her for a month. But she kept seeing him because he promised to divorce his wife and marry her, which he did. "I was intrigued by him keeping his word. He was the only man who said he was going to do something and did it. That was the attraction for me," Mildred recalled. Mildred Muhammad called her husband's Gulf War experience the cause of his "transformation from a loving husband to an angry, controlling man." Because of these changes, he became threatening toward her. She claims that he promised to kill her.[52]

In addition to his domestic charges, Muhammad faced an investigation by Antiguan authorities. They conducted a probe into Muhammad's role in producing and selling false documents, such as birth certificates and passports. (This criminal activity may explain Malvo's apparent ease of entry into this country.) Muhammad had an unusual exit from Antigua. He spent two nights in jail, then walked out of a police station after one of the two guards unexpectedly went home at 11:39 A.M. The remaining guard noted that Muhammad left at 11:40 A.M.[53]

CONCLUSION

The DC Sniper crimes were communication based when we consider the diversity and significance of communication acts present in this case. The extortion attempt relied entirely on communication between the DC Sniper and the police. When the initial telephone contact attempts failed, the third note became necessary, as did subsequent telephone calls.

The first note was on the tarot card. It was a very important part of the DC Sniper's communication plans and overall murder/extortion system. It included the phrase "I am God," which was used in the second note to verify the authenticity of that second communication. The second note was the extortion demand, the key to the crimes and the motive for the shootings.

In addition to these explicit, purposive communications with the authorities, the perpetrators reportedly recorded the DC Sniper murders. The computerized diary allegedly kept by the snipers did more than exemplify the use of computer technology in serial murders; it also manifested the tendency of these killers to maintain written records of their exploits.

These communications provided the means that led to the arrest and conviction of the DC Sniper suspects. Without the information from the telephone calls, the police had no suspects. Coupled with the telephone calls, the killers' desire to keep a record of their exploits aided the authorities in ending a community's season of fear.

3 The Mad Butcher

He was probably the most effective major American serial killer, though he is unknown to most people. He was never "officially" caught, although one possible suspect died in a mental hospital. Another committed suicide in jail. He successfully evaded detection at the hands of Eliot Ness, famed for putting Al Capone in prison and cleaning up Chicago. He sent Ness taunting cards and letters. He announced in a letter to the Cleveland chief of police that he had moved to Los Angeles. He made a taunting late-night call to the home of a detective working on his case. He also carved an enigmatic message into the torso of a victim.

He did not just murder his victims. They were decapitated, dismembered, subjected to unknown chemical processes, and scattered throughout Kingsbury Run, Lake Erie, and adjacent parts of Cleveland, Ohio, between 1934 and 1939. In addition, a series of similar crimes occurred in New Castle, Pennsylvania, between 1925 and 1939. A trio of bodies—decapitated and dismembered—was found in a boxcar not far from Cleveland in August 1940. One of the corpses had the word "Nazi" carved into it. In 1950, more than a decade after the earlier Cleveland murders, a similar crime was discovered in Kingsbury Run. Samuel Gerber, the coroner who handled the prior cases remarked, "The work resembles exactly that of the torso murderer."[1]

The communication theme of the Mad Butcher messages initially conveyed the killer's contempt and disrespect for the police and press. Then the most important single message, a letter, announced that the Butcher had left Cleveland for Los Angeles. And apparently he did.

THE KILLINGS BEGIN

It is uncertain precisely how many murders the Mad Butcher committed. The offender's success in disposing of remains in Lake Erie and throughout Kingsbury Run complicated this task, as did the occurrence of a number of similar crimes at the same time and later that may or may not have been related. We simply do not know, and as John J. Badal pointed out, it is not a definite fact that one killer was responsible for murdering all of the victims who are commonly considered to have been killed by the Mad Butcher. This Mad Butcher historian noted eight similar crimes during the same period, but committed elsewhere and not counted as Mad Butcher victims.[2] Steven Nickel, another expert on this case, realized that "it is impossible to determine" precisely how many Mad Butcher victims there were. He recognized the official total of twelve victims, but added that related killings increased the number of murders to at least twenty.[3] After the discovery of the McKees Rocks, Pennsylvania, bodies, Detective Peter Meyerlo told a reporter, "I think it is safe to say that the Mad Butcher's victims now total twenty-three."[4] Detective Meyerlo later estimated that there were at least thirty-four Mad Butcher murders, and perhaps as many as forty.

Parts of a woman were discovered on September 5, 1934, in the sand of Euclid Beach. She never was identified. Frank LaGassie of Beulah Park, near Cleveland, found the remains on the Lake Erie beach at East 156th Street. According to one account, all that was found was the decaying bottom half of a female torso, with the legs cut off at the knees. It was estimated that the woman was in her mid-to-late thirties, and was about five feet, six inches tall, and weighed approximately 115 pounds.[5] The body had been subjected to some type of chemical process. The skin was described as being red-hued, and relatively tough. Dr. W. H. Hay, Director of the City Chemical Laboratory, speculated that the chemical used was calcium hydrochloride or chloride of lime.[6]

About two weeks prior to this discovery, Joseph Hejduk of North Perry, Ohio, had found what he thought were human remains on the same stretch of beach. When told by a policeman that it was only an animal carcass, he buried the material. After reading of the September 5 finding, he again called the authorities, who eventually disinterred the remains and found that they matched the parts found by LaGassie.

About a year later, on September 23, 1935, two boys stumbled upon the decapitated and dismembered remains of two victims. One was identified as Edward Andrassy. The head of the other corpse was buried, and hair poked through the surface of the dirt so it would be found.

Sixteen-year-old James Wagner and his twelve-year-old friend Peter Kostura saw one body from the top of weed-covered Jackass Hill. Wagner told Kostura, "There's a dead man with no head down there."[7] Wagner had seen Andrassy's body. He had been decapitated and emasculated, and was lying on his side, nude except for black socks. His head was found about twenty feet away.[8] Andrassy was five feet, eleven inches tall, weighed 150 pounds, and had a light complexion and brown hair.

A second body was located about twenty to thirty feet away from the first body by the police searching for the rest of Andrassy. This unidentified victim was badly decomposed and had been treated with the same chemical as was the body of the dismembered woman. The head of this victim was found about seventy feet away from the body. The victim was five feet, six inches tall, and weighed 165 pounds. He had perfect teeth, brown eyes, and dark brown hair.

There were a couple of interesting aspects of this dual murder crime scene. First, the bodies were displayed; the scene was deliberately staged by the killer. The bodies were lying side-by-side, posed with their arms at the sides and their legs and feet together. Both men's genitals had been cut off and were found in a pile near the unidentified victim's body.

AN INITIAL COMMUNICATION?

A note was discovered at one of the early crime scenes. Cleveland Police Department Detectives Orley May and Emil Musil interviewed Jerome Kacirek. The twenty-five-year-old, who lived on East 49th, had found a bloodstained, typed note at the crime scene on September 24, the day after the bodies were discovered. Interestingly, the note contained precise instructions for cremating a human body.[9]

It is difficult to know what to make of this note. Although it does not explicitly refer to the decapitation/dismemberment deeds, it was found at a crime scene within twenty-four hours of the discovery of remains. And, it was bloody and referred to techniques for body disposal. It seems extremely unlikely that this was only a coincidence.

MORE MAD BUTCHER KILLINGS

On January 26, 1936, a butcher found parts of a woman's body in a basket near his shop. More of her body was located on February 7 in a different neighborhood, but her head was never found. The winter of 1936 was one of the coldest on record in the Midwest, and this killing was discovered in the heart of the prolonged cold spell. Barking dogs signaled the grim packages at the back of the White Front Meat Market at 2002 Central Avenue. The lower half of a woman's torso, both thighs, and a right arm and hand were discovered carefully wrapped and packed inside two half-bushel baskets.[10]

The body was identified as that of Flo Polillo. Born in Ashtabula, Ohio, she was a woman of many names: Florence Geneveive Sawdey, Florence Grant, Clara Dunn, Florence Martin, Clara Martin, Florence Gallagher, and Florence Davis. Polillo had been arrested for prostitution in Cleveland in 1931, and for solicitation in Washington, D.C. in 1934. She was convicted of illegal liquor sales in Cleveland in 1935. She was about five feet, seven inches tall, weighed 160 pounds, and had a light complexion. She had dark chestnut hair and eyes, but her hair was dyed red. The forty-one-year-old woman lived at 3205 Carnegie Avenue in Cleveland. She was last seen on January 24, at 8:30 P.M., by her landlady.[11]

When parts of Polillo's body were found, they were wrapped in newspaper. Nickel claimed that, "Some of the parts were wrapped in newspapers dated January 25, 1936 [the previous day] and August 11, 1935."[12] Another account suggested that the body parts were wrapped in pages of an old newspaper.[13] In addition to the paper wrapped around the body parts, detectives found a two-piece set of white cotton underwear wrapped in the *Cleveland News* of November 19, 1935.

A man's head was discovered in Kingsbury Run on June 5, and the rest of his body was discovered the next day, but he was never identified. Louis Cheeley, eleven, and Gomez Ivey, thirteen, found the head at about 8:20 A.M. The head was partly obscured from sight, partially wrapped in some trousers; it was lying on its side, eyes closed, mouth open. The head was described as belonging to a male, aged twenty to thirty-five, with brown eyes, thick reddish-brown hair, and five missing teeth.[14]

The body was found the next day. It was located about one thousand yards from where the head was discovered, and a distance less than that from where Andrassy and the unidentified man had been located. Unlike other Mad Butcher victims, this man was not a vagrant, but a well-built, well-nourished man who had his nails neatly trimmed and an undigested meal of baked beans in his stomach at his death.[15]

Seventeen-year-old Marie Barkley was walking in the woods at 11:30 A.M. on July 22, 1936, near West 98th Street and the Rayon plant.

She stumbled on the nude, badly decomposed, decapitated body of a white male. Later that day, Cleveland Police Department Sergeant James Finnerty located the head ten to eighteen feet away from where the body had been discovered.[16] The victim was killed where he was found, unlike the earlier victims who had all been killed elsewhere and relocated after death.[17]

This man was about forty years of age, and was five feet, five inches tall, weighed 145 pounds, and had long brown hair and blue eyes. The body was found chest-down, less than one hundred yards from railroad tracks. Reportedly, the head was only a skull with a few strands of hair still attached.[18]

A seventh victim—or parts of him—were observed in and recovered from a large stagnant pond in Kingsbury Run on September 10. Jerry Harris, a vagrant from St. Louis watching a train in hopes of catching a ride, noticed the body at 11:15 A.M. The upper half of a human male body was missing its arms and head. The lower portion of the trunk, with legs amputated at the hips, was located nearby. According to Coroner Arthur J. Pearse (or Pearce), the emasculated victim was twenty-two to twenty-eight years old, about five feet, nine inches or five feet, ten inches in height, and weighed 150 pounds, and had brown hair.[19] Pathologist Reuben Strauss offered slightly different estimates, describing a victim who was between twenty-five and thirty years old, at five feet, ten inches tall and weighing 145 pounds.[20]

Newspapers also figured prominently at this crime scene. Police found a man's blue denim workshirt at the site where they believed the body parts were dumped into the water. The shirt was wrapped in the September 4, 1936, edition of the *Cleveland Plain Dealer*.

On February 23, 1937, part of a woman's torso was found on Euclid Beach, at the same spot where the first remains were found. Robert Smith discovered her body in Lake Erie while collecting driftwood.[21] Another version has Smith checking on his sailboat when he made the horrible discovery.[22] He found the top part of a woman's torso, without her head and arms. It was approximately 1:40 P.M. when he noticed the grisly object, grounded just offshore in the cold green Lake Erie water. More of her body turned up on May 5, while her head remained missing.

She was in her mid-twenties, it was estimated, and between five feet, five inches and five feet, seven inches tall. She weighed between 100 and 120 pounds, and had brown hair and a fair complexion. Experts disagreed over whether or not she had borne children: Gerber said she had one or two children, while Strauss thought she was childless.[23]

On June 6, the decapitated skeleton of a black woman named Rose
Wallace was found. Fourteen-year-old Russell Lever found the gruesome objects at 5:40 P.M. A skull, and then other parts of a skeleton, were
discovered in a trash-filled field. Wallace, forty, was a full-time prostitute living at 2027 Scoville Avenue. She was last seen on August 21,
1936, almost a year before parts of her bones turned up. Coroner Gerber
disagreed that the victim was Wallace, but most others accept that
identification based on dental records, other physical similarities, and
the fact that Wallace never was seen after that date.[24] Pathologist
Strauss described the deceased as a black female, about five feet tall,
weighing one hundred pounds, and approximately thirty to forty years
of age.[25]

Wallace was discovered in a burlap bag, which contained her bones
along with some tattered clothes and an advertisement from the *Cleveland Plain Dealer*. Cleveland Detective David Cowles reportedly used
ultraviolet light scans to discern fingerprints on the three-week-old
newspapers and the rest of the items discovered in the burlap bag, but
without success.[26]

Exactly one month later, John Smith, a private in the 147th Infantry,
spotted a bobbing object in the Cuyahoga River. Smith and his fellow
soldiers were in Cleveland because of an impending strike of steel
companies. At 5:30 A.M., Smith saw the white object, as did fellow Private Edgar M. Steinbrecher. The next day, the forearms were found,
and, subsequently, the right upper arm was discovered on July 10, with
the right lower leg and foot found on July 14.[27]

The victim was described as a forty-year-old, well-built man. He was
between five feet, eight inches and five feet, ten inches tall, and weighed
between 150 and 160 pounds. The victim had been disemboweled, and
his heart was removed.

A one-hundred-pound burlap bag of Purina Chicken Feed was pulled
from the river later that day. Inside the bag was part of a human torso.
It was wrapped in newspapers that were three weeks old.

A year later, between April 8 and May 2, 1938, parts of a woman
were fished from the Cuyahoga River. Her head and some appendages
never were found. Steve Morosky, thirty-five, discovered a body part
floating in the Cuyahoga River at about 2:15 P.M. on April 8. He saw the
lower half of a human leg, amputated at the knee and ankle. On May 2,
two burlap bags floating in the river were spotted by Albert Mahaffey,
the West 3rd Street Bridge tender. The bags contained two large pieces
of a woman's torso. Both thighs were included, as was the left foot.
According to the autopsy, this victim was between twenty-five and

thirty years of age. She had been flat chested, and stood between five feet, two inches and five feet, three inches tall and weighed between 115 and 120 pounds. She had most likely given birth to two children.[28]

THE MAD BUTCHER CALLS THE POLICE

On April 10, 1938, the *Cleveland Plain Dealer* reported a serial killer telephone call incident. ''Someone telephoned Peter Meyerlo at 4:00 A.M. and teased him with an undisclosed sexual revelation that the caller described as 'something for your investigation.' '' The brief call was described as an insulting and taunting, obscenity-laced series of rude claims about the murderer's prowess and the ineffectiveness of the police.[29]

Was this phone call from the Mad Butcher? I believe that it was, since Meyerlo would not have told the press about the call unless he gave it credence. Whoever called knew details of the sexual torture inflicted on one of the Mad Butcher's victims, details that were not divulged to the press or to anyone else. One thing is certain. The kind of taunting, disrespectful communication behavior manifested in this call was entirely consistent with the body carving, letters, and crime scene note left by the Mad Butcher.

ANOTHER DOUBLE DISCOVERY

James Dawson, Edward Smith, and James McShack made the grim find in a field at Lakeshore Drive and East 9th Street on August 16, 1938. The female torso, wrapped in paper and a quilt, was found buried in garbage. The head, also wrapped in brown paper, was discovered a few feet away. Her arms and legs were wrapped in brown paper, secured with rubber bands, and protected from the elements in a handmade cardboard carton. She was in her mid-thirties, about five feet, four inches tall. She probably weighed between 120 and 125 pounds, and had very long, light brown hair. Interestingly, she had unusually small hands and very large feet (size 9).

Todd Bartholomew, thirty-nine, and his wife, Cecilia, spotted a second body in the same field at about 7:30 that evening. Within an hour, the skull and more than forty additional pieces of bone were discovered. This second August 16 victim was described as a male in his mid-to-late thirties. He was five feet, seven inches tall and had wavy brown hair. He had suffered a broken nose earlier in life.

A MAD BUTCHER LETTER

There were some letters of potential importance to the Mad Butcher case. The *Cleveland Press* published this letter, which was mailed from Los Angeles in January of 1939:

Chief of Police Matowitz:

You can rest easy now, as I have come to sunny California for the winter. I felt bad operating on those people, but science must advance. I shall astound the medical profession, a man with only a D. C.

What did their lives mean in comparison to hundreds of sick and disease-twisted bodies? Just laboratory guinea pigs found on any public street. No one missed them when I failed. My last case was successful. I now know the feeling of Pasteur, Thoreau and other pioneers.

Right now I have a volunteer who will absolutely prove my theory. They call me mad and a butcher, but the truth will out.

I have failed but once here. The body has not been found and never will be, but the head, minus the features, is buried on Century Boulevard, between Western and Crenshaw. I feel it my duty to dispose of the bodies as I do. It is God's will not to let them suffer. X.[30]

Meyerlo was initially convinced of the authenticity of the letter, but had a change of heart. "He felt the letter was genuine and one of the best solid leads authorities had in the case, but within a year he dismissed it as the ravings of a crank," Badal recalled.[31] Charles DiVere was reportedly identified as the letter-writer in the 1940s, but the police found he was no murderer.

If this controversial letter proved authentic, its content included several salient facts. Perhaps most important item was the alleged killer's reassurance to the people of Cleveland that "You can rest easy now, as I have come to sunny California for the winter." As it turned out, there was at most only one later Cleveland-area killing, besides the McKees Rocks, Pennsylvania, case.

There were numerous allusions to medicine. The killer professed, "I felt bad operating on those people, but science must advance." He noted "hundreds of sick and disease-twisted bodies," and compared himself to famous healers, "I now know the feeling of Pasteur, Thoreau and other pioneers." He added, "Right now I have a volunteer who will absolutely prove my theory." Was the Butcher subtly indicating that he was a doctor?

Perhaps in a slip, or perhaps deliberately, the letter-writer referred to himself by his common nickname, "They call me mad and a butcher, but the truth will out." The killer also admitted to having erred in Los Angeles, "I have failed but once here." This failure resulted in the decapitation and dismemberment of his victim, as he indicated in the letter. The letter ended with a religious justification for the murders.

The style of this missive was relatively sane and low key. It was somewhat informative, with explanatory overtones. The sentence structures were relatively effective and correct, and the vocabulary was that of an educated person. A prominent aspect of the style was its boastfulness, as he promises to "astound" and confound the authorities.

Despite Meyerlo's reservations, I accept the authenticity of this letter. The fact that the Black Dahlia and related murders began in Los Angeles shortly after the Mad Butcher claims to have relocated there authenticates the letter. The significance of this letter is in the writer's confidence that he would not be caught (he was correct), and his felt need to communicate with the police, to tease and torment them and prove his superiority—his rhetorical themes.

THE McKEES ROCKS MURDERS

On May 3, 1940, three decapitated bodies were found in boxcars at McKees Rocks, Pennsylvania, near Pittsburgh. The Pittsburgh & Lake Erie Railroad was conducting an inspection of railroad property at the suburban Pittsburgh railyard when a strong stench led them to a grisly discovery. A burlap sack in a corner of a boxcar contained a human body cut into seven pieces. Only the head was missing. Within minutes, a second horrible finding occurred. Three railcars away, police found a decapitated naked corpse lying in a boxcar. There was no trace of the man's head. This second victim was later identified as James Nicholson. (You will learn more about his death and subsequent body defilement later in this chapter.) A final victim was discovered in a boxcar at the end of the train. A woman had been cut apart. She was sliced into sections at her neck, waist, hips, and shoulders. Her head was missing, like the other two McKees Rocks' victims. Parts of her body appeared to be charred.

This grim finding elicited considerable interest in Cleveland, and a delegation was dispatched immediately to investigate any link to the Mad Butcher. Included in this group were Assistant Safety Director

Robert Chamberlin, Deputy Inspector David Cowles, and Cleveland Police Department Detectives Peter Meyerlo and Lloyd Trunk. One interesting finding from the autopsy of the McKees Rocks' victims, according to Pittsburgh Deputy Coroner Anthony Sappo, who conducted the autopsy, was that "The killer had a definite knowledge of surgery."[32]

The same deliberate, intentional use of newspapers was reported in the McKees Rocks, Pennsylvania, case. Nickel noted that numerous bloody pages from the December 11, 1939, edition of the *Youngstown Vindicator* lay around and under the bodies.[33] This seemed to link these crimes to the Mad Butcher and demonstrated his apparent interest in newspapers. This characteristic use of newspapers as funeral shrouds may have been a sarcastic statement by the killer about the interest of the press in his deeds, as the press intensely "covered" the murders.

A BODY MESSAGE

The Mad Butcher carved the word "NAZI" into Nicholson's chest, the "I" ended just below the neck and the "Z" was intentionally inverted. Local authorities, without exception, attributed the crimes to Cleveland's butcher, Newton recalled.[34] It was widely believed that the Mad Butcher had left Cleveland for McKees Rocks. Or had he returned from California, if the January 1939 letter was authentic?

Nicholson was convicted of burglary in Illinois at the age of twenty, and he received a ten-year sentence, of which he served half. Convicted a second time of burglary, in Wisconsin, he served only a year before earning early release from Waupan State Prison as a model prisoner. He was arrested once for trespassing on railroad property and twice for vagrancy in Greenville, South Carolina, in July 1938. The Mad Butcher is believed to have sought victims in railroad cars, another fact that seemed to link Nicholson's death to those of the Torso Slayer.

Despite its extreme brevity, we can examine both the content and the style of this body message. The single word, "NAZI," might have been more than merely an arbitrary selection. This murder took place in 1940, when Nazi Germany was succeeding in its conquest of Europe. Was this a political message? We do not know anything about Nicholson's politics, only that he was reportedly a homosexual and a former convict. In light of Nicholson's sexual preference, some police speculated on a sexual motive behind the Mad Butcher.

The style of this body message was definitely brief, as a one-word sentence, without punctuation, was employed. The word was carved in five-inch-tall letters, on the victim's chest. I conclude that the carving was a fundamentally expressive act, a succinct, attention-getting verbalization designed to taunt and confuse the police and to horrify the public.

A LETTER FROM THE YMCA

One other letter attributed to the Mad Butcher warrants attention. According to the top of the letter it was sent from Albany, New York. The date given was Saturday, January 24, 1942, and at the top of the letter was written, "A killer at large." The brief letter, with errors intact, read: "Sir/Is their any reward for the so called mad butcher of Kingsbury Run if so rit at once." The letter was signed, "Norman Carter, Railroad YMCA, 607 Broadway, Albany New York."[35]

Mad Butcher case detectives gave this letter some credibility. Again, in an instance of serial killer communications serving to authenticate each other, detectives noticed that there were substantial similarities in penmanship between this letter and the Nicholson body carving. "Something about the formation of the letters—especially the 'A'—attracted Meyerlo's attention; they bore a strong resemblance to the word 'NAZI,' with the inverted 'Z' carved into the chest of one of the three McKees Rocks victims," Badal reports.[36]

The content of this letter was interesting in that it referred to the serial killer by name, calling him "the so called mad butcher of Kingsbury Run." The use of the qualification, "so called," is potentially important. Was the writer debunking somehow the notorious serial slayer? Or was he merely "having fun," with the police, communicating with them incognito?

The letter was written for one purpose: to enrich the writer, if possible. He expressed interest in whether or not there was a reward. To facilitate payment of the reward, the author included a name and address in the letter. Or was there a more subtle rhetorical purpose?

The style of this letter differed considerably from the letter mailed from Los Angeles. It was much briefer, a bare thirty-one words. The New York letter seemed to be the work of a near-illiterate. The writer used "their" instead of the correct "there," and spelled "write" as "rit." But relatively difficult-to-spell words like "reward" and "once" were spelled correctly, so it is possible that the writer deliberately tried to appear less intelligent and literate than he was, "fooling" the police.

THE FINAL CLEVELAND MURDER

The police worked this case throughout the 1930s and 1940s. There were no solid leads, and thousands of interviews produced no results. It was thought that the Mad Butcher was history. Then, on July 23, 1950, the body of Robbie Robertson, forty-four, was located in downtown Cleveland. His murder was confirmed as belonging to the Mad Butcher pattern. It was the final such case in Cleveland.

The six-foot-tall Robertson had long brown hair and blue eyes. He had a checkered past, for the times, as a homosexual former convict. He had been arrested a dozen times for public intoxication. Police noted that some previous Mad Butcher victims shared either Robertson's criminal history, sexual preference, or both, but found no solid link between the victims.

Robertson's torso, both arms, and both legs were hidden beneath a steel girder. The body was found when a dog began playing with the other leg. Robertson's head was found under a pile of wood four days later, only twenty feet away from where the rest of the body was discovered.

THE NEW CASTLE MURDERS

The New Castle murders began before the Cleveland murders and were still being committed after the Mad Butcher left Cleveland for good. Investigators pursuing the Mad Butcher were astonished to discover that someone had been committing crimes involving decapitation and dismemberment for ten years in New Castle, Pennsylvania, a small town in western Pennsylvania near Youngstown, Ohio. The total? Seven gruesome decapitation and dismemberment murders were committed in New Castle's "Murder Swamp." Three were almost identical to the Mad Butcher crimes.

In 1921, a woman living in West Pittsburgh, Pennsylvania, near Murder Swamp was found dead in her home, nearly decapitated. Nothing was taken, and nothing in the house had been bothered. Two years later, a young woman's dismembered torso was found floating down a river near the swamp. In the next decade, terrified but angry New Castle residents watched as five more gruesome discoveries of corpses were made in this isolated location.

There was a cessation of Mad Butcher–style murders in New Castle between 1934 and 1939. Then, between 1939 and 1942, the mysterious killer struck six times. John R. Flynn, an assistant to Eliot Ness, was dispatched by Ness to investigate the New Castle crimes and any possible similarity or link to the Mad Butcher murders. Flynn believed that the Cleveland Mad Butcher had either expanded his criminal activities and killing grounds or was emulating the Pennsylvania murderer.[37]

Cleveland investigator, Deputy Inspector David Cowles, arrived at very similar conclusions. He was a forensic expert who noted definite similarities between the most recent New Castle murders and the Cleveland crimes. He admitted, however, that there were no facts linking the two sets of murders.[38] Mad Butcher case investigator Peter Meyerlo was not so reticent, however. He wrote in his memoirs that the New Castle and Cleveland decapitation murders were undoubtedly committed by the same maniac. In fact, Meyerlo reportedly had always believed that the New Castle killings were committed by the Mad Butcher.[39]

A railroad inspector discovered a naked male corpse in an unused boxcar on July 1, 1936, in New Castle, Pennsylvania. The decapitated corpse lay on top of pages from both the *Cleveland Plain Dealer* and *Pittsburgh Press*. Both papers were from July 1933.

THE SWEENEY CORRESPONDENCE

Eliot Ness had a suspect in the crimes. Frank Sweeney was a mentally ill former doctor who inundated Ness with a large volume of threatening notes, that only ended on Sweeney's death. In fact, Ness considered these cards to be important enough to save, instead of disposing of them as crank communications. That is why Ness saved the "greeting cards," sent by Sweeney anonymously.[40]

These cards have been examined by Badal, who described the curious manner in which the cards were addressed: "The sender decorated four of the cards by pasting on pictures clipped from newspapers or magazines. These cards, all sent from Dayton in the mid-1950s to Eliot Ness's office in the Union Commerce Building, are variously addressed to '*Eliot* (Esophogotic) *Ness*,' '*Eliot-Am-Big-U-ous Ness*,' '*Eliot (Head Man) Ness*,' '*Eliot-Direct-Um-Ness*,' and simply '*Eliot-Ness*'."[41]

Does it appear that Sweeney wrote and dispatched these cards? The cards were signed, after a fashion (a demented fashion, at that). Badal noted that "Three of the five cards bear a name, most likely the sender's. Beside the picture of the Deeds Carillon stand the words,

> "A-signature
> The-Sweeney-boy
> R-member,"

and a message next to the pansy ad reads,

> "Good-cheer
> The-American
> Sweeney."

Besides the ad for the poisoner handbook stands the stark pronouncement,

> "F.E. Sweeney-M.D.
> Paranoidal-Nemesis
> The-Better-Half-of-Legal-Exaction
> Will-upon you one day?"[42]

The following Sweeney letter was sent to Eliot Ness from the Veteran's Hospital in Dayton, Ohio, on February 14, 1954:

> Enclosed a few items for your, Personal Perusal, as to Hermacy Reference, "Per Se", should all or any have no significant application— Would that you Present to Special Agent McCord for a Personal Extraction herefrom and if again in the negative, tis no doubt as of some, Perverted, information having Dominant Dwelling, a loft in my, "Wind Sheets," I trust that we shall meet again Amongst more favorable "Federal Issues"?" P.S. 'Phony,' criminalization—Is tough, at any monetary Bargaining? As well as Phony Pschotization?

The letter was signed, "Frank E. Sweeney MD."[43]

Since Sweeney actually signed this letter, we do not have to rely on cryptic self-references and allusions to identify the writer. While it did not directly link Sweeney to the murders, it further demonstrated his precarious mental situation. Taken collectively, the Sweeney letters and cards can be assessed as a body of rhetoric. The content can best be characterized as irrational.

The style of these written messages revealed an intellectual and witty person who was also very disturbed. Written partly in verse and partly in prose, the vocabulary and sentence structure were those of an educated and intelligent person. However, there was a vaguely disquieting tone to these mildly threatening letters, which were intended to upset Ness, his family, and associates. Later in this chapter we learn why Ness suspected this former doctor of being the Mad Butcher.

THE MAD BUTCHER

Here is part of a 1930s-era psychological offender profile, as constructed by Cleveland coroner Samuel Gerber to help in the search for the Mad Butcher:

> He is a person of more than average intelligence, with definite professional knowledge of anatomy but not necessarily a man of surgery. He is large and strong. He probably lives in the section bounding Kingsbury Run where he comes and goes without attracting attention. In all probability he belongs to a higher social stratum than his victims, but can mingle with vagrants without arousing their suspicion. His murders are committed mostly in a laboratory near the Run. He is a pervert who sometimes drugs his victims and may lead a normal life when not absorbed with his sadistic passion.[44]

The Mad Butcher may have been seen—repeatedly—as he sunbathed over the remains of Robbie Robertson. Workers at Norris Brothers Company, movers, located at 2138 Davenport Avenue, saw a heavy-set man in his mid-fifties with thin, graying hair. He sunbathed for twenty minutes a day, every day, for six weeks, on the same year-and-a-half-old pile of scrap steel girders. Suddenly he stopped coming. And at about that time, workers began to notice a sickening odor coming from that same pile; Robertson's body was found there on July 22.

This criminal was known only by media-bestowed nicknames, since he was never conclusively identified or apprehended. The press referred to the unknown murderer as the Torso Murderer, the Mad Butcher, the Horrible Headhunter, and the Phantom of Kingsbury Run. Another list of nicknames mentioned the Headhunter, and the Torso Murderer.[45] A different list of newspaper-coined nicknames was described by Badal. He referred to terms such as fiend, maniac, maniac killer, crazed killer, and human butcher.[46]

A summit meeting of investigators and interested stakeholders was held on September 14, 1936, after the discovery of the sixth body. This

ad hoc group arrived at seven likely generalizations about the unknown killer:

1. All six Torso killings were the work of a single individual operating alone.
2. The killer, while obviously demented and psychotic, was not
   recognizably insane.
3. The killer possessed a definite knowledge of human anatomy
   and some surgical skill, but he had not displayed evidence of
   any actual medical training.
4. The killer was "large and strong."
5. The killer probably lived in or near the Third Precinct or another area close to Kingsbury Run.
6. The killer probably kept a private "workshop" or "laboratory"
   in which he conducted his butchery.
7. The killer preyed upon individuals of the "lower classes."[47]

A lengthy sociological psychological profile was produced by Coroner Gerber years after the crimes had ceased. He concluded:

> Therefore, the murderer ... was at one time or another associated with
> people in the upper strata of life but through unfortunate incidents either
> sank to association with persons in the lowest strata of life or has
> himself become a member. He may have been a doctor or medical stu-
> dent sometime in the past, butcher, osteopath, chiropractor, orderly,
> nurse, or hunter in order to be able to accomplish the dissection with
> such perfect finesse.
>
> The murderer undoubtedly gained the confidence and probably the
> friendship of the victims before killing them. ...
>
> From the anatomical examinations of the twelve so-called "Torso
> Murder Victims" ... the murderer may possibly be a schizophrene,
> considering the cold-blooded method of killing and then the dissection of
> the body.[48]

Many believed that the killer was a doctor, or had some type of
surgical knowledge or experience. Gerber, for instance, referred to the
killer having been "highly intelligent in recognizing the anatomical
landmarks as they were approached, or ... a person with some knowledge of anatomy.[49] His opinion was supported by that of Dr. Hubert
S. Reichle, City Hospital's head of pathology. He concluded that the killer
"clearly knew something about anatomy."[50] Gerber's predecessor as

coroner, Arthur J. Pearce, testified that the Torso Slayer knew a good deal about human anatomy. His knife incisions were professional, and in each case there was evidence of surgical skill. The killer may have obtained his training and experience in medical school. However, it is also possible that he was a butcher.[51] Brady referred to forensic scrutiny of the bodies, which showed that the decapitation, dismemberment, and organ removal were accomplished skillfully, suggesting that the killer possessed both the anatomical knowledge and surgical experience of a butcher or surgeon.[52]

The killer removed the genitalia from some of the victims. This fact was one of the reasons that the killer was suspected of being a surgeon. The body of the ninth victim surprised the autopsy doctors, who found that the victim's heart was removed, along with the sexual organs. Dr. Bradley H. Kirschberg, the New York State Police Scientific Laboratory director, observed, "The absence of certain organs pointed to the possibility of operation by a sex maniac either before or after death."[53]

There was considerable speculation about the personality of the killer. According to Nickel, the Mad Butcher was a patient man, who was careful and had an orderly personality.[54] The lead detective on the case, Peter Meyerlo, offered this assessment of the culprit:

> I am of the opinion that the murderer is a sex degenerate suffering from necrophilia, aphrodisia, or erotomania, who may have worked in the pathology department of some hospital, morgue or some college where he had the opportunity to handle a great number of bodies, or may have been employed in an undertaking establishment, and that he had a mania for headless and nude bodies. The murderer procured his sexual gratification while watching the blood flow after cutting the jugular vein of his victim.[55]

The motive behind these crimes has long been debated. Gerber disagreed with Meyerlo's assessment of the murders as sex crimes, but offered no alternate motive. Nickel observed the importance of the motive issue to the investigation, calling it one of the major unanswered questions about the Torso Murderer. The Cleveland police also puzzled over the murderer's mysterious motive from the beginning of the case. One problem complicating the assignment of a motive was the number of possible motives. Besides sex crimes, revenge was another motive considered by the police. Badal recalled that police initially looked at revenge involving mobsters or perhaps a lover's triangle as a motive.[56]

Another motive can be considered. Some suggest that the murders were a diversion to distract Eliot Ness from his crusade to clean up the notoriously corrupt Cleveland Police Department. Corruption was everywhere in the Cleveland police, from the top levels of police leadership to the cop on the beat, Nickel recalled. He added that Ness had evidence that Cleveland police officers were routinely accepting bribes, and even sometimes serving as informants or agents for the mob. Ness prepared an eighty-six-page report documenting the corruption, which described findings on twenty crooked cops, including a deputy inspector, two captains, two lieutenants, and three sergeants. After an investigation, at least two hundred police officers were forced to resign and 122 others were demoted and reassigned, including one captain and twenty-seven lieutenants.[57]

Ness devoted his attention to rooting out this corruption in his own department. According to Nickel, Ness checked each lead and its source himself. This resulted in an all-consuming investment of Ness's time. Some investigation was assigned to top assistants, but Ness did most of his own investigating.[58]

Ness had tried to stay out of direct involvement in the Mad Butcher case. But his anticorruption efforts were likened to a "witch hunt," and public pressure forced him to abandon his probe for the serial slaying case. Ness was criticized for spending time and police money investigating cops who were basically honest but imperfect, instead of investing police time, energy, and resources to capture the Mad Butcher.

We have already learned of suspicions that the Mad Butcher was a doctor, or possibly a butcher. Other observers have arrived at different analyses of the killer's likely occupation. Brady asked, "Could the Mad Butcher have been a uniformed policeman, a railway worker or a woman, as was speculated by many?"[59]

Over the years, there were two main suspects. Frank Dolezal allegedly confessed to one of the murders, that of Flo Polillo. He supposedly committed suicide in jail, however, before his trial could take place. None of the investigators believed that Dolezal was the Mad Butcher.[60] Ness favored Sweeney as the culprit. Sweeney, however, was a cousin of prominent U.S. Congressman Martin Sweeney. Meyerlo reportedly cleared Sweeney of any possible involvement in the crimes, but Ness nevertheless was adamant in his belief.[61] Sweeney allegedly had been observed mutilating corpses during war service as a medic, and later as a practicing physician. Alcoholism exacerbated his underlying mental difficulties, resulting in his divorce and civil commitment to a mental institution on more than one occasion. Sweeney reportedly failed a polygraph examination administered by polygraph authority Leonard Keeler.

Despite the horrible murders and mutilations, the Mad Butcher has been all but forgotten. Nickel claimed, "The Torso Murderer remains curiously unrecognized in the annals of crime."[62] According to Brady, "Yet the 'Mad Butcher of Kingsbury Run' is practically forgotten, rating hardly a mention in the annals of criminal history."[63] One more thing might be noted about the Mad Butcher. Ness withheld from the media an important aspect of these crimes: The Mad Butcher was a necrophiliac.[64]

CONCLUSION

In light of the elements of display present where the Mad Butcher's victims were found, and the repeated communication acts engaged in by this offender, there is little doubt that rhetorical motives were present in this case. But what exactly was the Mad Butcher trying to say? Enlightened speculation is possible based on careful study of the Mad Butcher messages.

Defiance of and disrespect for law enforcement might have been an intended message. That would explain the telephone call to Meyerlo. However, the Los Angeles letter served an informative function, as the writer explained his motive (vaguely), and said goodbye to Cleveland. The letter writer also taunted the authorities, declaring his invincibility.

It is difficult to know what the "NAZI" body carving meant. The Sweeney letters are similarly hard to fathom. Both sets of communication acts might merely have been the expressive but meaningless (literally, without any intended meaning) acts of a deranged serial killer. The communication itself was irrational.

Newspapers found at each dump site signified the killer's contempt for the press, I believe. They were used to wrap body parts and as covers under which corpses were kept. In light of their presence at virtually each crime scene, we cannot disregard their intentional use.

Unlike other serial killers, the Mad Butcher's rhetorical style was subtle. The body carving was enigmatic, and the letters and telephone call lacked the explicit self-promotion of the messages of other serial killers such as the Zodiac or the Black Dahlia Avenger. Despite our difficulty in grasping his message, his expressions of contempt and disrespect for the police clearly constitute the dominant theme.

4 The Unabomber

It is frequently suggested in expert accounts of serial murder that the offenders are typically very intelligent. That certainly was true of the Unabomber, Theodore John (Ted) Kaczynski. He earned a graduate degree in mathematics from the University of Michigan and was succeeding in a tenure-track mathematics teaching position at the University of California at Berkeley before something "snapped." He abruptly quit that position. Before his personal and professional transformation was complete, he would live in a crude cabin by himself in the Montana forest, building bombs and brooding about technology. Self-exile is an accurate term.

Kaczynski lovingly crafted his bombs, building most components by hand. He sanded, polished, and machined bomb components, and assembled them in his cabin, taking the time to etch the initials "FC" onto bomb parts. FC was his self-bestowed acronym, standing for the domestic terrorist organization he claimed to represent. But he lied about that—it was only him.

The Unabomber made phone calls, sent letters, and left notes at crime scenes. His manifesto may be his most memorable artifact. He extorted the *New York Times* and *Washington Post* into publishing the 35,000-word sociopolitical and cultural critical diatribe in September of 1995. In this chapter, I first discuss the crimes and communication of this killer. Then we examine the killer. The Unabomber murders were merely media events meant to publicize his cause. His communication—the manifesto in particular—directly led to his apprehension.

THE INITIAL UNABOMBS

The Unabomber's first bomb exploded on May 26, 1978. Mary Gutierrez discovered a brown package in the Northwestern University Science & Engineering Department parking lot. It was addressed to E. J. Smith, a rocket science professor at Renssaeler Polytechnic Institute in Troy, New York. The return address indicated that the package was from Professor Buckley Crist, a prominent computer science professor at Northwestern University's Technological Institute. Gutierrez tried to mail the package, but it would not fit in the mailbox, so she called Crist. He sent a messenger for the package, who retrieved it from Gutierrez. When Crist did not recognize the package when it arrived, he called campus police. Officer Terry Marker responded and was injured slightly when the bomb exploded as he examined it.

Was this a Unabomb? Reportedly, Kaczynski had moved back to Illinois shortly before this bombing, after an extended trip to Montana. He applied for an Illinois driver's license about a month and a half after this crime.

Almost exactly one year later, on May 9, 1979, John Harris, a Northwestern University mathematics graduate student, was injured by a second Unabomb. The explosion took place in a student meeting room at Northwestern University's Technological Institute. Harris noticed a "Phillies" cigar box left between two study carrels. Curious, Harris opened the box, resulting in an explosion and fire. He was taken to Evanston Hospital, but released an hour later.

Six months later, on November 15, 1979, a bomb exploded on American Airlines Flight 444 from Chicago Midway Airport to Washington National Airport, necessitating an emergency landing as the plane's cabin filled with smoke and the pilot struggled to keep control of the partly depressurized airplane. After pilots heard a thump, they noticed a reduction in the cabin pressure. Within minutes, the plane was filled with smoke and it was diverted to Dulles International Airport for an emergency landing. Twelve passengers were treated for smoke inhalation at Washington, D.C.-area hospitals. This bomb was another relatively sophisticated device. It was attached to an altimeter and set to detonate at 34,500 feet, well into the flight. After this incident, the Federal Bureau of Investigation (FBI) entered the case. Their top bomb expert, James C. Roney, was assigned to the Unabomb investigation.

United Airlines president Percy Wood was injured by a Unabomber device he received on his birthday, June 10, 1980. Wood and his family lived in Lake Forest, an affluent Chicago suburb. The bomb was contained in a hollowed-out book, Sloan Wilson's novel *Ice Brothers*. Wood received numerous cuts on his face and right leg.

A LETTER FROM ENOCH FISHER

Wood had received a letter in early June of 1980 from an Enoch Fisher. It promised him a book "you will find of great social significance." The letter stated that the impending arrival was "a book that should be read by all who make important decisions affecting the public welfare."[1]

This letter's content, although not fully disclosed, contained three noteworthy aspects. First, it tried to "tease" the recipient to be on the lookout for the arrival of the promised book. A second factor was the reference to the "great social significance" of that book, which I believe was a veiled reference to the intended bomb consequences. Finally, the choice of victim was not accidental, as wordplay involving "wood" occurred throughout the Unabomber's career and correspondence. Hence, Percy Wood was an ideal target.

Two aspects of the style of this partial letter can be discussed. It was reportedly very brief, and as mentioned previously, there was a tongue-in-cheek aura about it. The letter promised the recipient would receive something worth waiting for, in this case, a potentially lethal explosion.

Investigators who analyzed the Wood bomb fragments noticed something peculiar. The initials "FC" were inscribed on a metal plate that had been inserted into the bomb. The inscription had been painstakingly crafted, as tiny holes had been punched through the metal to form the letters.

MORE NONLETHAL BOMBS

Authorities intercepted a 1981 bomb left in a building at the University of Utah. A student leaving the business lecture hall on October 8 spotted a large package in the hall. Fearing a bomb, he called campus security. The university police called in the city police bomb squad, which detonated the device in the women's restroom on that floor. Investigators studied the bomb in a search for clues to the Unabomber's identity. A metal plate stamped FC had been placed in this bomb as well.

On May 5, 1982, a package addressed to renowned Vanderbilt computer expert Professor Patrick Fischer exploded, injuring Janet Smith, a staff secretary. The return address was that of Professor Leroy Wood Bearnson, another noted computer science authority. The package had been mailed to Fischer's former address at Pennsylvania State University and forwarded by Penn State staff to Fischer's Vanderbilt address. When Smith opened the package the bomb exploded, causing serious burns and eye injuries.

Another account of this bombing contends that the "addresser," Bearnson, was actually the intended target; the Unabomber meant for the package to be returned to him as undeliverable. It is worth noting that Bearnson's middle name is Wood.[2]

The Unabomber celebrated Independence Day of 1982 two days early, when his bomb detonated at the University of California–Berkeley's Department of Electrical Engineering and Computer Science. The explosion occurred at approximately 8:00 A.M. in the fourth floor faculty lounge of Cory Hall. (Kaczynski had once taught mathematics in Campbell Hall, near to the site of this bombing.) The bomb exploded and nearly killed Diogenes J. Angelakas, vice chair of the Department of Electrical Engineering and Computer Science, who saw what he thought was a can, perhaps left by a construction worker or student.[3] According to another report, Angelakas found a strange package with a handle, which he proceeded to lift. According to author Alston Chase, Angelakas was the director of the Electronic Research Laboratory at Berkeley.[4] Whatever his title or the exact nature of the package, there was no doubt about the effect of the bomb on the victim; his right hand was shredded and arm badly burned. Because of his injuries, Angelakas could not care for his sick wife, who died a month later.

Inside the bomb was a note, "Wu—it works! I told you it would—R. V."[5] The content of this note was characterized by self-congratulation, as the author wrote "I told you it would"; apparently he had some doubt that the bomb would work. A receiver was identified, Wu, as was the author, R. V. The style of this note was brief and smug.

Three years passed before a May 15, 1985, second Unabomber bombing at the same Cal–Berkeley department, when a blast shook room 264 of the Computer Science Building. John Hauser, a U.S. Air Force captain on special assignment, was severely injured by this explosion. Two arteries in his hand were severed, and the bomb also devastated several fingers. Hauser also lost partial vision in one eye. Ironically, the victim in the previous Unabomber bombing, Diogenes Angelakas, saved Hauser's life by applying a tourniquet and stopping his bleeding.

Hauser had seen a black vinyl spiral binder sitting on top of a plastic file box on a table in the middle of the room. The bomb apparently sat there for several days before it was detonated by Hauser.

A month later, a Unabomber parcel was intercepted at the Boeing Aviation mailroom in Auburn, Washington. It reportedly had been lost in Boeing's internal mail system for some time. The package was not addressed to any particular individual, so it was rerouted a number of times, before sitting in the mailroom for a while. Finally, a Boeing mailroom employee began to open the package before recognizing it as a bomb. He called security, and the bomb was successfully defused by the King's County Sheriff's Bomb Squad. The package had been mailed from Oakland, California.

THE McCONNELL LETTER

On November 15, 1985, Nicklaus Suino opened a package and was injured by a bomb. It was addressed to James McConnell, a University of Michigan professor. An envelope glued to the package's exterior contained a note, signed by Ralph C. Kloppenburg, explaining that the parcel contained his dissertation. The bomb was postmarked in Salt Lake City.

Suino was McConnell's teaching assistant. After he opened the box at the McConnell home, an explosion rocked the room, seriously hurting both men. McConnell lost a degree of hearing. Suino suffered shrapnel wounds and powder burns on his arms and legs.

There were two Unabomber messages associated with this bombing. First, it bore the by-now familiar, metal plate initials identification; the initials FC were imprinted on the end of the pipe plugs. And there was another Unabomber letter. "I'd like you to read this book. Everybody in your position should read this book," read the note.[6] The content of this letter included two salient items. First, the note suggested that the recipient should read the allegedly enclosed book. In addition, it was implied that McConnell represented or symbolized a certain class of person: the writer referred to "Everybody in your position." The style of this note was brief, patronizing, and accusatory. The suggested implied that somehow McConnell and a certain class of people had a lesson coming, which would be administered by the Unabomber campaign. The overall rhetorical theme was one of threats.

DEADLY BOMBINGS

Shortly thereafter, on December 11, a Unabomb killed Hugh Scrutton, thirty-eight, in Sacramento, California. The Berkeley graduate owned a small computer store, Rentech. He walked out his the back door of his store and saw what looked like a block of wood with some nails pounded into it, sitting in the parking lot. "Oh my God, help me," he cried after the blast in the fleeting seconds before his death.[7] Scrutton's assistant, Dick Knight, who heard a loud pop and ran outside, said, "His right hand was missing, and his heart was half out of his chest."[8] Knight had also noticed the object, which he said was disguised to look like a road hazard.

The Unabomber sent a message with the bomb. The letters FC were found on a piece of metal contained in the bomb. Again, the bomb was "signed."

In Salt Lake City, Gary Wright was injured by a Unabomb on February 20, 1987. Wright owned CAAMS (or Caams), a computer store. Wright had noticed a relatively small wooden object with nails protruding on the ground near the rear entrance to his store.[9] Another account reported that the bomb was disguised to look like a two-by-four, with nails sticking out.[10]

Although Wright survived, he was badly hurt. The blast lifted him off his feet, and filled his body with wood and metal shrapnel. His face was disfigured, and the explosion tore apart his left hand and arm, resulting in permanent nerve damage.

THE UNABOMBER WALL WRITING

The Unabomber mailed a bomb on June 20, 1993, and the indicated sender was James Hill, a chemistry professor at California State University–Sacramento. This resulted in Hill's apprehension, and intensive interrogation. Once he was cleared, he assisted the task force in trying to track the bomber down. That spring, unusual graffiti had been spray-painted on the side of the science building where Hill taught and on other nearby walls. In each of these instances of graffiti, a peace sign-like circle included the letters FC inside. Some of the graffiti included the word "ANARCHY" written outside of the circle.

There is no direct evidence that Kaczynski produced the graffiti near Professor Hill's office, but I am strongly inclined to suspect that he was responsible. The initials FC figured prominently in Unabomber communication, one of the Unabomber packages was meant to implicate Hill, and the FC-signed graffiti turned up adjacent to both Hill's office and classroom building. In light of the Unabomber's manifest communicative tendencies, displayed through a variety of media, there is little doubt that wall writing was another Unabomber serial communication tactic.

THE BOMBINGS RESUME AFTER A HIATUS

Six years passed before the Unabomber assaulted Charles Epstein, a prominent scientist, at his Tiburon, California, home on June 22, 1993. The geneticist researched at the University of California at San Francisco Medical Center, where he was a world-renowned expert on Down's Syndrome and Alzheimer's disease research. The explosion was a notable one. According to one report, Epstein was thrown across the room, and the telephone was blown off the wall.[11]

David Gelernter, a computer sciences professor at Yale University, was severely injured by a Unabomb two days later. The package arrived with the outer appearances of a dissertation. Gelernter recalled thinking, "Bombs must be going off all over campus this morning."[12] The Unabomber bomb severely injured his right eye, abdomen, chest, and right hand, which was "smashed beyond repair."[13]

A PERSONAL CALL

Less than two hours after the bombing, an anonymous call was made to the hospital where Gelernter's brother Joel practiced psychiatry. "You are next," he was told.[14]

There are two aspects of this call that merit comment. First, there was the making of an explicit threat against the call's recipient, the brother of a Unabomber victim. Second, the purpose of the call, judging by the content, clearly was to terrorize. The style of this brief call was taunting and menacing.

MORE UNABOMBER LETTERS

The next Unabomber letter was received at the *New York Times* on June 24, 1993. Addressed to Warren Hoge, an editor, the letter stated:

We are an anarchist group calling ourselves FC. Notice that the postmark on this envelope precedes a newsworthy event that will happen about the time you receive this letter, if nothing goes wrong. This will prove that we knew about the event in advance, so our claim of responsibility is truthful. Ask the FBI about FC. They have heard of us. We will give information about our goals at some future time. Right now we only want to establish our identity and provide an identifying number that will ensure the authenticity of any future communications from us.[15]

A number was provided, "553-25-4394." This number was the Social Security number of a man incarcerated in a California prison. The man had a tattoo, "Pure Wood."[16]

The content of this letter included noteworthy references to the FBI and to an unspecified event for which FC would be responsible. FC was described as an anarchist group, and an identifying number was provided to guarantee the authenticity of future FC communication. The style of this note was brief, informative, and low key. The theme was one of subtle boasting.

MORE MURDER

A Unabomb killed public relations executive Thomas Mosser on December 10, 1994. Mosser was misidentified by the Unabomber correspondence as a Burson-Marsteller executive, when in fact he had moved to Young & Rubicam, another respected public relations firm. According to Mosser's widow, when he opened the package at their New Jersey home, a tremendous explosion rocked the house. She recalled that her husband was lying on his back with his face burned, bloody, and blackened, and his stomach ripped open.[17]

APRIL 19, 1995

It has been alleged that Kaczynski was motivated to accelerate his activity by the bombing of the Alfred P. Murrah Federal Building in Oklahoma City, Oklahoma, on April 19, 1995. The next day, the Unabomber mailed a bomb that killed Gilbert Murray, and he also dispatched four letters and made a phone call to the Association of California Insurance Companies. Fred Rosenthal, a San Francisco psychiatrist, suggested that "All the reports of the Oklahoma bombing, all the attention they received, may have stimulated the Unabomber to do something he had been planning all along but for which he hadn't picked a date."[18] Gibbs, Lacayo, Morrow, Smolowe, and Van Biema offered their opinion: "The Unabomber, it seemed, wanted to bump the Oklahoma blast off the front pages and regain his rightful position as America's pre-eminent terrorist."[19]

The FBI concluded that the Unabomber had, in fact, been motivated by the Oklahoma City bombing. Former FBI profiler John Douglas provided an extended description of the FBI reasoning:

> We felt quite strongly that the timing was far from coincidental. Just five days before, the Murrah Federal Building in Oklahoma City had been destroyed, along with massive casualties, with a very crude bomb, but in a crime that dwarfed anything the Unabomber had done. And yet, the Unabomber must have seen himself as more artistic, more committed, more successful. After all, he'd been doing this for more than a decade and hadn't been caught. Losing center stage was an intolerable situation to him, we were sure, and he had to grab back the limelight in the only way he knew how—writing outrageous letters and killing people.[20]

THE UNABOMBER CALLS AGAIN

The day after the bombing of the Murrah building the Unabomber made a business call. At 10:52 A.M. the Association of California Insurance Companies, in Sacramento, received an anonymous call by a man with a gravelly voice. "Hi, I'm the Unabomber, and I just called to say hi," the caller said to the answering machine.[21]

There were a few content items in this call, beginning with the Unabomber's greeting. The caller proceeded to identify himself as the Unabomber, and he reiterated that his purpose was merely to say hello. There was a second, implied purpose: to show that the Unabomber was unafraid of the police and free to do as he wished—and call whom he pleased. The style of this brief call was taunting and mocking. In a way, it was also lighthearted, frivolous, and somewhat amusing.

A FINAL KILLING

Gilbert P. Murray, president of the California Forestry Association, was murdered in late April 1995. That was the last known victim of the

Unabomber. The bomb was actually addressed to Murray's predecessor, William Dennison, who had served the then-Timber Association of California as president. This package was mailed from Oakland.

On April 24, Murray opened the box, and the detonation ripped his arm off and exploded his face. There were small, bloody body parts throughout the room. There was a new element in this Unabombing, "a huge fireball."[22] Murray's body was so devastated by the explosion that it took eleven body bags to contain all of the small pieces that were recovered.

THE COMMUNICATION CAMPAIGN BEGINS IN EARNEST

David Gelernter was injured by a Unabomber-sent bomb in June of 1993. On April 20, 1995, he received a taunting and insulting letter from the Unabomber, under the signature FC. The letter read:

Dr. Gelernter:

People with advanced degrees aren't as smart as they think they are. If you'd had any brains you would have realized that there are a lot of people out there who resent bitterly the way techno-nerds like you are changing the world and you wouldn't have been dumb enough to open an unexpected package from an unknown source.

In the epilog [sic] of your book, "Mirror Worlds," you tried to justify your research by claiming that the developments you describe are inevitable, and that any college person can learn enough about computers to compete in a computer-dominated world. Apparently people without a college degree don't count. In any case, being informed about computers won't enable anyone to prevent invasion of privacy (through computers), genetic engineering (to which computers make an important contribution) environmental degradation through excessive economic growth (computers make an important contribution to economic growth) and so forth.

As for the inevitability argument, if the developments you describe are inevitable, they are not inevitable in the way that old age and bad weather are inevitable. They are inevitable only because techno-nerds like you make them inevitable. If there were no computer scientists there would be no progress in computer science. If you claim you are justified in pursuing your research because the developments involved are inevitable, then you may as well say that theft is inevitable, therefore we shouldn't blame thieves.

But we do not believe that progress and growth are inevitable.

We'll have more to say about that later.

FC.

PS. Warren Hoge of the New York Times can confirm that this letter does come from FC.[23]

The content of this letter included several noteworthy dimensions. In another example of Unabomber wit, the return address on the package was the FBI Headquarters in Washington, D.C. The letter also implied that Gelernter was not intelligent enough to avoid being hurt in the bomb blast, and essentially blamed Gelernter for his own injuries.

Much of the letter was critical of computers. Computers were blamed for invasions of privacy, genetic engineering, and environmental degradation caused by economic growth. In addition, the Unabomber recognized the existence of the digital divide. He noted Gelernter's claim that any college graduate could use a computer, and responded that "Apparently people without a college degree don't count."

The letter said that the advent of the computer age was a result of "techno-nerds" like Gelernter, and that computerization was not naturally inevitable. The Unabomber also denied that economic growth and progress were inevitable phenomena. He concluded with the assertion that a *New York Times* editor could confirm the authenticity of FC. Thematically, this moderate-length missive was both argumentative and insulting. The letter insulted the recipient's intelligence and refuted Gelernter's promotion of computers.

The *New York Times*'s Hoge received a Unabomber missive that same day. His declared:

This is a message from the terrorist group FC.

We blew up Thomas Mosser last December because he was a Burson-Marsteller executive. Among other misdeeds, Burson-Marsteller helped Exxon clean up its public image after the Exxon Valdez incident. But we attacked Burson-Marsteller less for its specific misdeeds than on general principles. Burson-Marsteller is about the biggest organization in the public relations field. This means that its business is the development of techniques for manipulating people's attitudes. It was for this more than for its actions in specific cases that we sent a bomb to an executive of this company.

Some news reports have made the misleading statement that we have been attacking universities or scholars. We have nothing against universities or scholars as such. All the university people whom we have attacked have been specialists in technical fields. (We consider certain areas of applied psychology, like behavior modification, to be technical fields.) We would not want anyone to think we have any desire to hurt professors who study archaeology, history, literature or harmless stuff like that. The people we are out to get are the scientists and engineers, especially in critical fields like computers and genetics. As for the bomb planted in the Business School at the U. of Utah, that was a botched operation. We won't say how or why it was botched because we don't want to give the FBI any clues. No one was hurt by that bomb.

In our previous letter to you we called ourselves anarchists. Since "anarchist" is a vague word that has been applied to a variety of attitudes, further explanation is needed. We call ourselves anarchists because we would like, ideally, to break down all society into very small, completely autonomous units. Regrettably, we don't see any clear road to this goal we leave into the indefinite future. Our more immediate goal, which we think may be attainable at some time during the next several decades, is the destruction of the worldwide industrial system. Through our bombings we hope to promote instability in industrial society, propagate anti-industrial ideas and give encouragement to those who hate the industrial system.

The FBI has tried to portray these bombings as the work of an isolated nut. We won't waste our time arguing about whether we are nuts, but we certainly are not isolated. For security reasons we won't reveal the number of members of our group, but anyone who will read the anarchist and radical environmentalist journals will see that opposition to the industrial-technological system is widespread and growing.

Why do we announce our goals only now, though we made our first bomb some seventeen years ago? Our early bombs were too ineffectual to attract much public attention or give encouragement to those who hate the system. We found by experience that gun-powder bombs, if small enough to be carried inconspicuously, were too feeble to do much damage, so we took a couple of years off to do some experimenting. We learned how to make pipe bombs that were powerful enough, and we used these in a couple of successful bombings as well as in some unsuccessful ones.

Since we no longer have to confine the explosives in a pipe, we are now free of the limitations on the size and shape of our bombs. We are pretty sure we know how to increase the power of our explosives and reduce the number of batteries needed to set them off. And, as we've just indicated, we think we now have more effective fragmentation material. So we expect to be able to pack deadly bombs into ever smaller, lighter and more harmless-looking packages. On the other hand, we believe we will be able to make bombs much bigger than any we've made before. With a briefcase-full or a suitcase-full of explosives we should be able to blow out the walls of substantial buildings.

Clearly we are in a position to do a great deal of damage. And it doesn't appear that the FBI is going to catch us any time soon.

The FBI is a joke.

The people who are pushing all this growth and progress garbage deserve to be severely punished. But our goal is less to punish them than to propagate ideas. We are getting tired of making bombs. It's no fun having to spend all your evenings and weekends preparing dangerous mixtures, filing trigger mechanisms out of scraps of metal or searching the sierras for a place isolated enough to test a bomb. So we offer a bargain.

We have a long article, between 29,000 and 37,000 words, that we want to have published. If you can get it published according to our requirements we will permanently desist from terrorist activities. It must be published in the *New York Times, Time* or *Newsweek*, or in some other widely read, nationally distributed periodical. Because of its length we suppose it will have to be serialized. Alternatively, it can be published as a small book, but the book must be well publicized and made available at a moderate price in bookstores nationwide and in at least some places abroad. Whoever agrees to publish the material will have exclusive rights to reproduce it for a period of six months and will be welcome to any profits they may make from it. After six months from the first appearance of the article or book it must become public property, so that anyone can reproduce or publish it. (If material is serialized, first installment becomes public property six months after appearance of first installment, second installment, etc.) We must have the right to publish in the *New York Times, Time* or *Newsweek*, each year for three years after the appearance of our article or book, three thousand words expanding or clarifying our material or rebutting criticisms of it.

This article will not explicitly advocate violence. There will be an unavoidable implication that we favor violence to the extent that it may be necessary, since we advocate eliminating industrial society and we ourselves have been using violence to that end. But the article will not advocate violence explicitly, nor will it propose the overthrow of the United States Government, nor will it contain any obscenity or anything else that you would be likely to regard as unacceptable for publication.

How do you know that we will keep our promise to desist from terrorism if our conditions are met? It will be to our advantage to keep our promise. We want to win acceptance for certain ideas. If we break our promise people will lose respect for us and so will be less likely to accept our ideas.

Our offer to desist from terrorism is subject to three qualifications. First: Our promise to desist will not take effect until all parts of our article or book have appeared in print. Second: If the authorities should succeed in tracking us down and an attempt is made to arrest any of us, or even to question us in connection with the bombings, we reserve the right to use violence. Third: We distinguish between terrorism and sabotage. By terrorism we mean actions motivated by a desire to influence the development of a society and intended to cause injury or death to human beings. By sabotage we mean similarly motivated actions intended to destroy property without injuring human beings. The promise we offer is to desist from terrorism. We reserve the right to engage in sabotage.

It may be just as well that failure of our early bombs discouraged us from making any public statements at that time. We were very young then and our thinking was crude. Over the years we have given as much attention to the development of our ideas as to the development of bombs, and we now have something serious to say. And we feel that just now the time is ripe for the presentation of anti-industrial ideas.

Please see to it that the answer to our effort is well publicized in the media so we won't miss it. Be sure to tell us where and how our material will be published and how long it will take to appear in print once we have sent in the manuscript. If the answer is satisfactory, we will finish typing the manuscript and send it to you. If the answer is unsatisfactory, we will start building our next bomb.

We encourage you to print this letter.[24]

This lengthy letter was a major component of the Unabomber communication campaign. The content began with an explanation of the attack on public relations executive Thomas Mosser, formerly of Burson-Marsteller, a major American public relations firm. Burson-Marsteller was criticized for its work on behalf of Exxon during the aftermath of the Exxon Valdez tragedy. The Unabomber generalized that all public relations activity was inherently manipulative and therefore worthy of destruction. Next, the letter reassured scientists and academics that they were in no danger, media reports notwithstanding. Only scientists in "dangerous" fields, related to technology, computers, and economic growth. In a curious mention, the letter called the failed bombing attempt at the University of Utah "botched," but refused to explain further for fear of assisting the FBI. In a separate paragraph, the letter addressed the Unabomber's explanation of the type of anarchy espoused by FC.

This letter denied the FBI characterization of the Unabomber as "an isolated nut," by referring to the mounting crescendo of public criticism of environmental and technological policies, and the very existence of the environmental movement. Two different parts of the letter explained why, after more than a decade and a half of bombing, the Unabomber had only recently begun to communicate.

Bombs were mentioned in several ways. The letter described how FC was able to create much larger, more powerful devices capable of more destruction. However, bomb making and testing was described as a difficult life, and FC proposed a "bargain," which involved the extorting major American periodicals into publishing the Unabomber's manifesto. In return, the bombing would cease. FC tried to persuade readers that it would honor the "bargain" (it did not), and the letter promised that FC would not advocate violence in subsequent messages intended for public consumption. The letter drew a distinction between sabotage and terrorism, and claimed that FC would continue sabotage activity. The letter ended with a threat if the "bargain" was not complied with by the appropriate authorities in law enforcement and the publishing industry.

There were numerous themes here. The superiority of FC, the evils of technology and computers, and the incompetence of the FBI were emphasized repeatedly.

The style of this extraordinarily lengthy letter was intellectual, with an air of superiority and a controlling manner. It was explicitly organized, as in one paragraph where the three qualifications of the "bargain" were numbered. Overall, it was a professional-sounding yet pathological communication.

Exactly two months later, on June 24, Kaczynski sent the manifesto to the *New York Times* and the *Washington Post*. The cover letter declared:

> We have no regrets about the fact that our bomb blew up the wrong man, Gilbert Murray, instead of William Dennison, to whom it was addressed. Though Murray did not have Dennison's inflammatory style, he was pursuing the same goals, and he was probably pursing them more effectively because of the very fact that he was not inflammatory. It was reported that the bomb that killed Gilbert Murray was a pipe bomb. It was not a pipe bomb but was set off by a homemade detonating cap. (The FBI's so-called experts should have been able to determine this quickly and easily, especially since we indicated in an unpublished part

of our last letter to NY Times—that the majority of our bombs are no longer pipe bombs).[25]

THE MANIFESTO

Kaczynski wanted publicity for his anti-industrial message. He prepared an elaborate document to advocate his position on public policy issues ranging from economic development, energy generation, and population policy to agrarian concerns and social psychology. The 232 numbered paragraphs and thirty-six footnotes, along with a list of corrections, made for formidable reading. Unfortunately for him, this document led to his identification and arrest.

"Industrial Society and Its Future" was how his manifesto was titled. It was a mega-sized term paper in academic prose, which argued a fundamental thesis: The industrial technological revolution and its side effects have been a disaster for the human race. His critique would not have been noticed, but he found a lethal way to get the people's attention. The manifesto's one unforgettable sentence declared, "In order to get our message before the public with some chance of making a lasting impression, we've had to kill people."[26]

The manifesto was co-published by the *New York Times* and the *Washington Post*. It appeared as an eight-page special supplement, an insert in the September 19, 1995, edition of the *Washington Post*. The cost of the printing was estimated at $40,000. The full text of the Unabomber treatise was also made available on the Internet.[27]

The manifesto was, in my opinion, the reason for the killings. Kaczynski did not seek fame, personal benefit, or any individual reward for his acts. He considered himself a messenger against an imperiled human future in a globe endangered by industrialization and technology. Kaczynski said precisely that, admitting that killing people was the only way he could command media and public attention. The manifesto was his message. He extorted free front-page space in America's most respected newspapers, besides generating a massive amount of free publicity for his message.

Five content aspects of the manifesto warrant examination. First, it was essentially an anti-industrial diatribe, concerned with the consequences of industrialization on individuals, society, and especially the environment. A second main theme was technology, which aided and abetted industrialization. Third, computers were identified as a major danger to mankind's future. Fourth, genetics research and

development were cited as substantial ethical and practical problems. Finally, the proposed solution was an agrarian, anti-industrial
revolution.

The style of the manifesto has been criticized repeatedly. It
was lengthy and very academic in the writing and documentation style.
It was repetitive and meticulous; there was even a typed list of corrections, useful in the pre-word processing days of the typewriter.
Overall, the tone was intellectual, although a bit haughty and superior.

MORE UNABOMBER LETTERS

The Unabomber wrote to the *San Francisco Chronicle* about two
months later, on June 27. To verify the authenticity of the missive, the
author gave the first two digits—55—of the nine-digit code number he
had earlier shared with the *New York Times*: "WARNING: the terrorist
group FC, called Unabomber by the FBI, is planning to blow up an
airliner out of Los Angeles International Airport sometime during the
next six days. To prove that the writer of this letter knows something
about FC, the first two digits of their identifying number are 55."[28]

Several content dimensions of this brief letter are worthy of our
consideration. The letter's author was identified as the terrorist group
FC, and two digits of an identification number were supplied to authenticate the communication as being a genuine FC message. The letter
claimed that the group would blow up an airplane leaving Los Angeles
International Airport (LAX) within six days of the posting of the letter.
The letter also mentioned the FBI. The style of this brief letter was
threatening, yet intellectual.

A day later, the *New York Times* received a missive:

> Since the public has such a short memory, we decided to play one last
> prank to remind them who we are. But no, we haven't tried to plant a
> bomb on an airline (recently).
>
> In one case we attempted unsuccessfully to blow up an airliner. The
> idea was to kill a lot of business people who we assumed would
> constitute a majority of the passengers. But of course some of the pas-
> sengers likely would have been innocent people—maybe kids, or some
> working stiff going to see his sick grandmother. We're glad now that the
> attempt failed.
>
> We don't think it is necessary for us to do any public soul-searching in
> this letter.

But we will say that we are not insensitive to the pain caused by our bombings.

A bomb package that we mailed to computer scientist Patrick Fischer injured his secretary when she opened it. We certainly regret that. And when we were young and comparatively reckless we were much less careful in selecting targets than we are now.[29]

The content of this letter focused on three things, with the main topic being the cancellation of the LAX airliner threat. The letter also mentioned an earlier unsuccessful attempt to blow up an airplane, and that FC regretted accidental injury, when people besides the FC target were hurt. The style of this letter was light, and subtly humorous.

Tom Tyler, a professor of social psychology at the University of California–Berkeley, received a letter and a copy of the Unabomber's manifesto on June 30, 1995. Here is the text of that letter:

Dr. Tyler:

This is a message from FC. The FBI calls us "unabom." We read a newspaper article in which you commented on recent bombings, including ours, as an indication of social problems. We are sending you a copy of the manuscript that we hope the *New York Times* will get published for us.

The trouble with psychologists is that in commenting on what people say or do they often concentrate exclusively on the non-rational motivations behind the speech or behavior. But human behavior has a rational as well as an irrational component, and psychologists should not neglect the rational component. So if you take the trouble to read our manuscript and do any further thinking about the "unabom" case, we suggest that you should not only consider our actions as a symptom of some social or psychological problems; you should also give attention to the substance of the issues that we raise in the manuscript. You might ask yourself, for example, the following questions:

Do you think we are likely to be right, in a general way, about the kind of future that technology is creating for the human race?

If you think we are wrong, then why do you think so? How would you answer our arguments? Can you sketch a PLAUSABLE [*sic*] scenario for a future technological society that does not have the negative characteristics indicated by our scenario?

If you think we are likely to be right about the future, do you consider that kind of future acceptable? If not, then what, if anything, do you think can be done about it?

Do you think our analysis of PRESENT social problems is approximately correct? If not, why not? How would you answer our arguments?

If you think we have identified some present social problems correctly, do you think anything can be done about them? Will they get better or worse with continual growth and progress?

We apologize for sending you such a poor copy of our manuscript. We can't make copies at a public copy machine because people would get suspicious if they saw us handling our copies with gloves.[30]

Kaczynski licked the stamp he used on the Tyler envelope, leaving his DNA. It was successfully retrieved by the police.

Several content dimensions of this letter deserve mention. First, the letter was attributed to FC. The initial paragraph explained that FC read a quotation attributed to Tyler in a newspaper article on recent bombings. Tyler was asked to put the bombings in perspective, and the letter proceeded to ask his opinion about a number of the Unabomber's arguments. He was asked his opinion of the FC assessment of the dangers posed by technology and social problems. Tyler was asked if he could offer any counterarguments to the Unabomber's basic antitechnology public policy position, and if he thought that American social problems were amenable to solution.

The letter also included an apology. FC explained that it could not make a copy of the manifesto at a public copy machine, because the use of gloves while handling the document might alert suspicions. The result of this reticence was a poor-quality copy of the manuscript.

UNABOMBER WRITTEN RECORDS: DIARY AND LAB NOTEBOOKS

Kaczynski's diary supplied direct evidence of his murderous motivation. In fact, he wrote on Christmas Day in 1972 that he had already planned and attempted a murder, but that his plans went awry: "About a year and a half ago I planned to murder a scientist—as a means of revenge against organized society in general and the technological establishment in particular. Unfortunately, I chickened out. I couldn't work up the nerve to do it."[31]

His diary described many of the Unabomber crimes, and his feelings about these crimes, in some detail. After his second bombing effort, he wrote, "I had hoped that the victim would be blinded or have his hands blown off or be otherwise maimed. . . . At least I put him in the hospital, which is better than nothing. But not enough to satisfy me. No more match head bombs. I wish I knew how to get hold of some dynamite."[32]

The Unabomber journal celebrated his successes. For instance, one entry recalled, "Berkeley bomb did very well for its size. It was sprung by air-force pilot, 26 yr old, named Hauser. He probably would have been killed if so positioned relative to bomb as to take the fragments in his body."[33]

Five dimensions of the diary's content deserve analysis. First, the diarist's personal thoughts and feelings were expressed, along with plans for and the recorded results of bombings. Second, revenge against others was a constant diary theme. Third, numerous entries pertaining to the bombings, along with murder plans, were included. Fourth, killings and injuries were carefully documented, along with reports of collateral damage to buildings and other property. Finally, a great deal of the author's self-realizations were recorded at various places in the diary.

The style of the diary was candid and revealing. A great deal of bitterness was evident, as was anger at many individuals and toward industrialization and technology in general. A self-centered perspective was revealed, along with the author's vindictive and retaliatory nature.

There was a third Unabomber written record, his laboratory notebooks. Kaczynski painstakingly recorded the results of his criminal enterprises. Chase recalled that Kaczynski maintained lab notebooks, written partly in Spanish, in which he documented the preparation and effects of approximately 254 bombs.[34] These lab notebooks were typical, standard academic paraphernalia, except that they recorded murder plans instead of benign experiments. The content included precise, detailed information on the design, construction, and deployment of Unabombs. The style of the notebooks was objective and dispassionate, detailed scientific instruments of a decidedly perverse nature.

THE CRIMINAL

What could have led the Unabomber, Ted Kaczynski, the son of literate, well-read, first-generation Polish immigrant parents to embark on a twenty-year odyssey of sending bombs to unsuspecting people? The Kaczynski home does not provide obvious clues to his future. The family was atheistic and lived in a Chicago neighborhood known as the Back of the Yards. The "Yards" referred to the nearby stockyards where animals were processed and slaughtered.

When he was about six months old, however, a significant incident occurred that might have had profound developmental and psychological consequences for Kaczynski. After a severe allergic reaction to medicine, he was kept in total sensory and tactual isolation for several weeks. Because of the therapeutic protocol and institutional regulations, he was deprived of the love and comfort needed by all infants: "Hospital rules did not allow his parents to hold him or hug him."[35] His parents, Theodore and Wanda Kaczynski, noticed a change in their son when they brought him home from the hospital. They quickly saw different behavior. Their once-expressive and joyous infant now was desensitized, apathetic, and withdrawn.[36]

At the age of six, he scored in the 160–170 range on the Stanford-Binet intelligence test. He had the I.Q. of a genius, according to A 2 Z of Serial Killers.[37] He enjoyed, and memorized, the parliamentary procedure guide Robert's Rules of Order. He read Scientific American at the age of ten, and the next year he taught himself calculus. He earned an undergraduate degree from Harvard and a master's degree from the University of Michigan.

Those who crossed or offended him provoked his wrath, which in time would prove to be lethal. He developed romantic feelings in 1978 for Ellen Tarmichael, a supervisor at Foam Cutting Engineers, Inc., in Addison, Illinois, where his father and brother, David, also worked. Eventually he asked her out. However, Tarmichael has since publicly denied any romance.

After one dinner and an apple-picking and pie-baking get-together, Tarmichael told Kaczynski that there would be no future relationship. Angered, he began to retaliate by writing and placing rude, sexually suggestive limericks all around their workplace. Ted's brother was his supervisor, and he told Ted to stop harassing Tarmichael. At that, Ted walked from his workstation to David's and slapped a limerick on his machine. So, David fired him.[38]

There was a potentially ominous postscript to the Tarmichael incident that combined Kaczynski's brooding, retaliatory nature with his habit of communicating. Kaczynski's family members say he wrote a threatening letter saying he might hurt Tarmichael. She denies ever receiving any such letter.[39]

Using analysis and evidence, Ted Kaczynski tried to warn America about the technological and industrial dangers inherent in the modern world. He sent out letters and articles. They explained what a bad idea funding scientific research was and discussed their negative consequences, especially with genetic research. He sent his writings to newspapers around the country, cautioning all about technological dangers. He wanted to get at least one essay published and publicly discussed that would result in a new generation of sympathetic supporters. But no one seemed to care. None of his submissions was accepted for publication.

COMMUNICATION CAUSES CAPTURE

When Ted Kaczynski was arrested, it was the result of an investigation initiated because his brother, David, recognized Ted's characteristic rhetoric in the prose of the manifesto. Thus, in this case, serial killer communication clearly and directly led to apprehension. "The clues in a killer's message can jog someone's memory and ultimately identify him, as in the published manifesto recognized by the brother of Unabomber Theodore Kaczynski," noted one media report.[40]

Former FBI profiler John Douglas described the specific details of David's identification of his brother: "David Kaczynski, a social worker in upstate New York, was haunted by the similarity of the Manifesto to certain ideas and phrases put forth by his strange and estranged older brother, Theodore." So he contacted retired FBI agent Cliff Van Zandt, who, based on writing comparisons, estimated a 60 percent probability that his brother was the Unabomber.[41] Ohio State University crime historian Roger Lane agreed, adding, "The manifesto, an odd mixture of the sophisticated and the naive, was nearly unique as a fingerprint; it was his younger brother's recognition of characteristic thoughts and phrases that led him to suspect Kaczynski's identity and turn him in."[42]

CONCLUSION

These serial murders were communication-based offenses. Kaczynski used communication as a tactic to attain communication as an end, or objective. That is, he used a variety of channels of communication, such as letters, phone calls, his manifesto, and wall writing, to convey his anti-industrial, technology-is-bad message. This serial killer's ultimate purpose, the motivation behind the crimes, was to draw attention to his cause and to attract media and public attention to his message.

But there was also a personal aspect to the Unabomber communication. This body of rhetoric was also exemplified by emotional cruelty and immature acts of retaliation. He meant to cause fear in and pain to the recipients of some of his telephone calls and letters.

In a sense, two different themes emerged from the Unabomber rhetoric. On one level, intellectual arguments based on altruism and utilitarian philosophy were advanced. Yet, on a more personal level, some Unabomber messages were ugly personal taunts and insults. One thing is certain. Communication was significant to the Unabomber crimes. Waits and Shore referred to Kaczynski's "archive of his written word." They added, "Organized in volumes of scratchpads, pocket notebooks and three-ring binders were some 22,000 pages of his life's script." "It was as if he was fulfilling a basic human need to communicate, to tell someone about his life's deeds in succinct and descriptive handwritten notes, even if it were only himself."[43]

5 The Zodiac

It is no exaggeration to describe the Zodiac as a master criminal, perhaps a genius. He outsmarted law enforcement and was never apprehended, despite sending authorities and media outlets a steady stream of messages. He killed and called and was never caught.

Intellectual ability and mental diversity characterized the Zodiac's interactions with police, the media, and other serial murder stakeholders. He wrote witty satirical comments about Gilbert and Sullivan operas and created coded messages so secure that the American experts in cryptoanalysis at the National Security Agency and Naval Intelligence could not decode them. He displayed sophisticated knowledge of maritime communication codes, complex engineering concepts, and law enforcement techniques.

No one except the Zodiac knows how many victims he killed.[1] Some controversy surrounds this issue, as not all observers agree that Cheri Jo Bates was a Zodiac victim. The Zodiac body of communication puts this issue to rest, however, as there was undeniable contemporary evidence that the Zodiac did kill Bates. He wrote and called the police, the press, and Bates's parents, taking credit for the murder soon after the events.

The Zodiac was an effective killer and a prolific communicator. He called the police, the media, and victims' families regularly. He left a crime scene note on the car door of an intended victim and carved a bizarre message into a school desk after the Bates murder. He signed his letters "Zodiac," giving himself the name by which he would forever be known. He wrote sometimes under his chosen pen-name and sometimes anonymously. His rhetorical themes included self-praise, criticism of the police, and threats.

THE ZODIAC CRIMES BEGIN

Cheri Jo Bates was an eighteen-year-old Riverside City College coed and cheerleader. And, on October 30, 1966, she probably became the Zodiac's first murder victim. Bates had graduated from Riverside's Ramona High School in the spring of 1966. The official police account of her murder, summarized in Riverside Police Department Report # 352-481 and filed on October 31, 1966, placed the attack on Bates at about 9:30 P.M.[2] One of the strangest aspects of this crime was the lengthy interlude shared by the killer and his victim. Police knew what time she left the Riverside City College library that evening and what time she was killed. There was an hour and a half unaccounted for in the interim.

The injuries to Bates were severe. She was slashed three times in the chest, once in the back, and seven times in her throat. Bates's throat wound was so extensive that she was nearly decapitated. Her larynx, jugular vein, and carotid artery were badly sliced and slashed, and she was also choked, beaten, and repeatedly cut in the face. The knife used in the assault was described as a relatively small one, with a blade measuring three and one-half inches long and one-half inch wide.

The Riverside Police Department had a suspect in this case, a man who was not associated with the Zodiac crimes. They denied a link between Bates and the Zodiac. But others disagreed. The *Los Angeles Times*, for instance, ran a banner headline, ''ZODIAC LINKED TO RIVERSIDE SLAYING,'' on November 16, 1970.

THE KILLER COMMUNICATES

The killer wrote to the police, taunting them about the crime. The following letter was received by the Riverside Police Department on November 19, 1966:

> SHE WAS YOUNG AND BEAUTIFUL
> BUT NOW SHE IS BATTERED AND
> DEAD. SHE IS NOT THE FIRST
> AND SHE WILL NOT BE THE LAST
> I LAY AWAKE NIGHTS THINKING ABOUT MY
> NEXT VICTIM. MAYBE SHE WILL BE THE
> BEAUTIFUL BLOND THAT BABYSITS NEAR
> THE LITTLE STORE AND WALKS DOWN THE

DARK ALLEY EACH EVENING ABOUT SEVEN.
OR MAYBE SHE WILL BE THE SHAPELY BLUE
EYED BRUNETTE THAT SAID NO WHEN I
ASKED HER FOR A DATE IN HIGH SCHOOL.
BUT MAYBE IT WILL NOT BE EITHER. BUT I
SHALL CUT OFF HER FEMALE PARTS AND
DEPOSIT THEM FOR THE WHOLE CITY TO SEE.
SO DON'T MAKE IT SO EASY FOR ME. KEEP
YOUR SISTERS, DAUGHTERS AND WIVES OFF
THE STREETS AND ALLEYS.
MISS BATES WAS STUPID. SHE WENT TO
THE SLAUGHTER LIKE A LAMB. SHE DID
NOT PUT UP A STRUGGLE. BUT I DID.
IT WAS A BALL.
I FIRST PULLED THE MIDDLE WIRE
FROM THE DISTRIBUTOR. THEN I WAITED FOR
HER IN THE LIBRARY AND FOLLOWED HER OUT
AFTER ABOUT TWO MINUTES. THE BATTERY MUST
HAVE BEEN DEAD BY THEN. I THEN
OFFERED TO HELP. SHE WAS THEN VERY WILLING
TO TALK WITH ME. I TOLD HER THAT MY CAR
WAS DOWN THE STREET AND THAT I WOULD GIVE
HER A LIFT HOME. WHEN WE WERE AWAY FROM
THE LIBRARY WALKING, I SAID IT WAS ABOUT TIME.
SHE ASKED ME, "ABOUT TIME FOR WHAT?"
I SAID IT WAS ABOUT TIME FOR YOU TO
DIE. I GRABBED HER AROUND THE NECK WITH
MY HAND OVER HER MOUTH AND MY OTHER HAND
WITH A SMALL KNIFE AT HER THROAT. SHE
WENT VERY WILLINGLY.
HER BREASTS FELT VERY WARM AND FIRM
UNDER MY HANDS. BUT ONLY ONE THING WAS ON
MY MIND. MAKING HER PAY FOR THE BRUSH OFFS
THAT SHE HAD GIVEN ME DURING THE YEARS PRIOR.
SHE DIED HARD. SHE SQUIRMED AND SHOOK.
AS I CHOKED HER, AND HER LIPS TWITCHED
SHE LET OUT A SCREAM ONCE AND I KICKED
HER HEAD TO SHUT HER UP. I PLUNGED THE KNIFE
INTO HER AND IT BROKE. I THEN FINISHED THE
JOB BY CUTTING HER THROAT. I AM NOT SICK.
I AM INSANE. BUT THAT WILL NOT STOP

THIS GAME. THIS LETTER SHOULD BE PUBLISHED
FOR ALL TO READ IT. IT MIGHT JUST SAVE THAT
GIRL IN THE ALLEY. BUT THAT'S UP TO YOU.
IT WILL BE ON YOUR CONSCIENCE. NOT
MINE. YES, I DID MAKE THAT CALL TO YOU
ALSO. IT WAS A WARNING. BEWARE.
I AM STALKING YOUR GIRLS NOW.
CC. CHIEF OF POLICE.
     ENTERPRISE.[3]

There are several noteworthy aspects of the content of this letter. It claimed that Bates was not the killer's first murder victim, and would not be the last. The writer claimed that he would cut out and publicly display his next victim's sexual organs. Most of the letter described how he killed Bates, beginning with his disabling of the distributor cap on her car so it would not start. The actual murder was described in great detail. Revenge for past brush-offs was said to be the killer's motive. The letter writer encouraged the authorities to publish the letter, which might avert future murders. The letter acknowledged that the writer had also made crime-related telephone calls and ended with the reminder that he was stalking victims for his next murder.

The style of this lengthy letter is graphic and detailed. It was intended to terrify and horrify, and a vindictive and vengeful tone is displayed throughout. The rhetorical themes included bragging and making threats. The Riverside Police Department dismissed it as a crank letter.

A SECOND ZODIAC LETTER: IN TRIPLICATE

One day after the six-month anniversary of the Bates murder and the publication in the local paper of an anniversary story, an identical letter was received by Joseph Bates, father of Cheri Jo Bates, the Riverside Police Department, and the local newspaper. The penciled note read, "Bates had to die. There will be more," and was signed with the letter "Z." The letter was mailed with the characteristic Zodiac extra postage, a common trait of the Zodiac letters. The letter explicitly named Bates and noted that she had to die, for an unexplained reason. More murders were threatened.

Two dimensions of this letter's style are worthy of consideration. It was a brief, eight-word message with a low-key, matter-of-fact tone.

The real theme was subtextual, the infliction of emotional pain on Joseph Bates and the humiliation of the police.

A MYSTERIOUS DESK POEM

Sometime during the fall of 1966, someone—perhaps the Zodiac—using a blue ballpoint pen scratched a message into a Riverside City College desk located in the library. According to school maintenance workers, the desk had been in the school library at the time of the Bates murder.[4] The message read:

> Sick of Living/Unwilling to Die
>> cut.
>> clean.
>> if red/
>> clean.
>> blood spurting
>>> dripping
>>>> spilling;
>> all **over** her new
>> dress.
>> oh, well,
>> it was red
>> anyway
>> life draining into an
>> uncertain death.
>> she won't
>> **die**.
> this **time**
> Someone ll find her
> Just wait till
> next time
>> rh.[5]

Noteworthy content dimensions can be identified within the message. The idea of a "cut" was mentioned prominently. Similarly, blood was specified once and implied a second time. A red dress was included, as was the idea of death. Finally, a threat of future killing ended the poem. Three words were darker than the rest: over, die, and time.

The style of this poem can best be characterized as free-form verse. For the most part, it used one-word stanzas. The poem seemed somewhat vague and abstract, although there seemed to be an implied or perhaps partly expressed threat. There was an overall evil ambience, a disquieting pathological tone about this poem. The theme of this message centered on a woman wearing a red dress. She was cut and bled on the dress. Her relatively imminent future death was predicted.

ZODIAC KILLS AGAIN. . . AND AGAIN

The Zodiac struck again a little more than two years later, on December 20, 1968, when he killed two victims at once. Betty Lou Jensen and David Faraday were shot to death as they sat in a parked car at a lover's lane in Vallejo, California. The couple had told her parents they were going to attend a local Christmas concert, but instead they ate dinner and then drove to the secluded place.[6] According to Solano County Sheriff's Office Report V-25564, the assault occurred at 11:15 P.M. Faraday, seventeen, was "shot once in the head at point-blank range and died within minutes." His date, Betty Lou, "was shot five times in the back and killed instantly." She was only sixteen years of age, and this was her first date with Faraday.[7]

When police reconstructed the crime based on the crime scene information, they discovered an unusual fact. The killer had apparently tried to force the occupants of the car to exit the vehicle. The police report observed, "Shots were fired into the vehicle in an apparent attempt to force them out." The Jake Wark of Crime Library agreed, adding that Jensen fled the car and began to run to the road; she was found within thirty feet of the rear bumper.[8] Zodiac letters later included details of this attack that would be known only to the murderer.

A ZODIAC POST-HOLIDAY MURDER

Darlene Elizabeth Ferrin was her full name. Her escort for the drive was Michael Renault Mageau, who for some unknown personal reason was wearing two pair of pants on a warm and humid evening. According to Vallejo Police Department documents, Crime Report # 342-146 suggested that the shooting had taken place at 12:10 A.M. on July 5, 1969.[9] Ferrin, who was twenty-two years of age at the time of her death, was shot five times. Mageau, nineteen years old, was shot four times.

Somehow, through a miracle perhaps, Mageau survived the attack. He described to investigators how he and Ferrin had seen a brown 1958 or 1959 Ford Falcon approach their car as they sat in the parking lot of the Blue Rock Springs Golf Course. The driver said something to Ferrin, but Mageau could not hear what was said. The Falcon then drove off, returning ten or fifteen minutes later.

The shooter was described as being a white male, between five feet, eight inches and five feet, nine inches in height. He was between twenty and thirty years old, and had a stocky build, weighing approximately 195 pounds. He had a round face, and brown hair.[10] Mageau's description of his attacker was the first eyewitness portrait of the Zodiac, who took credit for the murder in a phone call and letter.

As time passed, Mageau offered different versions of events. He later remembered that after being shot, he turned on the car's directional indicators to try and attract attention. He also tried to get out of the car, but because of his injuries, he "tumbled to the pavement."[11] He later decided that the killer's car was either a light-brown Ford Mustang or Chevrolet Corvair.[12]

CALLING INSTEAD OF KILLING

The phone rang at the Ferrin's residence at 1:30 A.M., shortly after the Zodiac murdered Darlene Ferrin. When her husband, Dean, answered, the only sound he could hear was someone's heavy breathing. At about the same time, Dean Ferrin's parents and brother also received prank calls. These anonymous calls to relatives of Darlene Ferrin were made within an hour and a half of her murder, before the crime was announced in the local media. Only the Zodiac had a motive to make these calls, as only he knew of Darlene Ferrin's then-unpublicized death.

In April 1970, Dean Ferrin again heard from the Zodiac. Ferrin had begun to receive crank calls about his wife's murder by the Zodiac. That was about eight months after her killing. Again, these calls provided details of the crime known only to the killer and the police.

The Zodiac shared crime-related communication with the police on several occasions. According to Graysmith, the July 5, 1969, phone call to the Vallejo Police Department began with the words, "I want to report a double murder." Graysmith added his description of the remainder of the call, "If you will go one mile east on Columbus Parkway to the public park, you will find kids in a brown car. They were shot with a 9-millimeter Luger. I also killed those kids last year. Goodbye." Initial police reports of the Ferrin murder did not mention the telephone call. The Vallejo Police Department was able to make a voiceprint of Zodiac's voice from the recording of the telephone call.[13]

THE "CIPHER" AND COVER LETTER

If the Zodiac did not kill Cheri Jo Bates, then the first Zodiac letters were sent on August 1, 1969, to three recipients: the *San Francisco Chronicle*, the *San Francisco Examiner*, and the *Vallejo Times-Herald*. The letters were basically the same, and each newspaper received one-third of a coded message, or cipher. Here is the complete text of the letter sent to the *Chronicle* (errors have been retained in all quoted material):

Dear Editor:
This is the murderer of the
2 teenagers last Christmass
at Lake Herman & the girl
on the 4th of July near
the golf course in Vallejo
To prove I killed them I
shall state some facts which
only I & the police know./
Christmas
    1. Brand name of ammo
       Super X
    2. 10 shots were fired.
    3. the boy was on his back
       with his feet to the car
    4. the girl was on her right
       side feet to the west
4th July
    1. girl was wearing paterned
       slacks
    2. The boy was also shot in
       the knee.

> 3. Brand name of ammo was
>   western
> (Over)
> Here is part of a cipher the
> other 2 parts of this cipher are
> being mailed to the editors of the Vallejo times & SF Exam
> iner./
> I want you to print this cipher
> on the front page of your
> paper. In this cipher is my identity./
> If you do not print this cipher
> by the afternoon of Fry 1st of
> Aug 69, I will go on a kill ram
> Page Fry. night. I will cruise
> around all weekend killing lone
> people in the night then move
> on to kill again, until I end
> up with a dozen people
> over the weekend.[14]

The content of this letter included noteworthy items. The letter admitted that the author had murdered David Faraday and Betty Lou Jensen on December 20, 1968, and Darlene Ferrin on July 4, 1969. The letter included considerable detail about the Faraday/Jensen murders, as well as a great deal of information about the death of Darlene Ferrin. The letter referred to the enclosed "cipher"; in a sense, this letter was a cover letter for the coded communication. The letter claimed that the killer's identity was revealed in the cipher, and it suggested lethal consequences if the cipher was not printed in the selected newspapers.

The style of this very lengthy letter was characterized by a threatening tone. It was composed of short stanzas, and internal organization was provided through spacing. It was extremely detailed, and there was a confessional but simultaneously bragging undertone. The self-perceived superiority of the writer was implied throughout the letter. Self-congratulation was the dominant rhetorical theme.

The cipher was beyond the best efforts of the experts employed by the American federal government. It was solved, however, by a secondary school teacher and his wife. Salinas High School teacher Donald Gene Harden and his wife, Bettye Jean, successfully decoded the cryptogram:

I LIKE KILLING PEOPLE
BECAUSE IT IS SO MUCH
FUN. IT IS MORE FUN THAN
KILLING WILD GAME IN
THE FORREST BECAUSE
MAN IS THE MOST DANGEROUE
ANAMAL OF ALL TO KILL
SOMETHING GIVES ME THE
MOST THRILLING EXPERIENCE
IT IS EVEN BETTER THAN GETTING
YOUR ROCKS OFF WITH A GIRL
THE BEST PART OF IT IS THAE
WHEN I DIE I WILL BE REBORN
IN PARADICE AND THEI HAVE
KILLED WILL BECOME MY SLAVES
I WILL NOT GIVE YOU MY NAME
BECAUSE YOU WILL TRY TO SLOI
DOWN OR ATOP MY COLLECTIOG OF
SLAVES FOR AFTERLIFE
EBEORIETEMETHHPTIT.[15]

The cipher's content was relatively remarkable. It explained that the author liked to hunt people because of the challenge. In the writer's opinion, killing people was more exciting than sex. The letter suggested that the murders were committed so that the killer could use the victims as slaves in the afterlife. Despite the previous claims, the true identity of the Zodiac was not revealed in the cipher. However, the final eighteen characters in the cipher were never decoded.

The style of this moderately lengthy message was dominated by the coded nature of the communication. The writer created the alphabet code himself, compiling individual characters from naval codes, mythological symbols, and other sources. The tone was arrogant and boastful. The rhetorical themes included fantasy and threats. The coded message emphasized the author's enjoyment of the act of murder. There was also a vague, foreboding sense of danger.

POLICE PROVOKE A ZODIAC LETTER

The next Zodiac letter was elicited or provoked by the police. After the receipt of the August 1 letter, the authorities decided to take advantage of the Zodiac's apparent interest in communicating with them. Vallejo Police Department Chief Jack E. Stiltz publicly challenged the Zodiac to write again, requesting "a second letter with more facts to prove it."[16] Within a week, on August 7, the Zodiac responded:

> Dear Editor:
> This is the Zodiac speaking.
> In answer to your asking for
> more details about the good
> times I have had in Vallejo,
> I shall be very happy to
> supply even more material.
> By the way, are the police
> haveing a good time with the
> code? If not, tell them to cheer
> up, when they do crack it
> they will have me./
> On the 4th of July:
> I did not open the car door. The
> Window was rolled down all ready
> The boy was originally sitting in
> the front seat when I began
> fireing. When I fired the first
> shot at his head, he leaped
> backwards at the same time
> thus spoiling my aim. He end-
> ed up in the back seat then
> the floor in back thrashing out
> very violently with his legs;
> that's how I shot him in the
> knee. I did not leave the cene
> of the killing with squealing tires
> & raceing engine as described in the
> Vallejo papers.
> I drive slowly away so as not to
> draw attention to my car. The man who
> told police my car was brown
> was a negro about 40–45 rather shabbily
> dressed. I was in this phone booth
> haveing some fun with the Vallejo
> cop when he was walking by.

When I hung the phone up the
dam thing began to ring & that
drew his attention to me and my car./
Last Christmass
In that epasode the police were
wondering as to how I could
shoot & hit my victims in the
dark. They did not openly state this,
but implied this by saying it was a
well lit night & I could see
silowets on the horizon.
Bullshit that area is srounded
by high hills & trees. What
I did was tape a small pencil flash
light to the barrel of the gun. If
you notice, in the center of the beam
of light as you aim it at a wall or
ceiling you will see a black or
darck spot in the center of the
circle of light about 3 to 6 in.
across.
When taped to a gun barrel, the
bullet will strike exactly in the
center of the black dot in the light.
All I had to do was spray them.
No address.[17]

Several content dimensions of this letter deserve mention. First, the writer explicitly acknowledged writing in response to Chief Stiltz's request. This letter mentioned the previous coded cipher and teased the police for being unable to decode it. Details of the Ferrin murder were provided, along with additional information about the Faraday/Jensen slayings. This letter also offered details about a black man who saw the killer talking on the telephone with the Vallejo Police Department.

The style of this lengthy missive was taunting and defiant. It was very detailed and, in some respects, argumentative. The stanzas were comprised of short lines, and there were numerous misspellings; "haveing," "all ready," "fireing," "cene," "raceing," "dam," and "christmass." The rhetorical themes at the core of this lengthy Zodiac letter included the correction of misreported crime facts, taunting the police, and boasting about his intellect and crime successes.

BACK TO MURDER

Cecilia Shepard saw him first, the strange squat man who seemed to be spying on them. As the couple relaxed together, she lay with her head on Bryan Hartnell's shoulder. When the stranger at last approached, they were captivated by his hood. It was square on top, and it hung down almost to his waist. A three-inch square on the front contained a cross over a circle, the Zodiac insignia. Pleasant Lake Berryessa was about to turn terribly tragic. For the first time in the Zodiac murders, there was direct communication between killer and victims. "Time's running short. I'm an escaped convict from Deer Lodge, Montana. I've killed a prison guard there. I have a stolen car and nothing to lose. I'm flat broke," Hartnell quoted the killer as telling the couple before he attacked them.[18]

Napa County Sheriff's Department Report # 105907 documented the attack on the couple, which it said occurred at 6:15 P.M. on September 27, 1969. Shepard, twenty-two, was stabbed ten times, five in the front and five in the back. Hartnell survived despite six deep stab wounds in his back. A wood-handled knife was used, with a blade of between ten and twelve inches in length.[19]

Again, there was a survivor who was able to offer investigators a description of the killer. He was about six feet tall, with a heavy build, Hartnell recalled.[20] The hood prevented a more detailed description of the offender.

ANOTHER ZODIAC CALL

The gruff-voiced killer called the Napa police on September 27 to report another double killing. The Zodiac told the police officer, "I want to report a murder—no, a double murder. They are two miles north of Park Headquarters. They were in a white Karmann Ghia. I'm the one that did it." Officer Dave Slaight, who took the call, described the caller's vocal mannerisms: "It sounded like the voice of a man in his early twenties. The voice was calm." The last part of the message was "barely audible."[21] The Zodiac placed his call from a phone booth at 1231 Main Street, the Napa Car-Wash, near the police station.

The rhetorical theme of this call was explicitly informative and confessional. There was also, however, a subtext message threatening future terror.

A CAR DOOR MESSAGE

Before he left the Lake Berryessa crime scene, the Zodiac wrote a message on one of the doors of Hartnell's car. It read, "Vallejo," "12-20-68," "7-4-69," "Sept 27-69-6:30," and "by knife."[22] The message was written with a slight upward tilt, and a felt-tip marker was used. According to a California Department of Justice report issued on October 3, 1969, by the Department's Bureau of Criminal Identification and Investigation, "The suspect had handprinted numbers and letters on the passenger door of victim HARTNELL's vehicle. Additional investigation revealed that the person who had printed on the car door was the same individual who had sent letters to the *Vallejo Times Herald*, *San Francisco Examiner* and *San Francisco Chronicle* claiming to have killed three people in Solano County."[23]

Four noteworthy content aspects of this door-message should be mentioned. First, it seemed to represent a scorecard of some sort, a serial killer's running count of murders committed to date. Second, there were several dates, of the three known Zodiac murders at the time (but excluding Bates). Third, one place was indicated, and finally, the method of murder used in one crime was indicated.

There were meaningful aspects of the style of this message. It was relatively brief. It was so brief, in fact, that it was context-dependant. That is, one cannot understand the meaning of the message from the message alone, but must rely on previously known facts to form a context within which to interpret and understand the communication. Finally, the style, like the content, was intended to terrorize and horrify.

The car door writing served Zodiac's personal rhetorical purposes. It documented his responsibility for the crime, an important consideration when one realizes the Zodiac's ego needs. The Zodiac wanted prominent media attention. He wanted to be a success, and he wanted acknowledgment of his crimes. That sums up the rhetorical theme of the car door message.

A FINAL ZODIAC MURDER

The 9:55 P.M. shooting on October 11, 1969, was recorded by the San Francisco Police Department as Case # 696314. Paul Stine was killed at the corner of Washington and Cherry Streets. The twenty-nine-year-old cabdriver was shot once in the head, at point-blank range. The killer apparently left behind a pair of size seven black leather gloves.[24]

Stine had been parked in the taxi zone in front of the St. Francis Hotel when he was assigned his fatal cab fare. Three witnesses saw the crime unfold from a second-floor window across the street from the shooting. Their elevated position allowed them to see the killer lean forward in the backseat and press the gun against Stine's right cheek, directly in front of his ear. They witnessed the assailant take Stine's wallet and rip off a section of the dead cab driver's shirt. He also wiped down the cab's interior and exterior to remove his fingerprints, a task at which he was unsuccessful.

The three witnesses offered police their description of the Zodiac, and the result was a composite sketch of the killer. He was depicted as being a white male, between twenty-five and thirty years of age. He was between five feet, eight inches and five feet, nine inches tall, with a stocky build. He wore his reddish-brown hair in a crew cut, and wore heavy-rimmed glasses. The police dispatcher who took the call either misunderstood the witnesses' description of the killer or there was some other sort of mistake. Police were told to look for a black man in connection with the shooting. A squad car happened to encounter the Zodiac on Jackson Street, a short distance from the crime scene. Officers Donald Foulkes and Eric Zelms took no notice of him, however, since he was of the wrong race. The officers later described the man they saw as being between six feet and six feet, two inches tall, and weighing more than two hundred pounds. He had receding reddish-brown hair, and wore glasses.[25]

The Zodiac letter claiming responsibility for the murder of cab driver Paul Stine is the last one considered here. It was received at the *San Francisco Chronicle* on October 14, 1969, and included a piece of Stine's bloody shirt to verify that it was in fact genuine. The letter chided the police and added a frightening ending:

> This is the Zodiac speaking
> I am the murderer of the
> taxi driver over by
> Washington St & Maple St last
> night, to prove this here is
> a blood stained piece of his
> shirt. I am the same man
> who did in the people in the
> north bay area./
> The S. F. Police could have caught
> me last night if they had

searched the park properly
instead of holding road races
with their motorcycles seeing who
could make the most noise. The
car drivers should have just
parked their cars & sat there
quietly waiting for me to come
out of cover.
School children make nice targets. I think I shall wipe out
a school bus some morning. Just
shoot out a front tire & then
pick off the kiddies as they come
bouncing out.[26]

There were five memorable points in this letter. First, the letter's author was identified as the Zodiac, and second, he took credit for Paul Stine's murder. Third, he confessed to the "north bay killings." Fourth, much of the letter was devoted to extensive criticism of the police, whose incompetence let the Zodiac escape capture after Stine's murder. Finally, the letter ended with the threat to stop a school bus and shoot all of the children.

This message seemed to both brag and criticize others, in this case the police. This detailed letter was also arrogant and threatening in nature. Superiority was the rhetorical theme.

ZODIAC TV . . . AND MORE CALLS

At 2:00 A.M. ten days after the shooting of Paul Stine, the Zodiac contacted the Oakland Police Department by telephone. He asked for a private conversation with F. Lee Bailey or local attorney Melvin Belli. The caller also insisted that one of these two appear on a Bay Area morning talk show.[27] The caller convinced the Oakland Police Department, the FBI, and Zodiac investigators that he might be the Zodiac.

Author Brian Lane claimed that the Zodiac called the Oakland police to surrender—if he could be represented by Melvin Belli or F. Lee Bailey. He also demanded time on a Bay Area morning television talk show.[28]

Zodiac called the station thirty-five times that day. The first call was received at the station about 7 A.M. He continuously called, then hung up, then called back again. For several hours he kept hanging up and calling back, giving his name as "Sam" and sharing with Belli and local talk show host Jim Dunbar extensively about his headaches and how unhappy and lonely he was. A dozen of these calls were played on the Dunbar morning show. Later calls to Belli from this caller were linked to a psychiatric patient at Napa State Hospital.[29]

Zodiac called the *Palo Alto Times* in 1969. A man called the front desk and asserted, "This is the Zodiac. I had to leave San Francisco because I'm too hot there." The Palo Alto police chief described the anonymous telephone message as "extremely serious." He preferred to take no chances and contacted the district transportation supervisor. They provided armed guards for each of the system's twenty-five buses.[30] Providing information was the call's rhetorical theme.

RESUMED COMMUNICATION

Five years passed before the next Zodiac call. A Cordelia school-teacher received four anonymous crank calls at her Vacaville apartment in May of 1974. All that she heard was wind at the other end. She left the phone off the hook and spent time at her boyfriend's house. That prompted a letter from the Zodiac. It mentioned his seeing her at her apartment, and even at her boyfriend's house. Two lines in this three-line, brief letter referred to the phone calls: "I'm pretty angry because your telephone doesn't ring at night. Bad things will happen if you don't let it ring."[31]

There was a terrifying postscript to this incident. The badly frightened teacher drove all the way to El Sobrante that night to stay at her parents' home. Late that night, the phone rang there. All she heard was the sound of wind at the other end of the line.

Author Robert Graysmith believed that he was receiving Zodiac crank calls. In September of 1978, he was receiving breathing phone calls at work. They typically came at 10:30 A.M.[32]

A California parole officer believed he was hearing from the Zodiac as well. This parole officer had no idea that one of his parolees was a Zodiac suspect. The day he found out, he was home looking at copies of the Zodiac letters. He kept getting calls in which the caller would only breathe. The P. O. told his girlfriend, "I think that he knows that I know and that he knows that I know that he knows."[33] I believe that the rhetorical theme of these calls was intimidation.

THE CRIMINAL

Since he was never identified, all we know about the Zodiac we learned from his crimes and communication. And since he was clearly in control of both of those sets of behaviors, this means that we effectively know nothing that Zodiac did not want us to know.

The Zodiac probably lived in or near the Bay Area of northern California. With the exception of the Bates murder, all of the Zodiac crimes were committed in this general locale. He may have had a military background or personal connection to someone in the military. The fact that he left distinctive footprints made by a type of boot distributed only on California military bases allows me to arrive at this conclusion. In addition, his familiarity with military codes, as shown in his cipher, and other related knowledge makes this a reasonable inference.

The Zodiac had to have at least some knowledge of automotive mechanics. He disabled Cheri Jo Bates's car, so that she might accept his offer of help. This led to her brutal death. He similarly caused mechanical problems in another vehicle, but for some reason let the intended victim, Kathleen Johns, and her baby daughter escape.

His letters revealed knowledge of an engineering term known as "radians." This is not a word used by the general public, so it was assumed that his use of this concept indicated some knowledge of engineering. On June 29, 1979, he sent a letter to a newspaper claiming that he had buried a bomb near a school; he also gave police a map and directions on how to find the buried bomb. The map was a Phillips 66 service station map "customized" with his directions and other information. In a later letter, his postscript read, "PS: The Mt. Diablo Code concerns Radians & # inches along the radians."[34]

Both the letter accompanied by the map and the subsequent letter referred to Mt. Diablo, which is located across the Bay from San Francisco, in California's Contra Costa County. In the exact center of Zodiac's modified Phillips 66 map was the Naval Radar Station. In light of the knowledge of military codes manifested in the cipher, this fact was considered to be potentially significant at the time.

Was the Zodiac an opera fan? Perhaps he had a fondness for Gilbert and Sullivan musicals? Allusions to the *Mikado* in two Zodiac letters justify this speculation about the killer's literary preferences. In the *Mikado*, a character named Ko Ko is "The Lord High Executioner," or "Mikado," in Japanese. The Zodiac wrote two letters on July 24, 1970, a rather brief missive followed by one of his lengthier letters. The second letter included two lengthy references to the "The High Executioner's

Song," a famous song from the opera. Several stanzas speculated about all of the people Zodiac would do away with, in a whimsical and intelligent parody of the song. In a later letter, written on January 30, 1974, the word "titwillo," used in the *Mikado*, was adapted to Zodiac's poetic license.[35]

There has been one publicly identified Zodiac candidate, Arthur Leigh Allen. As Davina Willett pointed out for Court TV, Graysmith "believed the Zodiac was a man named Arthur Leigh Allen, a reported sociopath and convicted pedophile. He claimed that police had long suspected Allen as the Zodiac killer."[36] However, Allen was reportedly cleared of any involvement in the crimes, both by a contemporary police investigation and by subsequent DNA comparisons.[37]

Whoever he was, he was big. Eyewitness descriptions portray a relatively short (five feet, eight inches in some accounts) but rather heavy (190–220 pound) individual. Survivors Mageau and Faraday described a very big but not fat person, as did the three eyewitnesses to the Stine murder and the two policemen who saw the Zodiac shortly after that crime.

He also had big feet. The Riverside Police Department investigation uncovered the fact that the killer left footprints "with a military-style heelprint, indicating a size 8–10 shoe."[38] The Crime Library added, "Also found at the scene were the heel-print from a shoe that appeared to be close to size 10, as well as hair, blood and skin tissue found in the victim's hands and beneath her fingerprints."[39] Later, in the murder of Cecilia Shepard and attempted murder of Bryan Hartnell, "Size 10 1/2 Wing Walker shoe prints were recovered from the scene, indicating a suspect weighing more than 210 pounds."[40]

CONCLUSION

The Zodiac, like the Unabomber, successfully extorted major media companies into doing his bidding. Serial killers typically demand one thing in cases like this—publicity. In 1966 and between 1969 and the mid-1970s, the Zodiac told editors at newspapers in southern and northern California, respectively, that failure to run his letters would result in unspecified but undoubtedly lethal consequences.

Unlike the Unabomber, who had a political philosophy to advocate, the Zodiac messages were largely self-congratulatory ramblings and taunts aimed at the police. Both the Zodiac telephone calls and the letters carried remarkably similar themes: the Zodiac's superiority, the ineptitude of law enforcement, and the frightful nature of future planned Zodiac crimes. Taking credit for his crimes was perhaps the most dominant theme in the Zodiac's messages. The Zodiac made telephone admissions of responsibility after two of the crimes, and the October 14 letter linked Zodiac to a murder at a time when he was not already being considered as a suspect.

Verification of his involvement was another important element of the Zodiac's communication. In one letter, he cited crime scene facts known only to the police and the murderer to demonstrate that he was the killer, and he included part of Paul Stine's bloody shirt in another for the same reason. The Zodiac cared about his credibility.

The Zodiac telephone calls typified his pathology. He taunted, threatened, and tried to torment the recipients. Whether he called and said nothing or made explicit threats, these phone conversations were terrifying for the recipients. Taken collectively, we might consider these communications by categorizing the types of calls made, as well as examining aspects of the content and style of these messages.

There were four types of Zodiac calls: (1) credit taking, (2) silence, (3) discussion, and (4) information. The Zodiac called the Vallejo Police Department to take credit for his crimes, and he similarly placed a call to the Napa County authorities. The most frequent type of calls were those where the caller said nothing—only wind or breathing was heard. A schoolteacher, a parole officer, victims' families, and even author Robert Graysmith received such calls. The Zodiac called the *Jim Dunbar Show* to discuss his problems, and he called a newspaper to inform them of his whereabouts and the reasons for his departure from San Francisco.

Several dimensions of the message content of the Zodiac calls should be discussed. He reported murders he had just committed, taking credit for the crimes and even providing directions to the crime scene. He also provided other details of the murders, such as information about the weapon used and description of the victim's vehicle. The content of the silence calls was the sounds of wind, breathing, or simply nothing. The discussion calls focused on the Zodiac's unhappiness and his personal problems. The Zodiac also made an appointment to meet Melvin Belli, which he failed to keep.

The information calls covered a variety of topics. They identified the caller as the Zodiac and announced that he had left San Francisco. The reason given for the Zodiac's departure was the pressure being placed on him by the investigation into his murders.

The style of these calls varied, of course, especially between categories. Three unifying stylistic traits can be considered. The calls seemed to be planned or scripted. They were brief, and concise. Finally, many were intended to terrorize and frighten. However, others seemed to merely be informative, or even cathartic.

Zodiac's correspondence ranged from regular letters to cryptograms, and from plain paper to messages inscribed on greeting cards and even promotional brochures. Some were almost silly, as when he requested that people wear Zodiac buttons, to the deadly serious threat to ambush a school bus full of children. Newspapers were the favored recipients, as they attracted twenty of the twenty-three Zodiac letters. These communications may have gratified the Zodiac, but they also left potentially incriminating evidence behind. There are voiceprints of the Zodiac's telephone calls to the police, and numerous handwriting samples are available for comparison. It is conceivable that trace amounts of the Zodiac's DNA linger on the stamps, paper, and envelopes used in his written communication.

Dear Melvin

This is the Zodiac speaking I wish you a happy Christmass. The one thing I ask of you is this, please help me. I cannot reach out for help because of this thing in me wont let me. I am finding it extreamly dif-icult to hold it in check I am afraid I will loose control again and take my nineth & posibly tenth victom. Please help me I am drownding. At the moment the children are safe from the bomb because it is so massive to dig in & the triger mech requires much work to get it adjusted just right. But if I hold back too long from no nine I will loose ~~complet~~ all controol of my self & set the bomb up. Please help me I can not remain in control for much longer.

The Zodiac sent this letter to prominent attorney Melvin Belli. (Courtesy of the San Francisco Police Department.)

A woman told the FBI in 1969 that she recognized the voice of the Zodiac
and knew his identity. This memo explains why the FBI chose not to get
involved. (Courtesy of the Federal Bureau of Investigation.)

A Zodiac-coded communication sent to the *San Francisco Chronicle*
on November 8, 1969. (Courtesy of the *San Francisco Chronicle*.)

On February 7, 1941, retired Detective ███████████
contacted ████████████ psychologist, VICAP Unit, Quantico,
Virginia. ███████ was familiar with the Zodiac case. He was
informed of the investigation by Detective ███████████ in
1971, and the more recent information obtained from ████████
████████ in 1991. ███████ indicated that his experience
would show that the Zodiac killer probably gained as much
pleasure from taunting the police regarding his killings and
reliving the killings as he did of the killing itself, ████████

This declassified FBI document acknowledged the importance of serial killer communication to the Zodiac. This FBI analysis found that the Zodiac enjoyed his crime-related communication more than the murders themselves. (Courtesy of the Federal Bureau of Investigation.)

I am aware that the Zodiac wrote at least twelve letters to newspapers in San Francisco, Vallejo, and Los Angeles, and at least one letter to an attorney by the name of
████████████ These letters were primarily taunting the
police that they would never catch him and exhibiting a
score-indicating that he was beating San Francisco Police
Department. Some of these letters also contained cryptograms which were supposed to spell out the reasons for the
killings and the Zodiac's name. Numerous attempts have been
made to crack those cryptograms with dubious results. Al-

The Zodiac letters were discussed in this FBI document. (Courtesy of the Federal Bureau of Investigation.)

Sick of living / unwilling to die

cut.
clean.
if red /
clean.
blood spurting;
dripping;
spilling;
all over her new
dress.
oh well.
it was red
anyway.
life draining into an
uncertain death.
she won't
die.
this time
someone'll find her.
just wait till
next time.

r.h

This carving was made in a library school desk by the Zodiac. It is thought to refer to the murder of Cheri Jo Bates. (Courtesy of the Riverside Police Department.)

113

6 The BTK Strangler

Most serial killers stake out their killing territory in a major metropolitan area. This gives them a large target public from which to select their victims. It also affords them the anonymity that results from being one of great numbers of people.

Wichita, Kansas, is not a major metropolitan area. It is not a small town, either, but even in its own state there are bigger cities, and Kansas City is close by. Nevertheless, Wichita was the chosen hunting grounds for a 1970–1980s serial killer who called himself The BTK Strangler. He killed an entire family once. He locked the children of one victim in a closet while he murdered their mother. He killed single women living alone on two occasions.

Skilled as a killer, The BTK Strangler was also very interested in communication about his crimes. He made phone calls, wrote letters, and left a note at a crime scene, or potential crime scene. He engaged in mixed-mode messages. He called a newspaper editor to tell him to look for a letter in a certain library book. He complained about the lack of publicity afforded a previous communication, and he asked what he had to do to get media attention. He even suggested his own nickname: The BTK Strangler, with an uppercase "T" in "The." In March of 2004, after two decades of silence, he told a newspaper about his role in the unsolved 1986 homicide of Vicki Wegerle.

His communication was a central aspect of the BTK crimes. In fact, the murders might have been motivated by the killer's need for attention. Thus, his rhetoric was the key to the BTK murders and related crimes. If caught, however, his communication could convict him.

But he was never apprehended, despite a half-dozen major investigations. In this chapter, I discuss these crimes and the accompanying communication. Then we examine what little is known about The BTK Strangler and the investigation into his crimes and identity.

THE FIRST MURDERS

The first known victims of The BTK Strangler were four members of the Otero family, who lived in a small frame house at 803 Edgemoor Street in Wichita. Joseph Otero, thirty-eight, was found lying on the floor of his bedroom, at the foot of the bed, face down, tied at the hands and feet with an old venetian blinds cord. A cord was wrapped around his neck. Joseph's wife, Julie, lay on the bed, dead and similarly tied. Their lives ended on January 15, 1974.

Joseph II, the Otero's nine-year-old son, was found in his bedroom, also face down on the floor at the foot of his bed. He too was tied, and he also had a plastic bag over his head. In the basement, investigators found the Otero's eleven-year-old daughter, Josephine. Dressed only in her socks and a sweatshirt, she had been hung from a pipe. When police discovered Josephine's body, they noticed "evidence of torture."[1]

The Oteros's fifteen-year-old son Charlie discovered the murders when he arrived home after school. Both Joseph II and Josephine had stayed home from school that day because they were not feeling well. Their absences that day would cost them their lives.

The killer struck again three months later. On April 4, 1974, Kathryn Bright was murdered in her home, at 3217 E. 13th Street. The twenty-one-year-old was bound and strangled, but she was also stabbed repeatedly in the abdomen. The coroner determined that she had been stabbed three times. Clear signs of ligature strangulation were evident around her neck. She had been partially undressed.

THE BTK WRITES AND CALLS

The First Telephone Call

The first call was part of a multimedia informational campaign, as he alerted a newspaper editor where to find a letter. In October 1974, a newspaper editor received a call from the killer that directed him to an engineering textbook in the Wichita Public Library. The content of this telephone call centered on the location of a hidden letter. The newspaper editor was told to look in a certain book in a certain library for a letter. The caller specified a mechanical engineering textbook, to be located at a certain branch of the Wichita Public Library. The style of this brief, anonymous call could accurately be described as low key and calm in tone, with an informative intent. This call's rhetorical theme was an informative one.

The Initial Letter

That anonymous call to a newspaper editor led police to a long, single-spaced letter, found exactly as the killer had indicated in the telephone call. This letter described how the writer had murdered the Otero family, and stated, "Since sex criminals do not change their M. O. [modus operandi] or by nature cannot do so, I will not change mine. The code words for me will be . . . bind them, torture them, kill them, B.T.K."[2] Another section of the letter referred to "the monster within" the killer. The letter amplified this notion, adding, "When this monster enters my brain I will never know. But it is here to stay. How does one cure himself? I can't stop it, but the monster goes on, and hurts me as well as society."[3]

There are slightly different versions of The BTK Strangler's nickname. Respected crime writers Brian Lane and Wilfred Gregg contended that the letters in BTK stood for blind, torture, and kill. Davina Willett of Court TV agreed, declaring, "He signed his letters 'BTK,' which stood for Blind, Torture and Kill, his method, he explained, for killing his victims."[4] Most observers agree, however, that the correct word is "bind," the word he used in his first letter. For example, Wichita reporter Stan Finger noted, "The BTK Strangler" was "the killer's abbreviation for Bind, Torture and Kill."[5]

Several topical mentions in this initial BTK Strangler letter deserve consideration. First, the murders of the Otero family were described in graphic detail. The criminal implied that he was a "sex criminal" by noting that they seldom vary their M. O., and neither would he. He supplied investigators with a set of "code words" by which he could be identified: "Bind them, torture them, kill them." The letter repeatedly referred to the "monster" inside the killer, and the implication was that he was not responsible for his actions because the monster was in charge of the killings. The monster's residency was permanent, the letter claimed, and The BTK Strangler was unable to control himself. The letter acknowledged the damage caused to society and the writer lamented that fact.

I have found three noteworthy dimensions of the style of this letter. This mid-length missive was in some aspects very detailed and graphic, as when describing the Otero murders. On the other hand, parts of the letter seemed explanatory and rather low key. Different rhetorical themes emerged from this letter. The writer meant to terrify by predicting more murders. Yet other sections seemed intellectual and intended to inform.

THE BTK KILLS AGAIN

Shirley Vian was the next BTK Strangler murder victim. She was killed on March 17, 1977, at 1311 Hydraulic Street. The twenty-six-year-old mother of three was bound with the same material and in the same manner as the Oteros. She was stripped and strangled, and left with a plastic bag over her head and a cord around her neck. At least the killer had spared her children. They were locked in a closet while their mother was killed. Again, as in the case of Josephine Otero, Vian was found "also bound and strangled with other evidence of torture."[6]

Nancy Fox was the last consensus BTK Strangler victim. Her body was found on December 9, 1977, in her Wichita apartment at 834 South Pershing Street in Wichita. Unlike the other victims, she was fully clothed. The twenty-five-year-old Fox was found dead in her bedroom, with a nylon stocking twisted tightly around her neck. Investigators noticed a broken window and assumed that was the killer's means of entry to her apartment.

ANOTHER BTK CALL

After the Fox murder, The BTK Strangler called the police a second time. On December 9, 1977, the murderer called from a public phone to report the Nancy Fox murder. The caller simply stated, "Go to this address. You will find a homicide—Nancy Fox."[7] When the police arrived at the phone booth, the phone dangled from the receiver. Author Michael Newton recalled that an unnamed caller led police to the crime scene. Investigators traced the phone call to a downtown phone booth.[8] Weinman agreed, adding "Dormant for three years, he resumed killing in 1977, even going so far as to call the police to point them to a woman he'd just murdered."[9]

There are noteworthy content dimensions of this call. In a demonstration of the caller's superiority over law enforcement, the call directed police to a specified address. The killer had to assist the police in locating his victims, a fact of some satisfaction to the criminal. The fact that a homicide had been committed was mentioned, as was the homicide victim's name—Nancy Fox. The caller implicitly accepted responsibility for the murder by the fact that he was the only one who knew about it, although that claim was not explicitly made.

The style of this relatively brief anonymous call was similar to the other call, in some respects. It was low key and calm in tone, and there was an evident informative nature. At the end of the call, the caller did not hang up the telephone; instead, he left it dangling off the hook. The rhetorical theme of this call was a combination of superiority and helpfulness to the police.

BTK LETTERS WITH POEMS

A second missive was mailed to a local newspaper. But, things went awry. The BTK Strangler mailed a poem to the *Wichita Eagle-Beacon* on January 31, 1978, but it was accidentally sent to the advertising department and overlooked for days. Tomas Guillen, who coauthored a book on the Green River killer and has conducted a study of serial killer communiqués, described this communication, which included a short poem about victim Shirley Vian. The poem was based on a "Curley Locks" nursery rhyme. The second communication ended with this line, "P.S.: How about some name for me, its time: 7 down and many more to go. I like the following, How about you? 'THE B.T.K. STRANGLER'."[10] A *USA Today* report agreed, adding, "A killer operating in Wichita in the 1970s named himself the BTK Strangler. The initials meant bind, torture, kill."[11]

The content of this second letter, as far as it has been disclosed, indicated that the writer/killer requested a nickname. He then proceeded to offer his own preferred nom de plume, "The B.T.K. Strangler." The letter claimed that the writer had killed seven people to date, with "many more to go," in a sort of informal serial murder scorecard. The style of this second letter was low key and almost lighthearted. However, there was an underlying atmosphere of veiled threats. The style was characterized by the use of questions, instead of the more typical declarative sentences. Overall, the use of questions and the tone resulted in a dialogue-like style. The rhetorical themes were proclamations of superiority and threats of more murders.

A third BTK Strangler letter was received by KAKE-TV Channel 10 on February 10, 1978. It complained about the manner in which the previous communication was handled. "How many do I have to kill before I get my name in the paper or some national attention?" he asked. "You guess the motive and the victims," the letter taunted.[12]

A second poem was included, "Oh Death to Nancy." It was patterned after a poem ("Oh Death") taught in a class at Wichita State University. The accompanying letter provided graphic descriptions of how two victims were tortured and killed.

"I find the newspaper not writing about the poem on Vian unamusing. A little paragraph would have been enough. I know it [sic] not the news media fault. The Police Chief he keep [sic] things quiet," the letter announced.[13] "I'm sorry this happened to society. They are the ones who suffer the most. It's hard for me to control myself. When this monster entered my brain, I will never know. Maybe you can stop him. I can't. He has already chosen his next victim," the letter reportedly added.[14] Investigators were astonished at the enclosed illustration. The letter was accompanied by a professional-quality rendition of the Fox crime scene. It was so detailed that it was virtually identical to a police technician's photo of the crime scene. The police immediately requested that the letter be embargoed. In this standard public relations practice, information is held back for publication until a later date. It has not yet been made public; in fact, none of The BTK Strangler messages has been officially and completely released.

The writer complained of a lack of media attention. He told investigators that they would have to guess his motives and the number of victims. The writer expressed his realization that society suffered from his crimes, and he expressed some regret for this societal damage, but he said he could not control himself. According to the letter, the writer did not know when the "monster" entered his body, and he added that "maybe you can stop him. I can't." The letter concluded with the claim that the next victim had already been selected.

The style of this important letter was characterized at times by a whining, complaining tone. At other times, the letter conveyed a menacing and taunting sensation. Overall, the letter was explanatory and informative, with a section devoted to the author's rationalization about why his "monster" was responsible for The BTK Strangler crimes, not him.

This letter included several rhetorical themes. Criticism of the police was evident, as was the killer's superiority. I also think the writer intended to cause public terror and panic.

THE BTK NOTE AND LETTERS LADEN WITH SCARVES

In addition to those letters, it is believed The BTK Strangler also wrote a note that was left in the home of a sixty-three-year-old Wichita woman. The note, dated April 8, 1979, told her that he left after getting tired of waiting for her as he hid in her closet. "Be glad you weren't here, because I was," the note simply declared.[15]

There is some disagreement over the facts of this BTK Strangler communication. Author David Lohr suggested that the last verified BTK incident occurred on April 28, 1979. The BTK Strangler is believed to have waited inside a house in the 600 block of South Pinecrest Avenue for the abovementioned sixty-three-year-old owner to return. When she failed to come home in time, he became angry, left the premises, and later mailed a letter to the woman; enclosed was one of her scarves.[16] Some authorities believed that the elderly woman's daughter was the actual target of The BTK Strangler. Wichita police thought the killer might previously have seen the daughter at the house.[17]

There were some noteworthy aspects of the content of this crime scene note. Initially, it told the intended victim that she should consider herself very fortunate. Why? Because he had been hiding in her closet, waiting to kill her when she came home. He got bored and and left.

What can be concluded about the style of this note? It was relatively brief, consisting of a mere eight words. It was mildly threatening in tone, although undoubtedly extremely frightening for the intended victim. It was in general a relatively simple message in vocabulary, structure, and content. The explicit rhetorical theme was informative. However, the tacit subtext message was one of danger barely averted, and terror.

WERE THERE MORE BTK MURDERS?

The murders discussed so far were all of the crimes definitely attributable to The BTK Strangler. However, there may have been other BTK murders. Two such crimes are the murders of Shannon Olsen and the Fager family.

Shannon Olson was a fifteen-year-old girl who was killed in Wichita on October 31, 1987. She was found partly dressed, and her hands and feet were tied. She had been stabbed repeatedly and dumped into a pond in an industrial area. There were unreleased letters allegedly from The BTK Strangler claiming responsibility, but the case remains unsolved.

Exactly two months later, on the last day of 1987, Mary Fager returned to her Wichita home at 7105 East 14th Street after spending a couple of days out of town. She found her husband, Melvin, dead from two gunshots to the back. Both of her daughters were found strangled to death in the hot tub in the basement of the family residence. Kelli, sixteen years of age, was nude. There were no marks on her body, and she had not been bound. Drowning was the cause of her death. Her little sister Sherri's hands and feet had been bound. In addition, she was strangled nearly to the point of death, and then drowned. The killer used half-inch-wide black electrician's tape to bind and strangle her. She was wearing her pajamas. The killer closed the hot tub lid and left the two dead girls inside when he left. Melvin Phillip Fager was found in the family's living room. He had been shot twice in the back at very close range. He was found lying on his back with his feet pointing toward the door. He was fully clothed, still wearing a winter coat.[18]

Unlike previous BTK crime scenes, these victims apparently fought back as best they could. Wichita Police Department Captain John Dotson told a news conference, "I think it would be reasonable to say there was resistance. There is evidence in the home that something occurred." However, when pressed for details, "He wouldn't say which victims resisted, or what form that resistance took."[19] Nothing was taken from the house, and it had not been ransacked or damaged in any way. However, the family car—a gray 1983 Volkswagen Rabbit—was stolen.

WERE THERE LATER BTK LETTERS?

There has been recent activity in The BTK Strangler case. In February 1998, Wichita Police Chief Richard LaMunyon said that a typed, disorganized letter supposedly written by The BTK Strangler was sent to the police the week after the Fager murders.[20] It reportedly was not connected to the December 30, 1997, murders of Philip Fager and his children. The continuing police investigation has not confirmed whether The BTK Strangler sent the letter. LaMunyon added that the department occasionally receives letters from people who claim to be The BTK Strangler.

Did The BTK Strangler resume writing about his crimes after more than two decades of silence? Some think so. Someone claiming to be The BTK Strangler wrote a letter to Mary Fager shortly after her family was murdered. The letter denied that he had committed the Fager murders but said he was a fan of whoever had. FBI experts could not irrefutably tie the letter to BTK, but a Wichitian who was involved in the original investigation and who saw the letter himself declared that there is no doubt in his mind that it was authentic. "It made the hair stand up on the back of my neck," the source said.[21]

The *Wichita Eagle* recently received a BTK letter, postmarked March 17, 2004. It reportedly contained a photocopy of Vicki Wegerle's driver's license and three photographs of her murder scene. The sender was identified in the addressee information as Bill Thomas Killman, of 1684 Oldmanor, in Wichita.[22] Police were unable to locate Mr. Killman at that address. The elusive Mr. Killman's initials? BTK.

WHO WAS THE BTK STRANGLER?

The BTK Strangler was seen on two occasions. Neighbors of the Otero family reported seeing a strange-looking man in the area just prior to the murders. They notified the police and described the man.

The killer grew bolder over time. He reportedly had stopped one of Shirley Vian's sons in the street the day of her murder. He showed him a photograph of someone he claimed he was trying to locate in that neighborhood.[23]

He was a sexually maladjusted individual. The Wichita Police Department discovered evidence of semen in numerous places in the Otero home after their brutal murders. Wichita Police Department Captain John Dotson disclosed that the killer had masturbated on the victims. Guillen agreed, adding that while the victims were not sexually assaulted, investigators located semen throughout the house and on some victims' bodies. Another media report noted, "Someone had masturbated on some of the victims."[24]

The same perversion was practiced at the Nancy Fox murder scene. The autopsy ruled out sexual assault on the victim. But, semen was discovered at the crime scene.

The BTK Strangler apparently took items from the crime scenes, perhaps to serve as souvenirs or mementos of his criminal acts, something common to many serial killers. It was reported that Joseph Otero's watch was taken and was never recovered. Police suspected that the killer kept the watch as a souvenir. Similarly, Nancy Fox's driver's license was missing; to date, it has not been recovered.

THE BTK INVESTIGATION

Investigators pursuing The BTK Strangler have arrived at certain conclusions about their quarry, based on their assessment of the accumulated information in the case files. Wichita Police Department Captain John Dotson declared, "This type of personality doesn't stop voluntarily. This type of person continues to kill." Fellow BTK Strangler investigator Mike Hill, then Sheriff of Sedgwick County, Kansas, added this pessimistic prediction: "It's sad to say the only way that we'll ever find out who this individual is will be when we have a victim."[25]

Psychological Profiles

The Wichita Police Department accepted assistance in a variety of ways from a variety of sources. For example, a panel of local psychiatrists evaluated the letters and other messages sent by The BTK Strangler. According to Newton, "Psychiatrists who analyzed the letters felt the killer saw himself as part of some nebulous 'grand scheme'."[26] In addition, at least three psychological profiles of The BTK Strangler were produced, by two former FBI profilers and by the president of the Violent Crimes Institute.

John Douglas, a former FBI profiler and serial killer expert, developed a profile of The BTK Strangler for the investigators. Several of the Douglas profile predictions are worth our consideration. The killer used police jargon in his letters. He might have been a cop, or he impersonated one. He most likely read true crime magazines and probably owned a police badge. He would attempt to inject himself into the investigation, if possible. He would brag and hint about his crimes.

In other respects, the profile of The BTK Strangler is fairly typical of many serial killers. Douglas suggested that at the time of the 1970s killings, The BTK Strangler was a white male loner, in his twenties or thirties, who might have a record for petty crimes, like break-ins or voyeurism. The profile speculated on the reasons behind the apparent cessation of BTK Strangler activity: the killings may have ended because he was incarcerated or institutionalized, the killer might have died or become otherwise incapacitated, he might have become frightened, The BTK Strangler might have gone over the edge.[27]

A second profile of The BTK Strangler was created in August 2000 by Dr. Deborah Schurman-Kauflin, president of the Violent Crimes Institute. Several aspects of this profile are noteworthy. Dr. Schurman-Kauflin's initial conclusions were about the demographics and appearance of the offender. She described him as an unmarried white male, approx-imately twenty-eight to thirty years of age. He lived in the vicinity of the Oteros family or spent considerable time there, enough time to fantasize about Josephine Otero. He resided in a house, not in an apartment. He was relatively tall and physically fit; his general ap-pearance was neat, he had short hair, and he probably preferred dark clothes.[28]

The crux of the profile was conveyed in the next point—his pathol-ogy:

> Considered quiet and conservative by those who know him. Modest. I believe people would mistake him as kind because of his quiet demeanor. But he suffers from extreme pathology—psychopath.
>
> There are no voices or demons. This man knew exactly what he was doing.
>
> He was and, if alive, still would be an extremely sad individual. Sad for himself and his pain. Completely self-absorbed.
>
> Due to the fact that I did not have access to the letters, his job sta-tus is questionable to me. I do feel that his job was very secondary to him. Money was not important either. His compulsion to kill was and ALWAYS would be number 1. He would not be satisfied with fantasy. He would be forced to act. Therefore, I find it hard to believe that he did not kill between 1974 and 1977. If there were no murders in Kansas at that time, he was someplace else.
>
> He was very immature—the games, magazines, choice of child target. The fact that he did not sexually assault lends credence to this. He masturbated on his victims but did not rape.
>
> At the same time, he is very patient in his crimes, stalking and killing without detection. This makes him a paradox, which in and of itself would be disturbing even to him. I do feel like he is very comfortable with books and would have many of them in his home. Not just a few, many, many books. True crime as well as books which feed his fantasies. I feel as if they would be found all over his house. He was smart, very intelligent.[29]

The profile ended with these final main conclusions. The killer did not heavily abuse drugs and/or alcohol. He may drink occasionally, but that did not cause the murders. He owned a car, which would have been dark colored. However, he enjoyed walking around neighbor-hoods people-watching and searching for victims. Because he was immature, he would only socialize with much younger people. He did not have many friends, preferring to keep most people at a distance. Almost all of his interpersonal relationships would be superficial. He was unmarried, and his past history with women was frustrating and unsuccessful.[30]

After these specific profile points, Dr. Schurman-Kauflin speculated about the reasons behind The BTK Strangler's cessation of serial murdering: "This is not a person who would stop on his own. There are 3 reasons to stop. 1. Death. 2. Prison. 3. Too disabled or sick to kill. Period. This is a compulsive psychopath who enjoyed killing and wouldn't give it up."[31]

Another former FBI profiler, Robert Ressler, also created a psychological profile of The BTK Strangler. According to Ressler's analysis, the offender was an academic, either a professor or a graduate student at a Kansas university engaged in a criminal justice discipline. The profile also suggested that the killer "was most likely in his mid-to-late 20's at the time of the killings and was an avid reader of books and newspaper stories concerning serial murders, who had left the area, died or was in a mental institution or prison," because of the abrupt and complete cessation of BTK crimes and communication.[32]

The Investigation to Date

The BTK Strangler case is not officially closed. A 1986 BTK Strangler reinvestigation was christened, "The Ghostbusters Task Force," and it was based on a computerized analysis of a series of lists deemed salient to the BTK case. The motivation behind the reopening of the case in 1991 can be attributed to "a new lead in the BTK murders. Although the lead fizzled, Capt. John Dotson will not disclose the nature of the tip." Whatever the tip was, it prompted Mike McKenna, then a Wichita Police Department detective, to remark, "I believe he is still probably in this community."[33] The March 2004 BTK letter made McKenna's hunch look good.

One fact was clear to investigators from the start—the killer had pronounced and restrictive geographic preferences. All of the killings took place within a 3.5-mile radius; therefore, investigators assembled lists of each and every white male who resided within a quarter-mile of the Oteros's house in January of 1974. They also compiled comparable lists for the Vian, Fox, and Bright homes. Investigators considered geography the most important factor in their case. Wichita Police Department Lieutenant Kenneth Landwehr admitted, "The main crux of our search always was geographical. According to the behavioral scientists, the individual lived close to where he was striking."

A second salient list concentrated on an academic audience. Investigators listed all of the white males who had attended Wichita State University between 1974 and 1979.

The BTK Strangler composed poems about two of his murders, resulting in two lists. It was discovered that his poem about the Vian murder was a take-off on a "Curly Locks" nursery rhyme, recently published in *Games,* a puzzle magazine. Investigators obtained the magazine's subscription list. The Fox murder poem, "Oh Death to Nancy," turned out to be loosely fashioned after a poem called, "Oh Death," taught in a Wichita State University folklore class. Police obtained the class roster, another academic list to be checked out carefully.

The BTK Strangler left a letter to the authorities in a mechanical engineering library book. Investigators noted the eight people who had checked out that particular book from that library. This was by far the shortest list.

Once these lists were assembled and verified, a computer was used to collate and cross-reference the lists. As a result, the computer identified 225 potential suspects. Most of these individuals no longer lived in Wichita. The detectives systematically began to eliminate each of the possible suspects. They succeeded in locating more than two hundred of these individuals, and all but five agreed to provide blood and saliva samples. As a result, all but twelve of the suspects have been eliminated, including the five reluctant donors.[34]

Motives

What can be said of the possible motives behind these crimes? Since the criminal was never apprehended, we do not know for certain why these crimes were committed. Author Sarah Weinman suggested that the motive was conceit, referring to The BTK Strangler as "one of the most egotistical killers in years, maybe ever."[35] According to another study of these crimes, the murderer was attempting to emulate the Son of Sam: "The BTK Strangler has been said to have been following in the footsteps of Berkowitz."[36] However, since the first BTK murders took place in 1974 and the Son of Sam started killing in 1976, this particular explanation is relatively unconvincing.

A final motive possibility—Were the murders somehow tied to an occupation? Weinman posed the on-point question, "Was he a criminal justice professor at a nearby university, or a cop, as some theories have postulated?"[37] Ressler speculated that the killer was either a graduate student or a professor in a criminal justice–related field at Wichita State University, which was located in Wichita, and where the folklore class that taught the "On Death" poem was held.

Investigators considered a wide variety of possible motives, as well as several relatively improbable theories. "We tried a hundred thousand theories. We checked house numbers, the victims' length of residency, the phases of the moon, we read books, looking for arcane connections to mythology, witchcraft and demonology," declared former Wichita Police Department Lieutenant Al Stewart.[38] One thing about the M.O. of The BTK Strangler was certain: his habit of cutting the telephone lines to his victim's homes. Lohr recalled that, during the time The BTK Strangler was active, people returning home after work would check to see if their telephone lines had been cut.

Perhaps the most heinous thing about The BTK Strangler's crimes was the torture inflicted upon the victims before their death. Rose Stanley, who worked at a Wichita TV station at the time of the killings, recalled, "He would choke the person almost to the point of death. Then he would let them come back. Then he would strangle them to death."[39] In some cases, he would do this repeatedly.

One thing is certain. If The BTK Strangler ever is apprehended, it will be relatively easy to identify him as the culprit; he left traces of himself behind. A single fingerprint was found at the Otero crime scene, and semen was left at the Otero and Fox crime scenes. Tape recordings of what is believed to be his voice exist, as do the letters and note he wrote. Weinman also noted the communication-based array of evidence accumulated against The BTK Strangler, citing DNA samples, semen samples, handwriting samples, and voiceprints.[40] In fact, identification of The BTK Strangler from his biological deposits at crime scenes should be relatively simple, as his genetic characteristics place him in a distinctive category. The killer's semen is a type found in less than six percent of all males.

These were not spontaneous crimes. Rather, BTK investigators were certain that the killer had planned these murders carefully. Crime scene signs supported this belief. In the Otero crime, there was evidence of planning. The phone lines had been cut, and the killer brought the venetian blinds cord. Similarly, in the Vian murder, the same-day conversation with Vian's son demonstrated that The BTK Strangler was not acting out of some passion or spontaneous impulse, but that he planned his crimes. The police appraisal of the killer's personality described him as being anything but a raving lunatic: "Investigators call BTK fastidious, calculating and meticulous."[41]

Law enforcement took these crimes very seriously. Between the first crime in January 1974 and the last major reinvestigation in 1991, the Wichita Police Department devoted approximately 100,000 hours of detective time, in the course of a half-dozen separate major investigations of The BTK Strangler. The FBI refers to these crimes as a top unsolved case.

The BTK Strangler murders were "one of Wichita's most notorious unsolved crime sprees," according to a recent report in the *Wichita Eagle*.[42] Another story in the *Wichita Eagle* recalled, "BTK was the serial killer who claimed at least seven lives, who terrified the community for more than four years. And who has never been caught." Richard LaMunyon, the former Wichita police chief, remarked, "I think we grew up. We used to think, 'This is not New York or New Jersey or Los Angeles. This is Wichita'."[43]

AN ABUNDANCE OF COMMUNICATION CLUES

The BTK Strangler was never caught. However, at the time of the crimes, investigators tried to use the messages as clues to help locate the killer. The police played tapes of the phone calls for the public, hopeful that someone could identify BTK. They also had a panel of local mental health professionals read the letters and offer a collective analysis of their meaning.

His communication could incriminate him, if apprehended. Police have his voiceprints. Several BTK Strangler handwriting samples exist to compare with the writing of any suspect.

CONCLUSION

The BTK Strangler eluded authorities in Wichita, Kansas, as he murdered and communicated throughout the 1970s and 1980s, and in a letter as recently as March 2004. This serial killer has conducted a dialogue with Wichita law enforcement agencies through the media. In letters and telephone calls, The BTK Strangler pleaded for respect and appreciation. When asked to summarize the still-unreleased BTK Strangler letters, Wichita Police Captain John Dotson replied, "Here I am. Pay attention."[44]

Why did The BTK Strangler write and send poems and letters to the media and law enforcement agencies? Since all of these communications taunted and teased his ineffective pursuers, we might conclude that these rhetorical acts heightened the pleasure he experienced from the overall homicidal act. The BTK Strangler seemed to have an agenda, and murders were only part of the process. He felt the need to call and write the authorities, through the media, to engage them in pointed communication about his prowess and their ineffectiveness.

This criticism of the police, combined with their inability to apprehend the killer, resulted in a great deal of public and media pressure being exerted on the authorities. This is a typical feature of serial murder cases. Guillen concluded that the BTK communiqués hindered the police probe into the serial murders, because they were sent to newspapers and television stations, rather than to the authorities. This resulted in increased pressure on the police to apprehend the killer.[45]

He threatened future murders. One letter included a countdown of sorts: "7 down and many more to go." But the classic BTK Strangler line must be his frustrated, whining lament about being underpublicized and insufficiently feared: "How many do I have to kill before I get my name in the paper or some national attention?" In a nutshell, that line from a BTK Strangler letter characterized this killer's motivation and communication behavior. He killed and communicated in a symbiotic holistic package of rhetorical/homicidal activity that made perfect sense to him. One without the other, in his mind, would have been meaningless. Which brings us back full circle to the most recent BTK letter, which arrived as this book went into production.[46] To BTK, to kill and not to receive credit was empty, unfulfilling, and a hollow victory.

Why did the BTK Stranger send items to the police, linking him to another homicide, that of Vicki Wegerle? Until he communicated by sending the items, he was not a suspect in that case. For BTK, the communication consummated the crimes.

7 John Robinson Sr.

John Robinson Sr. became known as the Internet Slavemaster. He was a devotee of bondage, domination, and sadomasochism (BDSM), an extreme subgroup of the sadism and masochism (S&M) sexual proclivity. In this milieu, he was a "Slavemaster," and a "Teaching Master," or one who teaches "Masters" how to train their "Slaves."

The mayor of Kansas City and a Missouri state senator were taken in by one of his schemes, an exercise in self-aggrandizement in which he created an entire organization just to name himself "Man of the Year." He even fooled the *Kansas City Star*—for a day. He convinced women he met through Internet chatrooms that he would be a good "Master," and several of them journeyed to Kansas City to be his "Slave." Some died.

Other victims were obtained courtesy of nonprofit social service agencies. Robinson convinced the agencies that he was a suitable social services provider, and a young mother and her baby daughter were entrusted to his care. The woman vanished, and Robinson's brother adopted a baby girl. Similarly, a single mother and her wheelchair-bound daughter turned to Robinson for social services help. They disappeared, but their Social Security and disability checks continued to be cashed by "J. T." Robinson.

In this chapter, I discuss these crimes and the communication surrounding them. The criminal was bad, the crimes despicable. The communication facilitated the murders. But the communication also resulted in a criminal investigation and in Robinson's conviction at his three murder trials. The themes of Robinson's rhetoric involved deceptive efforts of help and deceptive attempts to conceal his crimes.

FIRST KILLING AND COMMUNICATION

No one besides John Robinson knows with absolute certainty how many people he murdered. I estimate at least eight and perhaps as many as fifteen lives were ended by this serial killer. Paula Godfrey was his first known victim, last seen on September 1, 1984.

Godfrey went to work for Equi-II, Robinson's management consulting firm. She was hired as a sales representative soon after her graduation from Olathe North High School. Robinson told her she was enrolled in a training seminar in Texas. The morning he picked her up at her parents' home for the ride to the airport was the last time she was seen alive.

A curious development in Godfrey's disappearance seemed to exonerate Robinson. Letters signed by Godfrey arrived, sent to the police and her family, stating that she had left town of her own accord. Sue Miller Wiltz of Court TV recalled, "Police investigated both the Godfrey and Stasi cases. In both, family members received typewritten letters bearing the signatures of the two women that said they had decided to move out of town. Those who knew them immediately suspected foul play."[1] An Associated Press account reported, "Robinson had forced some of his victims to write letters to family members telling them all was well, according to the prosecution's case. The correspondence eventually stopped, and the women disappeared."[2]

Paula Godfrey's family filed a missing person's report on her. They confronted Robinson about their daughter's disappearance. Shortly thereafter, a brief, handwritten note mailed from Kansas City, allegedly written by Paula, arrived at the Godfrey home. Although it assured her parents she was fine, Mr. Godfrey thought it "very out-of-character," and took it to the police.[3]

Soon afterward, the Overland Park Police Department was sent a handwritten letter, ostensibly from Paula, declaring that she was fine and extremely grateful to John Robinson. According to the letter, she was now residing in the western part of Kansas, and she expressed her disinterest in seeing her family.[4] These messages were meant to mislead. Their rhetorical theme was deception. Robinson sought to create documentation for his defense if apprehended for Godfrey's murder.

MOTHER AND DAUGHTER MURDER

Lisa and Tiffany Stasi were next to fall prey to Robinson. January 10, 1985, was the last time Lisa was seen alive. Lisa, nineteen, and her four-month-old daughter simply vanished. Her baby daughter, Tiffany, was adopted by Robinson's brother, Donald, soon after the disappearance of the Stasis.

Lisa Stasi was separated from her husband, Carl. Robinson met her when she and Tiffany stayed at a Kansas City shelter for battered women. She told her family that a man named John Osborne (later identified as Robinson) had obtained a job for her in Chicago. In the meantime, he put her and Tiffany up in a hotel room.

Betty Stasi received a typed letter from her daughter-in-law, Lisa. This upset Betty, because Lisa could not type, and "she also clearly remembered her daughter-in-law saying that 'they' had made her sign four blank sheets of paper."[5] The letter to Betty Stasi reads:

Betty:

Thank you for all your help I really do appreciate it! I have decided to leave Kansas City and try and make a new life for myself and Tiffany. I wrote to Marty and told him to let the bank take the car back, the payments are so far behind that they either want the money or the car. I don't have the money to pay the bank all the back payments and the car needs a lot of work. When I wrote Marty about the car I forgot to tell him about the lock box with all my papers in the trunk. Since the accident I couldn't get the trunk opened. Please tell him to force open the trunk and get that box of papers out before the bank gets the car.

Thanks for all your help, but I really need to get away and start a new life for me and Tiffany. She deserves a real mother who works and take care of her. The people at Hope House and Outreach were really helpful, but I just couldn't keep taking charity from them. I feel that I have to get out on my own and prove that I can handle it myself.

Marty wanted me to go to Alabama to take care of aunt Evelyn but I just can't. She is so opinionated and hard to get along with right now I just can't deal with her. Marty and I fought about it and I know he will try and force me to go to Alabama. I am just not going there.

I will let you know from time to time how I am and what I am doing. Tell Carl that I will write him and let him know where he can get in touch with me.[6]

This letter's content included an expression of gratitude to the recipient for her help. Lisa's letter informed her mother-in-law that she was leaving Kansas City to start a new life with her daughter, Tiffany. There was an extended description of Lisa's car problems, and her request for her brother, Marty, to remove some personal items from it before it was repossessed by the bank. Her letter emphasized her desire for independence, and there was a lengthy account of Lisa's dispute with Marty, who wanted her to relocate to Alabama to care for their Aunt Evelyn. The letter concluded with the promise to stay in touch.

There were noteworthy aspects of the style of this letter. The tone of this moderate-length letter was low key, and calm. It seemed basically informative in nature, with a heavy element of self-justification for the decisions she had made.

Lisa Stasi supposedly sent another typed letter, this one to Cathy Stackpole at Hope House. Dated the day of her disappearance, it read (all errors will be retained in quoted material):

Dear Cathy:

I want to thank you for all your help. I have decided to get away from this area and try and make a good life for me and Tiffany. Marty my brother want me to go take care of my aunt but I don't want to. He is trying to take over my life and I just am not going to let him. I borrowed some money from a friend and Tiffany and I are leaving Kansas City. The people you referred me to were really nice and helped me with everything. I am greatful for everyones help.

I wrote to the outreach people, Carl's mother and my brother telling them all that I had made the decision to get a fresh start in life. If I stay here they will just try and run my life more and more like they are trying to do. I finally realized that I have a baby to take care of and she is my first responsibility. I asked my brother to tell the bank to pick up the car because the tags have expired and I am so far behind with the payments that I could never get them up to date, and with no job the bank wants the car or the money. I will be fine. I know what I want and I am going to go after it. Again thanks for your help and Hope House and thanks for telling me about outreach. Everyone has been so helpful I owe you all a great deal.[7]

The content of this letter was virtually identical to the one sent to Lisa Stasi's mother-in-law. The one main difference was that the letter to Cathy Stackpole included an additional paragraph about how Tiffany was Lisa's main responsibility and an important factor in Lisa's decisions. There were no substantial stylistic dissimilarities between these two letters. The rhetorical purpose of both letters was deception. By explaining the innocent nature of the victims' disappearance, both provided alibis for Robinson. Neither letter was true.

MORE MURDERS AND MISLEADING MESSAGES

Sometime around May or June of 1987, Katherine Clampett met her demise at the hands of John Robinson. Clampett was twenty-six or twenty-seven at the time of her disappearance, accounts vary.[8]

Robinson needed a secretary for his company, Equi-II. In 1987, Robinson advertised for one in a local newspaper. The lucrative position seemed too good to be true, with considerable traveling and even a generous wardrobe allowance. Clampett saw the ad in the morning paper and immediately called Equi-II to arrange an appointment for an interview. She was soon hired by Equi-II, and was traveling nationwide on Equi-II business soon after.

The Overland Park Police Department declared Katherine Clampett a missing person on June 15, 1987. After detectives questioned Robinson, they dropped the case because of insufficient evidence. Robinson reportedly had been the only suspect in her disappearance.

Beverly Bonner divorced her husband and abandoned her children to be with John Robinson. They had an illicit love affair behind prison walls when she worked as a volunteer in the library of the prison where Robinson was incarcerated for theft. She was probably killed during the winter of 1994.

Bonner's positively identified remains were found in a barrel on Robinson's property. She had moved from Cameron, Missouri, to be with Robinson, telling a friend that she had taken a job with Hydro-Gro, Inc., another Robinson company. Then, in January of 1994, she abruptly dropped out of sight.

Beverly Bonner's family and friends received typed letters from around the world, claiming that she was enjoying herself. The strange thing was that none of her letters mentioned the death of her eldest son, Randy, and she failed to return for his funeral. Both the Associated Press and Court TV reports confirmed this bogus letter-writing campaign.[9]

Later that year, Sheila and Debbie Faith died at the hands of Robinson. They were last seen alive in the summer of 1994. Sheila was a forty-one-year-old mother of a handicapped daughter, sixteen-year-old Debbie. The Faiths had moved to Kansas City from Pueblo, Colorado. Sheila's husband had recently died from cancer, and she was seriously overweight and lonely; Debbie was permanently confined to a wheelchair because of spina bifida.[25] Robinson misled the lonely widow. According to one report, Sheila told friends, "She had found her 'dream man,' who promised she'd never have to work. He'd take her on a cruise, take care of her daughter, and teach her to ride horses in Kansas."[10] Instead, she and Debbie were murdered and stuffed into a barrel hidden in a storage locker.

Izabela Lewicka, twenty-two, left college to be Robinson's sex "slave." She was most likely murdered in July of 1999. Lewicka, petite and with long brown hair, was a native of Poland and a freshman studying fine arts at Indiana University-Purdue University at Indianapolis. After she met Robinson through an Internet BDSM chatroom, she told her parents she was going to Kansas City to pursue a school-related internship.

Her body was discovered after Robinson's arrest in June 2000. The Associated Press reported, "a search of his rural property turned up the barrels and, in them, the bodies of Trouten, and Lewicka, 22."[11] Investigators surmised that Lewicka had probably been dead since 1999.

Lewicka vanished while in Robinson's company during the spring of 1999. Nevertheless, Izabela's parents in Indiana received letters over the next few months, all signed by their daughter, recounting her world travels. The Associated Press also described the bogus letters received by the Lewickas and others. This time, Robinson also used e-mail in his attempt to conceal Lewicka's murder. Wiltz concluded that, "While her parents never saw their daughter again, and authorities believe she was murdered around August 1999, they continued to receive e-mails purportedly from her up until Robinson's arrest."[12]

The final known Robinson murder victim was Suzette Trouten. She was last seen or heard from in March of 2000. The pretty twenty-seven-year-old had curly brown hair and brown eyes and worked as a nurse's aide. A report by Court TV observed, "In February, 2000, Trouten drove to Kansas City with her two Pekinese, calling her family on arrival to let them know she'd arrived safely and was staying at a hotel in the suburbs. On March 1, she called her mother for the last time." Trouten told her family that a man she met over the Internet had offered her $60,000 to care for his grandfather. The elderly man supposedly was diabetic and confined to a wheelchair.[13] According to a report by ABC News, Trouten was twenty-eight at the time, and she left her home in Monroe County, Michigan, to relocate to Lenexa, Kansas, to meet Robinson.[14]

Trouten's family reported her as a missing person in March 2000. Her mother, Carolyn Trouten, described her youngest daughter as a "mama's girl" and told the media, "We knew she was being kidnapped or held."[15] Her body was discovered in a barrel on Robinson's farm, and positively identified.

The Trouten family began receiving letters apparently from Suzette on June 1, 2000. Family members received computer-generated letters, supposedly from Suzette, with Mexican postmarks and her signature. These letters were in distinctive yellow-and-pink envelopes, Suzette's favorites. She said that she and "Jim Turner," were enjoying their trip, sailing around the world. She described how Peka and Hari stood on the bow of the yacht, excitedly barking at dolphins. She had quit smoking, and her life could not be better.[16]

Family and friends of Suzette Trouten also began receiving e-mails, purportedly from her. Testimony described how Suzette's family and friends immediately knew the e-mails they were receiving were not from Suzette because of the un-Suzette-like flawless spelling and writing.[17]

The day after Robinson killed Suzette, he took her computer to his trailer and read her e-mails, noting her passwords and address. Suzette's family received this "chain" e-mail on March 12, 2000:

> Well the wandering suz finally decided to drop everyone a note and say howdy. Sorry no e-mail up to now. No excuses just lazy. Peka, Hari and I are fine, they travel really well. I'm in California and getting rested up for sailing. Excited, what an opportunity. Promised mom I would send her a doll from every country we go to.
>
> I hope I didn't worry you at all. I really am having a great time, enjoying myself. I needed the change. Don't worry about me, I'm a big girl...bigger than I should be. Love to you all Suz.[18]

Suzette's aunt and uncle, Don and Marshella Chidester, also received an e-mail supposedly from Suzette. It declared that Suzette was preparing for the trip of a lifetime and was extremely excited. She had written her mom and dad each a letter, it noted, so everyone could quit worrying. She would not be online during this lengthy sojourn, but promised to keep her family and friends up-to-date on her trip at every opportunity. Her dogs, Peka and Hari, had adjusted well to life on a boat. At first, the e-mail admitted, she had feared that they might wander and fall overboard, but there were no problems.

The e-mails to Trouten's family shared content items. The author of the e-mail was identified as Suzette, and she claimed that she was fine, and the recipient should not worry about her. They noted that she would be out of regular communication for some time due to travel. She described past travels and plans for future trips. She also mentioned that her dogs were fine. The style of these moderate-length e-mails was chatty, informal, and informative. There was an excited, animated, and enthusiastic tone to the e-mails.

As with the bogus Paula Godfrey and Lisa Stasi letters, the real author was John Robinson. His rhetorical theme of deception attempted to divert attention away from him, and protect him from any blame of responsibility for the disappearances.

PSEUDO-SUZ'S E-MAIL

A friend of Suzette's named Crystal Ferguson began receiving e-mails signed by Suzette the day after Robinson killed her. The first read, "By the time you get this I off. My computer crashed yesterday and it took hours to get it working, you would laugh, station wagon full, the dogs in the back and off we go on the adventure of a lifetime." The e-mail ended, "Sees ya, Suz." But soon, the e-mails from pseudo-Suz took an ominous tone, as she was obviously cultivating Crystal as a new slave for her wonderful master, "J. T.," or "John Turner," a John Robinson alias. When Crystal told Suzette that she had left her former master, Suz wrote back, "Caught your message just before I unplugged. . . . If your interested in a MASTER who is really great, write him. He is a great MASTER. His email addy is *eruditemaster@email.com*. Wow, what news. . . . I'm off, love you, too, don't forget to write him!!! hugs, suz."[19] Crystal sent an e-mail to J. T., and he wrote her back almost immediately. He understood that she was a slave, he told her, adding that he was a MASTER with at least twenty years of experience who was looking for a trainable slave. He mentioned the end of her previous relationship with a MASTER, and she was instructed to send him a picture of herself.

J. T.'s next e-mail to Crystal acknowledged that he understood her relational situation because Suz had explained it to him. She had obediently sent him the photographs he had requested. He then added that he had told Suz to contact Crystal if she felt that Crystal was a good candidate. He was unsure about travel arrangements, but he wanted to explore the possibilities a bit more. He reminded her that if he accepted her she would be his slave and she should understand that her place would be at his feet, on her knees. There was no mercy shown. He was firm but fair, stern yet caring, a MASTER who adores his slave, he e-mailed her. He concluded by telling Crystal that she must e-mail him daily before 9:00 A.M. Central Standard Time. He also demanded a summary of her experience at BDSM.[20]

Crystal almost immediately heard from Suz, or someone claiming to be her. This e-mail declared that the MASTER Crystal was corresponding with was a teaching MASTER who assists other MASTERS to train their slaves efficiently and effectively. Suz and this MASTER were in Arizona at the time, traveling to California. They had stopped at a cafe that had an Internet-connected computer available for rent. Suz warned Crystal not to waste her opportunity to become J. T.'s slave, because he would make her toes curl.[21]

Robinson, pretending to be Suzette, actually sent these e-mails to Crystal. The content of these communications was characterized by extreme and unqualified praise for J. T., who was described as a wonderful master and human being. The writer urged Crystal to contact J. T. right away, and emphasized that not only was J. T. a master, he was a "teaching master." Suzette explained that her computer access was limited, by crashed computers, or by her travel, packing, and moving. She also claimed that her dogs were fine. The style of these relatively brief e-mails was enthusiastic and excited. The writer seemed genuinely thrilled that Crystal was considering becoming a slave to J. T. The rhetorical theme was persuasive, not informative, as the writer tried to influence Crystal to associate with J. T.

J. T. wrote to Crystal in late March. He told her that he was going to figure out how to handle their developing slave/master relationship. In an e-mail ending with "Hugs and Lashes," he assured her that she was going to fall in love with him.[22]

A COMMUNICATION TRAP

On March 29, a Lenexa Police Department Detective named Jack Boyer arranged a conversation with Crystal to discuss her e-mail conversations with J. T., and to enlist her assistance in a citizen-based sting operation. She briefed him on Suzette's disappearance and the strange e-mails. The detective asked Crystal to assist the task force by maintaining daily e-mail contact with Robinson. Boyer also wanted to see all of Robinson's e-mails as they were received. He promised to guide and protect her at all times.[23]

Crystal accepted the police invitation to assist in the investigation into Suzette's disappearance. She e-mailed J. T. the next morning, claiming that she wanted to visit him in Kansas as soon as possible. Her children would be at home with her husband, and she would be able to lavish her undivided attention on her master. She knew he would enjoy the experience as much as she would, Crystal declared in that e-mail message. J. T. e-mailed her back within an hour: "Hey, I'm in a jolly mood. Tell me when you want to come to Kansas."[24]

On April 8, J. T. e-mailed Crystal: "I have been trying to figure out when I can get you here ... grin. ... I've been busy as hell with all kinds of shit happening and then a bit of business too. Today's tasks were nipple training, tonight ice." About a week later, on April 14, J. T. again e-mailed Crystal: "Soon my slut, soon, you will begin your training and be completely obedient to your MASTER. ... Just know I am thinking about you."[25]

All of the e-mails J. T. sent to Crystal were similar, and there were numerous noteworthy content dimensions. Crystal was referred to as a "slave," and J. T. as a "master." And not just any master, but a teaching master with more than twenty years' experience training slaves. J. T. explained that he was seeking "a trainable Slave," and that since Crystal was available she should send him her picture. He told her he wanted to explore the possibility of Crystal becoming his slave, and if she was accepted, her place would be at his feet. He described his master philosophy toward slaves as "stern, but caring" and "firm, but fair." He cherished his slaves, he said, and then ordered Crystal to submit a summary of her BDSM experience to him.

The style of these e-mails was controlling and dominant. Crystal was characterized as a "slut" and a "slave," and she was degraded in other ways as well. There was a demanding element, as Crystal was ordered to send things to J. T. and to report to him daily at a specified time. At times he was transparently acting indifferent, as when J. T. claimed that his interest in Crystal was based entirely on Suzette's opinion and that he was merely going along with her. The themes of this electronic communication centered on Robinson's superiority and BDSM expertise. The messages revealed the author's desire for sexual and interpersonal power in relationships.

Robinson was the target of a citizen-based e-mail sting operation. The Lenexa police used e-mail to set Robinson up and catch him in the act of online victim solicitation, but federal agents got to him first.

SLAVE CONTRACTS

John Robinson earned the nickname "Internet Slavemaster." He murdered an unknown number of women and is perhaps best remembered for his Slave Contracts. These documents are part of the sexual lifestyle of an extreme fringe group of the bondage and sado-masochism (BDSM) population of the United States. John Robinson's Slave Contracts, which countless gullible and emotionally needy slaves would sign over the years, were not legally valid, although his slaves apparently did not realize this. One such document was featured on "The Slavemaster's" own International Council of Masters Web site as a prototype guide for young masters:

SLAVE CONTRACT
This is a basic contract that may be used
between a Master and Slave.

Of my own free will, as of this day {date}, I {name of Slave} {hereinafter called "SLAVE"}, hereby grant {Name of Master} {hereinafter called "MASTER"}, full ownership and use of my body and mind from now until I am released.

I will place my sobriety/emotional sobriety first in all considerations in this relationship.

I will obey my MASTER at all times and will wholeheartedly seek your pleasure and well-being above all other considerations. I renounce all my rights to my own pleasure, comfort, or gratification except insofar as you desire or permit them.

I will strive diligently to re-mold my body, my habits, and my attitudes in accordance with your desires. I will seek always to please you better, and will gracefully accept criticism as a means for growth and not a threat of abandonment.

I renounce all rights to privacy or concealment from you . . .

I understand and agree that any failure by me to comply fully with your desires shall be regarded as sufficient cause for possibly severe punishment.

I understand that for a training period indicated by you all punishment will be given at a 5 to 1 ratio to the offense.

Within the limits of my physical safety and ability to earn a livelihood, I otherwise unconditionally accept your prerogative anything that you may chose to do with me, whether as punishment, for your amusement, or for whatever purpose, no matter how painful or humiliating to myself.

I understand that if I use certain words which are deemed by you to be inappropriate for a SLAVE, the punishment will be automatic and then it is my duty to remind MASTER in the case that he forgets to remember.

I understand that at all times I am to be honest with you and communicate my feelings (even if I perceive that you may not approve).

I understand that no feeling I have can be wrong, and that they may indicate a situation which needs to be addressed.

Within the limits of my physical safety and my ability to earn a livelihood, I otherwise unconditionally accept as your prerogative anything that you may choose to do with me, whether as punishment, or your amusement, or for whatever purpose.

I understand that my MASTER has my ultimate physical, mental and spiritual well being in mind and will strive to be worthy of his pride in all my endeavors. I will at all times maintain a safe, sane and consensual relationship.[26]

Robinson's Slave Contracts first came to public light when he entertained a slave at an Extended Stay America hotel. After some time, hotel management became suspicious of Robinson's activities. Brad Singer, an assistant general manager, said that on one day, one of Robinson's women came to the front desk and asked to make copies of a document. One of the copies did not come out properly so he threw it away. After he made the copies, he gave them to the woman. His curiosity aroused, the hotel desk clerk pulled the defective copy out of the trash and was amazed at what he read. Singer said that it was a contract stating that Robinson had complete and total control of the woman's mind and body and, that he was entitled to do whatever he wanted to her. When a detective visited the hotel on another matter, he was given the copy of the contract. The detective was extremely interested, instructing the manager to call immediately if Robinson made another reservation.

The Slave Contract figured prominently in Robinson's crimes, and it is a fascinating document. There were several noteworthy aspects of the content of this legal-looking, but invalid, instrument. There was an early caveat that the slave's emotional and spiritual well-being be respected and promoted at all times, followed by the injunction that the slave must obey the master at all times. Slave behavior is controlled even to the extent of the master's prohibition of certain words. Slaves are required to self-report on their infractions, in case their master overlooks a slave mistake. The master/slave relationship was described as a "consensual" one, where the safety of the relational parties was the primary concern of the parties involved.

The Slave Contract's style was relatively formal and somewhat legalistic in tone. Judging by the vocabulary choices and syntax, this lengthy document was prepared by an intelligent and educated person.

The organization even simulated that of a legal contract, with clauses breaking the text into small, contract-like units.

What was the rhetorical theme of this document? It had two purposes. One was to explain the contract terms. A second, implicit theme was the justification and legitimization of the contract.

THE CRIMINAL

John Robinson qualifies as one of the most intelligent and interesting serial killers in U.S. history. It is quite likely that, had he turned his considerable intellect and ability to any legitimate profession or field of endeavor, he would have become famous and respected. Instead, he became infamous and detested. Others have investigated the Robinson cyber-serial murders and arrived at relatively similar conclusions. Serial murder expert Antonio Mendoza, for example, called Robinson another "pillar of the community" who in reality turned out to be a serial killer.[27]

Robinson devised, initiated, and successfully completed a campaign to have himself proclaimed "Man of the Year." In early November 1997, Robinson launched his campaign by writing to then-Kansas City mayor Charles B. Wheeler. He claimed to be representing the Kansas City Area Association of Sheltered Workshops. He invited the mayor to an awards luncheon to recognize Kansas City businesses that were committed to assisting sheltered workshop programs. Within about a month of the implementation of his plans, Robinson had managed to execute the scam. On Pearl Harbor Day, fifty Kansas City businessmen—as well as his wife, Nancy, and their children—attended the luncheon award ceremony, where a state senator gave John Robinson his "Man of the Year" award. The senator's speech was written by Robinson, who gave it to her when she arrived.[28]

Unfortunately for Robinson, the scheme was exposed within a matter of hours. The next day, the *Kansas City Star* ran a brief story about the award luncheon. The newspaper was soon inundated with calls complaining about the false story. As a result, "somewhat embarrassed," the *Star* investigated, and the "Man of the Year" award was revealed to be a crooked John Robinson scam.[29]

John Edward Robinson was arguably the first cybersex serial killer in history. He visited sadomasochist Internet chatrooms looking for gullible victims. Over a sixteen-year period, between five and eight women fell prey to his deadly schemes. Authorities had been investigating Robinson for fraud, but instead arrested him on July 6, 2000, for separate sexual assaults on two women he met in Internet chatrooms. After Robinson was arrested, police unearthed two, fifty-five-gallon barrels containing corpses from his property. Then investigators discovered three more dead women in a storage locker he rented in Raymore, Missouri.[30]

ROBINSON'S INCRIMINATING COMMUNICATION CLUES

Robinson's communication was meant to prevent his incrimination. He thought the letters and e-mails to victims' loved ones would provide him with an alibi. However, these messages, intended to keep him free, would instead be turned against him.

His communication became clues for the police, provoking the initiation of a sting operation. Robinson had been e-mailing a friend of one of his victims, trying to lure her to Kansas to be his slave. Police learned of this and enlisted her to keep up e-mail contact, but under their direction. Before these local police could spring their trap, Robinson was arrested by federal law enforcement agents on other charges.

At his trial, his communication was also used to incriminate him. Bogus e-mail and phony letters were persuasive evidence against him. These deceptive communications assisted the jury to reach a guilty verdict.

CONCLUSION

What made John Robinson's crimes especially terrible was his habit of preying on those vulnerable people who mistakenly thought he was a trustworthy social services provider. The *Law Enforcement News* declared that Robinson pretended to be a trustworthy philanthropist motivated to assist troubled individuals and families escape poverty. According to this criminal justice periodical, the Kansas-Missouri task force called Robinson America's first serial killer who used the Internet to obtain victims.[31]

As a child, Robinson seemed to have a fairly typical, middle-class upbringing in Chicago. He was the middle child of five in the household. His father, Henry, worked as a machinist at Western Electric, and was reportedly a binge-type alcoholic. Robinson's mother, Alberta, was a stay-at-home-mother. According to some familiar with the family at that time, she was the disciplinarian in the family.[32]

In 1957, Robinson's Eagle Scout troop traveled to England. There, they performed a concert for the Queen of England. He received a kiss from Judy Garland backstage at the event. The rest of Robinson's childhood was more mundane, culminating in his 1961 enrollment at Morton Junior College in Cicero, Illinois. He trained as a medical x-ray technician.

How many victims did Robinson silence forever? While an exact answer to this question is unavailable, expert estimates can be entertained. In 2003, Court TV suggested that Robinson owned the land and leased the locker where the bodies of six victims were found. He is suspected of having killed at least six women in Kansas and Missouri. Johnson County (Kansas) District Attorney Paul Morrison claimed, "What I'm going to say is he's certainly a suspect in all nine cases. We know that we've got five bodies; we know that all nine people have links to him, and you can probably draw your own conclusions."[33] Robinson was convicted of three murders, and pleaded guilty in 2003 to an additional five murders.

John Robinson's communication activity was central to his serial murders. He used communication as a tool in his homicidal schemes. He used communication to obtain victims, and he used communication to conceal the fact that he had killed his victims. There was an inherently sleazy quality to Robinson's communication. Whether we are talking about his Slave Contracts or his e-mails to potential slaves, the man was a cunning criminal. Sadly, many innocents perished as a result of his criminal desires.

8 Jack the Ripper

Jack the Ripper. That nickname has special meaning. It resonates among people of many nations, religions, and creeds as an exceptionally evocative emblem of evil. Now it is a symbol. Then it was a stark reality, an unexpected and unfamiliar terror for Victorian Britons. British police and civil authorities were unprepared to respond to such a homicidal menace. The name signified a particularly evil murderer.

No one is sure exactly how many victims fell prey to the Ripper's knife. No evidence remains of the Ripper crimes. No meaningful traces of the killer were left at crime scenes or dump sites, and there were no eyewitnesses. He strangled his victims first, some say, and then set about the grim task of using his knife to slit their throats prior to engaging in other heinous acts of bodily desecration. Two victims were quite nearly decapitated. Body organs, typically the uterus and surrounding tissues, were removed and taken by the killer. He also took half of a victim's kidney and another victim's heart. The killer later mailed the kidney fragment to an adversary, George Lusk, the head of a vigilante committee sworn to apprehend him.

Jack the Ripper was infamous in his time and retains that notoriety even today. Judging by public interest and the commercial outpouring of Ripper products—such as books, movies, and video and computer games—his fame has increased in the intervening years. To some, Jack the Ripper represents the archetype of evil.

Besides being perhaps the first serial killer and one of the first sex criminals, the Ripper holds another distinction: he was the first communicating serial killer. Although he is best known for the Jack the Ripper letters, he also engaged in wall writing and the transmission of body parts. To better understand this unique archetypal serial killer, we consider his crimes and his communication. But first, one preliminary point—the Ripper was probably a doctor.

JACK THE RIPPER, M.D.?

It is impossible to speak with much authority about Jack the Ripper because there is so little reliable information about him. There was much speculation at the time about his appearance, lifestyle, occupation, and other details, and the speculation continues to this day. But that is all it is—speculation—however reasonable and documented.

Jack was a doctor, it was said. In fact, with the exception of Elizabeth Stride, each of the Ripper victims' mutilations revealed signs of medical training. Ripper historian William Beadle noted the debate over whether or not the Ripper was a doctor. He stated that Dr. Timothy Killeen, who performed the autopsy on the Ripper's probable first victim, Martha Tabram, thought the killer revealed surgical skill.[1] F. E. Camps, famed British coroner and medical doctor, thought the autopsy physician was named Dr. Timothy Keens. Camps suggested that "Keens" also said he thought that Tabram's assailant showed elementary knowledge of surgery.[2]

Polly Nichols was the next Ripper victim. At the inquest into her savage murder, the attending physician, Dr. Rees Ralph Llewellyn, declared, "The murderer must have had some rough anatomical knowledge. He seems to have attacked all the vital parts."[3]

Annie Chapman was next to die at the hands of the Ripper. The coroner who conducted the inquest, Wynne Baxter, astonished the Coroner's Jury and everyone else who heard this statement in his summation:

> The body had not been dissected but the injuries had been made by someone who had considerable anatomical skills and knowledge. There were no meaningless cuts. The organ had been taken by one who knew where to find it, what difficulties he would have to contend against, and how he should use his knife so as to abstract the organ without injury to it. No unskilled person could have known where to find it or have recognized it when it was found. For instance, no mere slaughterer of animals could have carried out these operations. It must have been someone accustomed to the post mortem room.[4]

Dr. George Bagster Phillips was the physician at the Chapman autopsy. The British medical journal *Lancet* carried his statement about the Ripper's medical training, "Obviously the work was that of an expert—or one, at least, who had such knowledge of anatomical or pathological examinations as to be enabled to secure the pelvic organs with one sweep of the knife."[5]

Dr. Frederick Gordon Brown examined the body of Ripper victim Catherine Eddowes and concluded, "I believe the perpetrator of the act must have had considerable knowledge of the positions of the organs in the abdominal cavity and the way of removing them. It required a great deal of medical knowledge to have removed the kidney and to know where it was placed."[6] Mary Kelly was the next, and possibly last, woman to perish at Saucy Jacky's hand. Psychologist and serial killer consultant David Abrahamson claimed that the doctors who viewed Kelly's corpse thought that the killer had medical knowledge and experience.[7]

Historians and Ripperologists tend to accept that the Ripper may have had medical training. Richard Wallace pointed out that Doctors Llewellyn, Brown, and Phillips thought the killer showed medical skill, with Dr. Sequiera finding evidence of experience with knives.[8] In fact, six out of the seven police medical experts who were involved with this case at one time or another believed that the Ripper was a qualified surgeon, a Doctor of Medicine.[9] Respected Ripper scholar Phillip Sugden suggested that "most" of the doctors who examined the Ripper victims concluded that the murderer possessed some degree of anatomical knowledge.[10] Steven Knight, another important Ripper researcher, reported that more than twenty-five percent of the 103 published theories on the identity of Jack the Ripper claimed that he was a medical student or doctor.[11] Similarly, authors Colin Wilson and Robin O'Dell referred to the majority view that anatomical skill had been demonstrated by the Ripper.[12]

THE CRIMES BEGIN

In addition to the five victims generally attributed to the Ripper, I believe he in fact killed two more women, for a total of seven. His initial victim was Martha Tabram, sometimes called Turner. Her estranged husband, Henry Tabram, identified the body of the thirty-nine- or forty-year-old woman as his wife. They had been separated for about thirteen years because of her chronic alcoholism. She had two children with Tabram, he testified at the inquest. After her relationship with Tabram ended, she began a common-law marriage with a carpenter named Henry Turner, with whom she lived for approximately nine years. Their relationship ended less than a month before her death. Tabram was described as being five feet, three inches tall, with dark hair and complexion. She wore a green skirt with brown petticoat and stockings, under a long black jacket. She also wore a black bonnet and side-spring boots.

Martha Tabram met the Ripper early on the morning of August 7, 1888, in George Yard Buildings, in the East End of London. She was stabbed thirty-nine times with two different instruments. The excessive nature of the knife attack was conveyed by the *Illustrated Police News*: "The wound over the heart was alone sufficient to kill and death must have occurred as soon as that was inflicted. Unless the perpetrator was a madman, or suffering to an unusual extent from drink delirium, no tangible explanation can be given of the reason for inflicting the other thirty-eight stab wounds."[13] Tabram's murder was attributed to the Ripper by no less an authority than Dr. Robert Anderson, head of Scotland Yard's Criminal Investigation Division, who considered her to be the initial Ripper victim.[14]

Mary Ann Nichols, who was often called Polly, was the next Ripper victim. She died on August 31, 1888, in Buck's Row. Nichols was identified in the morgue by her father, Edward Walker, a retired smith who lived at 15 Maidwell-street, Albany-road, Camberwell. His daughter was forty-two years old when she died. Her husband, William Nichols, was a machinist who lived at Coburg-road, Old Kent-road. He testified at the inquest that he had been separated from his wife for more than eight years due to her habitual intoxication. Her last residence was a common lodging house located at 18 Thrawl-street, Spitalfields, where she lived until a week-and-a-half before her murder.

Nichols was eviscerated, with two slits running up from her pubic area to her breastbone. The *Manchester Guardian* provided a tactful and brief account: "A sensational crime was committed in Buck's Row, Thomas-street, Whitechapel, early yesterday morning. A woman of from 35 to 40 years of age, who has not been identified, having evidently been murdered in a barbarous manner."[15] Her body was discovered by Robert Paul, a carman on his way to work, at a quarter to four in the morning. Inspector John Spratling's report described the injuries to Nichols's body:

Her throat had been cut from left to right, two distinct cuts being on left side, the windpipe, gullet and spinal cord being cut through; a bruise apparently of a thumb being on right lower jaw, also one on left cheek; the abdomen had been cut open from centre and bottom of ribs along right side, under pelvis to left of the stomach, there the wound was jagged; the omentum, or coating of the stomach, was also cut in several places, and two small stabs on private parts.[16]

Nichols was buried in a polished elm coffin. It bore an inscription: "Mary Ann Nichols, aged 42, died August 31st, 1888."[17]

Next to die was Annie Chapman, who was found at 29 Hanbury-street on September 8, 1888. Chief Inspector Donald Swanson's report to the Home Office included basic facts about the victim, such as her alias, "Annie Siffey," and her age, forty-five. She was five feet tall, with wavy, dark brown hair and blue eyes. She had a thick nose and a fair complexion, and she wore a black skirt and jacket, with a striped petticoat and a crepe bonnet.[18] The *East London Advertiser* reported, "The woman's name was Annie Chapman, alias Sieve. She came from Windsor, and had friends residing at Vauxhall. Her home was a lodging house at 35, Dorset-street, in Whitechapel. Her husband was a veterinary surgeon, who allowed her 10s. [shillings] a week, but he died a twelvemonth ago, and the pension ceasing, she has since earned her living on the streets. She lived for a time with a man named Sieve."[19]

Medical evidence from the inquest revealed the extent of Chapman's injuries:

The throat had been severed. The incisions of the skin indicated that they had been made from the left side of the neck on a line with the angle of the jaw, carried entirely round and again in front of the neck, and ending at a point about midway between the jaw and the sternum or breast bone on the right hand. There were two distinct clean cuts on the body of the vertebrae on the left side of the spine. They were parallel to each other, and separated by about half an inch. The muscular structures between the side processes of bone of the vertebrae had an appearance as if an attempt had been made to separate the bones of the neck. There are various other mutilations of the body.[20]

The Ripper had tried to cut off Chapman's head. Inspector Swanson's report disclosed additional facts about Chapman's murder and mutilation: "Examination of the body showed that the throat was severed deeply incision jagged. Removed from but attached to the body & placed above right shoulder were a flap of the wall of the belly, the whole of the small intestines & attachments. Two other portions of wall of belly & 'Pubes' were placed above left shoulder in a large quantity of blood.'' The report disclosed that the Ripper took some body parts with him: "The following parts were missing:-part of belly wall including navel; the womb, the upper part of vagina & greater part of bladder.''[21]

THE RIPPER STARTS TO WRITE

Four September 1888 letters seem to be likely Ripper items. The first was not discovered until 1988, when Peter McClelland reportedly found it in the Public Records Offices files of originals where it had been overlooked. This letter, dated September 17, began with the typical "Dear Boss" greeting. It read (errors have been retained in all quoted material): "So now they say I am a Yid when will they lern Dear old Boss? You an me know the truth dont we. Lusk can look forever hell never find me but I am rite under his nose all the time. I watch them looking for me an it gives me fits ha ha I love my work an I shant stop until I get buckled and even then watch out for your old pal Jacky, Catch me if you can Jack the Ripper.''

The next genuine Ripper letter is somewhat questionable, but it shared enough traits with other valid letters to be seriously considered. Dated September 24, it began, "Dear Sir," and stated:

> I do wish to give myself up I am in misery with nightmare I am the man who committed all these murders in the last six months my name is so and so [silhouette of coffin] I am a horse slauterer and work at name [rectangle blacked out] and address [rectangle blacked out] I have found the woman I wanted that is Chapman and I done what I call slautered her but if any one comes I will surrender but I am not going to walk to the station by myself so I am yours truely [silhoutte of coffin] keep the boro road clear or I might take a trip up there photo of knife [drawing of a knife] this is the knife that I done these murders with it is a small handle with a large long blade sharpe both sides.

A third September Ripper letter is probably the most well known of the lot, the September 25 letter addressed to the Central News Office:

> Dear Boss I keep on hearing the police have caught me but they won't
> fix me just yet. I have laughed when they look so clever and talk about

being on the <u>right</u> track. That joke about Leather Apron gave me real fits. I am down on whores and I shant quit ripping them till i do get buckled. Grand work the last job was. I gave the lady no time to squeal How can they catch me now, I love my work and want to start again. you will soon hear of me and my funny little games. I saved some of the proper <u>red</u> stuff in a ginger beer bottle over the last job to write with but it went thick like glue and I cant use it. Red ink is fit enough I hope <u>ha ha</u>. The next job I do I shall clip the lady's ears off and send to the police just for jolly wouldn't you Keep this letter back till I do a bit more work then give it out straight. My knife's so nice and sharp I want to get to work right away if I get a chance, good luck. yours truly, Jack the Ripper Don't mind me giving the trade name wasn't good enough to post this before I got all the red ink off my hands curse it. No luck yet. They say I'm a doctor now <u>ha ha</u>.

The first of the so-called Liverpool letters was also sent in September. Dated September 29 and sent from Liverpool, this brief message declared, ''Beware I shall be at work on the 1st and 2nd inst. in the Minories at 12 midnight and I give the authorities a good chance but there is never a policeman near when I am at work. Yours, Jack the Ripper.''

THE KILLING RESUMES

The Ripper claimed two victims on September 30, 1888. It is commonly believed that the Ripper was interrupted while assaulting Elizabeth Stride, resulting in her not being mutilated, and the killer's motivation to strike again that morning. Stride's body was found at 1:00 A.M. at 40 Berner-street. Coroner Wynne Baxter revealed that Stride was born Elizabeth Gustoftroller on November 27, 1843, at Landaro, Sweden. Sven Olsen, a clerk at London's Swedish Church, gave her name as Elizabeth Gustafsdotter, and said she was born at Forslander, Sweden. She was married to John Thomas Stride, a ship's carpenter. She was about forty-five years old when she died. Her companion for the last three years of her life, Michael Kidney, was a waterside laborer who made the identification of the body.

Despite the paucity of time available to the Ripper in this case, Stride's wounds were nevertheless severe. The *Times* reported that, according to Dr. Frederick Blackwell, ''Her head had almost been severed from her body.''[22] Dr. George Baxter Phillips was called to examine the body at the crime scene, and he remarked, ''The throat was deeply slashed, and there was an abrasion of the skin about $1\frac{1}{4}$ in. in diameter, apparently stained with blood, under her right brow."[23] Phillips and the police estimated that there were at least two quarts of blood on the ground where she was slain.

Within an hour, Catherine Eddowes met the Ripper and lost her life. Eddowes was forty-three years old at her death, according to a report by the *Pall Mall Gazette*.[24] Her body was officially identified by John Kelly, her companion for the final seven years of her life, who knew her as Kate Conway. She was about five feet tall, with dark complexion, auburn hair, and hazel eyes. She wore a black cloth jacket with an imitation fur collar over a green chintz dress with a Michaelmas daisy pattern. She also wore a white vest, a light-drab lindsey skirt, a dark-green alpaca petticoat, and brown-ribbed stockings. She rather fancied her black-straw bonnet and a large white handkerchief.

Eddowes was severely mutilated. Her killer had disemboweled her, with parts of her internal organs arrayed on her body. Her uterus and left kidney had been removed and taken by the killer. Tiny nicks had been made around her eyes, an attempt had been made to sever her ears, triangles were cut into her cheeks, and numerous other cuts and slices were inflicted on her body. The *City Press* reported, "Her throat was cut half-way round, and blood had flowed out in great quantities from the wound, staining the pavement for some distance."[25] The *British Daily Whig* noted, "The second crime was committed 45 minutes later in Mitre-square, five minutes' walk from the scene of the first tragedy, and the victim was shockingly mutilated."[26] Dr. Frederick Gordon Brown, who was called to Mitre-square to examine the body, briefly described some of the wounds:

> The clothes were drawn up, the left leg was extended straight down, in a line with the body, and the right leg was bent at the knee. There was great disfigurement of the face. The throat was cut across, and below the cut was a handkerchief. The upper part of the dress had been pulled open a little way. The abdomen was all exposed; the intestines were drawn out to a large extent and placed over the right shoulder; a piece of the intestines was quite detached from the body and placed between the left arm and the body.[27]

Eddowes was laid to rest in a "handsome polished coffin with oak mouldings." A block plate contained the following inscription, in gold lettering, "Katherine [*sic*] Eddowes. Died September 30, 1888, aged forty-three years."[28]

Ironically, Eddowes had been in police custody the evening of her death, only to be released and subsequently murdered shortly thereafter. Constable George Henry Hutt, 968, of the City Police, was the gaoler (jail keeper) at the Bishopsgate Police Station. Hutt told the inquest that Eddowes had been jailed earlier that evening for public drunkenness, but she was released at about 12:55 A.M. because she seemed lucid and in control of herself. That police station was approximately four hundred yards from Mitre-square.[29]

THE WALL WRITING

Policemen searching for Eddowes's killer happened on a piece of her bloody apron in the street, left there by the Ripper. At that very spot, on the wall of a Jewish tenement, was a message written in chalk by the Ripper. The precise wording of the message is a matter of debate, because Metropolitan Police Commissioner Sir Charles Warren ordered that it be wiped out before it was photographed, and the handwritten versions of eyewitnesses differs from rendition to rendition. "The Juwes are the men that will not be blamed for nothing," is the most likely version.

Was the Ripper truly responsible for this outdoor message? Donald McCormick, one of the early Ripperologists, concluded that he was because "The writing on the wall had not been there at midnight."[30] Since a part of Eddowes's apron was found at that very spot, the police believed that the Ripper had done this since a few of the words were slightly smudged by bloodstains.

Other authorities also place the chalk in the Ripper's hands. Respected Ripperologist Paul Begg observed that the apron-piece was bloodstained. The torn fragment of material matched exactly the apron worn by Catherine Eddowes. There was, and remains, no doubt that the apron was deposited and the message written by the Ripper.[31]

Contemporary reports also claimed the writing to be the work of the Ripper. The *London Times* reported Coroner Crawford's assertion: "The writing appeared to be recently done," to which a juryman replied, "He assumed that the writing was recent, because from the number of persons living in the tenement he believed it would have been rubbed out had it been there for any time. There were about three lines of writing, which was in a good schoolboy hand."[32] An explanation of why the police attributed the graffiti to the Ripper was provided in Chief

Inspector Donald Swanson's report to the Home Office, dated November 6, 1888:

> At 2.55 A.M. he found in the bottom of a common stairs leading to No. 108
> to 119 Goldston-street Buildings a piece of a bloodstained apron, and
> above it written in chalk the words, "The Juwes are the men who will
> not be blamed for nothing," which he reported, and the City Police were
> subsequently acquainted at the earliest moment, when it was found that
> beyond doubt the piece of apron found corresponded exactly with the
> parts missing from the body of the murdered woman.[33]

Alfred Long, 254A, Metropolitan Police Force, told the Eddowes
inquest: "I was on duty in Goulston-street, Whitechapel on the 30th
September, about 2.55 A.M. I found a portion of a woman's apron which
I produce. There appeared blood stains on it, one portion was wet,
lying in a passage leading to the staircase of 108 to 119 Model Dwelling
House. Above it on the wall was written in chalk—The Jews are the
men that will not be blamed for nothing."[34] Long made an almost
identical statement in his police report, dated November 6, 1888:

> I was on duty in Goulston-street on the morning of 30th Sept. at about
> 2.55 A.M. I found a portion of an apron covered in blood lying in a pas-
> sage of the door-way leading to Nos. 108 to 119 Model Dwellings in
> Goulston-street.
>   Above it on the wall was written in chalk, "The Juews are the men
> that will not be blamed for nothing." I at once called the P. C. on the
> adjoining beat and then searched the staircases, but found no traces of
> any person or marks.[35]

Long was not the only eyewitness to the graffiti before it was
destroyed. Daniel Halse, a detective with the City Police, also saw it. He
testified at the inquest:

> I came through Goulston-street at 20 past 2 and accompanied Inspector
> Collard to the mortuary. I saw deceased stripped and saw a portion of the
> apron was missing. I went back with Major Smith to Mitre-square when
> we went ["back to Goulstone" {deleted}]. I then went with Detective
> Hunt to Leman Street police station. I and Detective Hunt went on to
> Goulstone-street and the spot was pointed out where the apron was found.
> I saw some chalk writing on the black fascia of the wall. I remained there
> and sent with a view to having the writing photographed.

Directions were given to have the writing photographed and during the time some of the Metropolitan Police said as it was Sunday morning it might cause a riot or an outbreak against the Jews and decided to have it rubbed out and it was rubbed out. When Hunt returned an enquiry was made at every tenement of the Building but we could gain no witness of any one going in likely to be the murderer.

About 20 past 2 I passed over the spot where the piece of apron was found. I did not notice anything. I suggested that the top line should be taken out of the writing on the wall. I took a note of the writing before it was rubbed out. The exact words were "The Juwes are not the men that will be blamed for nothing." The writing had the appearance of being recently written. I protested against the writing being rubbed out. I wished it to remain there until Major Smith had seen it.[36]

The Goulston-street graffiti is difficult to fathom. The majority opinion, then and now, is that the Ripper wrote the message. The proximity of the message to Eddowes's apron fragment accounts for this conclusion. The question is, what did the message mean? Unfortunately, that question is unanswerable. Did the Ripper want to inflame anti-Semitic passions by blaming Jews for the Ripper crimes, or was he trying to exonerate them with the enigmatic message?

What can be concluded about the content of this Ripper rhetoric? Despite the ambiguity of the message's content, two assertions can be advanced. Probably the most important aspect of the message was the identification of Jews as the focus of the graffiti. Although different eyewitnesses render the spelling of this key word in varying ways, such as Juees, Juuews, and Jews, there is no doubt about the intended meaning of the writer. Another topical conclusion is that the message was an effort to intensify already-prevalent Victorian English anti-Semitism.

We can offer more analysis of the style of this message than is possible for the content dimension. The graffiti was characterized by its brevity and by the unusual syntax used by the writer. Depending on the version of the message being used, there was an unusual negative phrase; either "the men that will not be blamed for nothing," or "not the men who will be blamed for nothing." This tortured syntax partially obscures the meaning of the message. All we know for certain is that the message was a simple declarative sentence. Most of all, the style of this graffiti was marked by its vagueness and planned ambiguity. What does it mean? No one has ever really suggested a concrete, documented answer.

MORE RIPPER CORRESPONDENCE

Perhaps there were no Ripper murders in October 1888 because he was too busy writing and sending threatening letters. There were at least thirty-seven Ripper letters sent that month, the largest monthly total of all. Here we consider the first seven October Ripper messages.

A postcard received by the police on the first of October sets the tone for the month: "I was not codding, dear old Boss, when I gave you the tip You'll hear about Saucy Jacky's work to-morrow. Double event this time. Number one squealed a bit couldn't finish straight off. Had not time to get ears for police. Thanks for keeping the last letter back till I got to work again Jack the Ripper."

The next day, a letter for "Dear Boss" was written:

> Since last splendid success. two more & never a squeal. oh I am master of the art. I am going to be heavy on a guilded whore now, we are some dutchess will cut up nicely.
>
> You wonder how! oh we are masters no education like a butchers no animal like a nice woman. the fat are best. On to Brighton for a holiday but we shant idle splendid high class women there my mouth waters. Good luck there. If not you will hear from me on West End. My pal will keep on at the east a while. When I get a nobility womb I will send it to C. Warren or perhaps to you for a keepsake O it is jolly George of the high Rip Gang. red ink still but a drop of the real in it.

Interestingly, the very next day another Ripper letter threatened killings in the West End. This one was sent to Sir James Fraser of the City Police:

> I will write to you again soon. Just a card to let you know that I shall (if possible) do some more of my business in the West part of London & I hope to be able to send you my victims ears. I was not able to last time. My bloody ink is now running out so I must get some more. It amuses me that you think I am mad you will see when I am caught but it is death to the first man who touches me. It will be most probaly the end of October or it may be before it all depends Jack the Ripper.

The Ripper wrote on a fourth consecutive day, as one of the two October 4 letters showed: "I beg to inform the police I am the White-chapel murder I intend to commit two murders in the Haymarket tonight take note of this Whitechape is to warm for one now my knife has not been found for I still have the knife I intend to keep it untill I finish 20 then try & find me." According to another letter of October 4, "Prepare for thy doom. For I mean to settle you You villain you've lived long enough. Yours truly Jack the Ripper."

A Ripper letter postmarked October 5 was addressed to "Dr. Boss," and it declared: "You have not found me yet I have done another one and thrown it in the river and I mean doing another one before the weeks out. You can put as many bloodhounds a you like but you will never catch me Yours truly Jack Ripper." The same day, a telegram was sent to Sir Charles Warren: "Dear Boss if you are willing enough to catch me I am now in City Road lodging but the number you will have to find out and I mean to do another murder in Whitechapel Yours Jack The Ripper."

Frequency analysis, the counting of how often certain content themes, phrases, and names were mentioned, of Ripper correspondence tells us precisely what was and was not in those letters. There were three dominant elements in the letters: the "Dear Boss," salutation (and implied class conflict), the merciless taunting of the police, and the predictions of and warnings about future murders and mutilations. Also very characteristic of the Ripper correspondence were the major content themes. These included giving the day/date/time of planned murders, giving the location (street and town) of planned murders, giving the police the Ripper's address, discussing the number of accomplished and remaining murders, and discussing the Ripper's travel plans.

THE LUSK PACKAGE

On October 16, 1888, George A. Lusk received a three inch-square cardboard box wrapped in brown paper. Lusk was a prominent figure in the Whitechapel Vigilance Committee, a group of citizens set up to help catch the Ripper. Inside the box were half of a human kidney, with an inch of renal artery still attached, and a letter. The letter read

> From Hell Mr Lusk, Sor I send you half the kidne I took from one woman prasarved it for you tother piece I fried and ate it was very nise I may send you the bloody knif that took it out if you only wate a whil longer signed Catch me when you can Mishter Lusk.[37]

Were the kidney and letter from the Ripper? Eddowes was murdered on September 30, about two and a half weeks before Lusk received his package. Her killer removed half of her left kidney, leaving half of it and two inches of renal artery. Nevertheless, at the time and subsequently, opinions differed on whether the letter and partial kidney were sent by the Ripper.[38] "Medical opinion was divided over whether... it belonged to Catherine Eddowes."[39] Eddowes was suffering from Bright's disease, commonly known as "ginny kidney," which would have killed her within a short time if the Ripper had not murdered her. Lusk sent the kidney fragment to Major Smith, who had two pathologists conduct examinations. Dr. Thomas Openshaw decided that the kidney was that of a forty-five-year-old woman suffering from Bright's disease. The other examination, by Dr. R. S. Reed, replicated those findings. The police and press "scoffed at what was seen as a hoax," but the laughter ceased when Major Henry Smith observed that the Lusk kidney fragment had one inch of renal artery attached. Why was that important? Female human renal arteries are generally about three inches long, and "two inches had been found in the corpse."[40] Respected early Ripperologist Tom Cullen confirmed that two inches of renal artery were discovered in the corpse of Catherine Eddowes, while one inch was still attached to the kidney portion delivered by the Ripper to Mr. Lusk. Major Smith added, "The kidney left in the corpse was in an advanced stage of Bright's disease. The kidney sent to me was in an exactly similar state."[41] "It is most likely that Lusk received Eddowes' kidney from the Ripper," Scott Palmer concluded.[42]

Press reports of this gruesome incident varied from small mentions to more extensive accounts. The *City Press* noted on October 20, 1888, that "MR. LUSK (of the Whitechapel Vigilance Committee) has received a parcel containing a portion of a human kidney, with a letter dated from an unmentionable place, and signed, 'Catch Me When You Can.' It has been handed over to the City Police. Dr. Brown will report on it."[43]

That same day, the *London Times* reported:

> The horrible incident of the box containing a portion of a kidney sent to Mr. Lusk, of the Whitechapel Vigilance Committee, is not generally regarded as a practical joke in view of the opinion given by two medical gentlemen, Dr. Openshaw and Mr. Reed. The box and its contents were taken from Leman-street to the City Police Office in Old Jewry, and Dr. Gordon Browne [*sic*], police-surgeon, will examine and make a report in due course. The extra police precautions are still in force.[44]

A day later, the *East London Observer* reported a very similar account of the Lusk kidney and Ripper letter incident:

> The only startling event worth chronicling is the following: From inquiries made at Mile End, we are enabled to give particulars, on the most reliable authority, concerning the receipt of certain letters and a parcel at the house of a member of the Whitechapel Vigilance Committee. A letter, delivered shortly after five o'clock on Tuesday evening, was accompanied by a cardboard box containing what appeared to be a portion of a kidney. The letter was in the following terms: "From Hell.—Mr. Lusk.—half the kidney I took from one woman. Prasarved it for you. Tother piece I fried and ate; it was very nice. I may send you the bloody knife that took it out, if you only wait a while longer."[45]

The Ripper sent his grim souvenir from the Eddowes slaying to Lusk because Lusk chaired a citizen's group aimed at catching him. He wanted to assume the offensive and put Lusk on the defensive. The Ripper sought to frighten and intimidate Lusk and cast a chill on the vigilance committee.

Several main content dimensions should be noted. Most important was the kidney fragment itself. The accompanying letter was provided to offer a verbal context and some explanation, but the rhetorical and psychological effect of the message was conveyed largely through the enclosure of the human organ. The letter was "From Hell," according to the author, and it was addressed to Mr. Lusk, who was again named as the addressee in the letter itself. The letter was essentially a cover or transmittal letter for the conveyance of the piece of kidney, a fact that was acknowledged explicitly in the opening sentence. The letter mentioned that the kidney fragment was taken from a woman, and added that the killer/author ate part of it, to his satisfaction. Finally, in what perhaps was an insincere offer, the writer promised to send "the bloody knif" at an unspecified future time.

What of the style of the Lusk letter? There are main generalizations to consider. First, this was a moderately brief letter, not terse, but not lengthy or chatty. It was clearly aimed at taunting the recipient, and it was intended to shock, horrify, and terrorize him and his Vigilance Committee, which had pledged to catch the Ripper. Most versions of the letter have "Sir" spelled "Sor," and "Mister" spelled "Mishter," perhaps to imply an Irish author. Numerous words were misspelled in most typical versions of the letter, including "knif" instead of "knife," "wate" for "wait," and "nise" in lieu of "nice." The word "preserved" was rendered as "praeserved."

THE MURDERS RESUME

Mary Kelly was the only victim known to have been killed indoors, giving the Ripper time and privacy to indulge his pathological desires to the fullest. She died on November 9, 1888, in her room at 13 Miller's Court. According to the *East London Observer,* she was "Marie Jeanette Kelly—a woman about 25 years of age—a blonde, of medium height, who was born in Wales, married a collier at sixteen years of age, and becoming a widow shortly afterwards, led a gay life ever since."[46] A slightly different tale was told by the *Illustrated Police News,* which reported that she was called "Mary Jane Kelly, alias 'Ginger.' She was a Welch woman, and it is believed was married, but separated from her husband."[47] Joseph Barnett, a laborer and fruit and fish porter who had lived with Kelly for about a year and eight months, moving out less than two weeks before the murder, officially identified the body.

Kelly's body was terribly mutilated. Her legs were skinned and her breasts cut off and placed on the table next to her, along with assorted internal organs and flesh cut from her legs. She was disemboweled, and one hand was placed into her open body. Her heart was missing. The *Eastern Post & City Chronicle* tersely reported, "A woman was discovered with her head entirely cut off from her body, and lying by her side."[48] Similarly, according to the *East London Observer,* "This much, however, is known, that the head, as in the case of the Mitre-square victim, is nearly, if not entirely, severed from the body, and that the abdominal wounds correspond in nearly all their details to those inflicted upon previous victims." "The mutilations were of a revolting description—the throat being deeply cut, the abdomen ripped open, many of the entrails taken out, a certain organ being reported missing, and the fleshy portion of the cheeks, breasts and thighs hacked away," the report added.[49] The *Illustrated Police News* provided an extended description of the injuries:

> The throat had been cut right across with a knife, nearly severing the head from the body. The abdomen had been ripped partially open, and both of the breasts had been cut from the body. The left arm, like the head, hung to the body by the skin only. The nose had been cut off, the

forehead skinned, and the thighs, down to the feet, stripped of the flesh. The abdomen had been slashed with a knife across and downwards, and the liver and entrails wrenched away. The entrails and other portions of the frame were missing, but the liver, etc., it is said, were found placed between the feet of the poor victim. The flesh from the thighs and legs, together with the breasts and nose, had been placed by the murderer on the table, and one of the hands of the dead woman had been pushed into her stomach.[50]

Unlike previous Ripper crimes, when the time of death was indicated rather precisely in each case, there was controversy over when Kelly died. The *London Times* recalled, "Great difference of opinion exists as to the exact time, or about the time, the murder of Mary Jane Kelly took place."[51] The traditional tale has Kelly being murdered and mutilated in the early morning hours of November 9. Dr. George Bagster Phillips examined the body shortly before 11:00 A.M., and estimated that death had occurred five or six hours earlier, placing the time of death at between 3:45 and 4:45 in the morning. There is one problem with this conclusion, however. Two witnesses saw Kelly alive between eight and nine o'clock that morning and were certain of the day, time, and person involved. One witness, Caroline Maxwell, saw Kelly twice between 8:30 and 9:00 A.M., and even spoke with her.[52]

Kelly was buried in a "polished elm and oak coffin, with metal mounts." A coffin plate read, "Marie Jeanette Kelly, died 9th Nov. 1888, aged 25 years."[53] Two crowns of artificial flowers sat upon the coffin, along with a cross made of heartsease.

Many believe that Jack the Ripper claimed at least one more victim, Alice McKenzie. She was killed on July 17, 1889, in Castle Alley, Whitechapel. Her throat had been cut, and there were zig-zag slash marks across her abdomen. Her killer escaped without being seen or heard. Dr. Thomas Bond, who performed a medical analysis of the Ripper victims at the behest of the British police, also examined McKenzie. He concluded, "I am of opinion that the murder was performed by the same person who committed the former series of Whitechapel murders."[54] Others were in agreement. James Munro, the Under Secretary of State who was the Home Office liaison for the investigation, remarked, "I need not say that every effort will be made by the police to discover the murderer who, I am inclined to believe is identical with the notorious 'Jack the Ripper' of last year."[55] The doctors who examined McKenzie at the crime scene concurred with Dr. Bond and Mr. Munro, as the *East London Advertiser* reported, "Meanwhile,

Dr. Phillips and Dr. Brown had been communicated with, and on their arrival they examined the nature of the wounds, and informed the police that the murder must have been done by the same person or persons who committed the series of previous murders in Whitechapel and Spitalfields."[56] However, there was some disagreement about this fact. Police Superintendent Thomas Arnold wrote to the Home Office, "The opinion formed by Dr. Phillips after his examination of the body, was that the wounds had not been inflicted by the same hand as in the previous cases, inasmuch as the injuries in this case are not so severe and the cut on the stomach is not so direct."[57]

Who was Alice McKenzie? Here is how she appeared to the officer who discovered her lifeless body at 12:50 A.M. on the last day of her life. According to Police Superintendent Arnold's report:

> He found a woman, age about 40 to 45, length 5ft 4in, complexion pale, hair and eyes brown, top of thumb of left hand deficient, also tooth deficient in upper jaw, dress red stuff bodice, patched under arms, and sleeves with marone [sic] coloured stockings, brown stuff skirt, kilted brown lindsey petticoat, white chemise and apron, paisley shawl, button boots, all old and dirty, lying on her right side with her clothing turned up to her waist exposing her abdomen, with a deep zig-zag cut extending across same, a quantity of blood was on footway.[58]

McKenzie was about forty years of age at her death, according to her companion of six years, John M'Cormick. He testified at her inquest that he did not know if she had any children. M'Cormick declared, "She worked very hard as a washerwoman and charwoman to the Jews."[59] M'Cormick and McKenzie reportedly met at Bishopsgate in 1881 or 1882, and they had lived together in lodging houses since then. A harsh description of McKenzie was offered by the *East London Observer*, "She was in all probability one of the lowest kind of prostitute."[60]

Dr. Phillips testified about McKenzie's injuries at the inquest into her death. Press coverage of his testimony reported, "The witness then described the wounds, of which there were several." Of the lethal injuries, it was noted, "The wound in the neck was 4 in. long, reaching from the back part of the muscles, which were almost entirely divided. It reached to the fore part of the neck to a point 4 in. below the chin. There was a second incision, which must have commenced from behind and immediately below the first."[61]

CONCLUSION

Jack the Ripper was not the most prolific serial killer of all time. He did not devise the cruelest tortures or cause the most suffering. But he is probably the best remembered and most feared of all serial killers to date. I attribute his notoriety to his communication prowess, which he displayed on many occasions and through a variety of media.

The Ripper was the first serial killer to engage the police and the public in sustained dialogue. More than three hundred letters were allegedly written by Jack the Ripper and sent to the police, the press, and a plethora of other parties. These letters taunted and teased the police, promising future murders and even specifying where and when they would occur. It is difficult to fathom completely the Goulston-street graffiti. Jack the Ripper wrote it, and then called attention to it with the apron-piece. But why? No one then or now has had a real clue as to what the message means.

The sending of part of Catherine Eddowes's left kidney to George Lusk, along with the accompanying letter and previous and subsequent letters to Lusk, demonstrated the rhetorical nature of the Ripper's crimes. He frightened Lusk, he knew it, and he meant to do it. The communication aspect of the murders heightened the enjoyment the Ripper received from his crimes.

In an article in *Public Relations Quarterly*, I argued that the Ripper crimes were actually a premodern public relations campaign. The crimes were media events that were publicized by the Ripper correspondence (news releases) and the wall writing (outdoor). The Lusk kidney was a specialty advertising piece, and the entire campaign was coordinated by a sophisticated media relations campaign.[62] While that is an argument beyond the scope of this chapter, there can be no denying the role of communication in the Ripper crimes.

25. Sept. 1888.

Dear Boss,

I keep on hearing the police have caught me. but they wont fix me just yet. I have laughed when they look so clever and talk about being on the right track. That joke about Leather apron gave me real fits. I am down on whores and I shant quit ripping them till I do get buckled. Grand work the last job was. I gave the lady no time to squeal How can they catch me now. I love my work and want to start again. You will soon hear of me with my funny little games. I saved some of the proper red stuff in a ginger beer bottle over the last job to write with but it went thick like glue and I cant use it Red ink is fit enough I hope ha. ha. The next job I do I shall clip the ladys ears off and send to the

The most famous and well-known Ripper letter, it gave the killer his nickname. (Courtesy of the British Public Records Office.)

police officers just for jolly wouldnt
you   Keep this letter back till I
do a bit more work. then give
it out straight   my knifes so nice
and sharp I want to get to work
right away if I get a chance.
Good luck.
                    yours truly
                    Jack the Ripper

Dont mind me giving the trade name

I get out with my hands
excuse it—
No luck yet-they
say I'm a doctor.
how ha ha

(continued)

Dear Sir

  I do wish to give myself up
I am in misery with nightmare
I am the man who committed
all these murders in the last
six months my name is ████ ████
I am a slauterer and work at
████████ ████████████ I
have found the woman I wanted
that is chapman and I done up if
I called slautered her but if
any one comes I will surrender but I
am not going to walk in the streets
by myself so I am your truly ████

This may have been one of the earliest Ripper letters. It was rediscovered in 1988 by Peter McClelland, who said he found it wedged inside another letter in the British Public Records Office. (Courtesy of the British Public Records Office.)

168

keep the B-oro road clear
or I might take a
trip up there.

phot.

of knife.

this is the knife that
I done these murders
with it is a small
handle with a large long
blade sharpe beth sides

This is the second page of the letter discovered by McClelland. (Courtesy of the British Public Records Office.)

From hell

Mr Lusk

Sor I
Kidne I took from one women
prasarved it for you tother piece I
fried and ate it was very nise I
may send you the bloody knif that
took it out if you only wate a whil
longer

signed
Catch me when
you Can
Mishter Lusk

This letter accompanied a piece of human kidney mailed to George
A. Lusk, a Ripper adversary. (Courtesy of the British Public Records Office.)

This letter was sent to a doctor who examined the kidney mailed by the Ripper. (Courtesy of the British Public Records Office.)

This letter bears Inspector Donald Swanson's declaration of authenticity in the upper-left corner. (Courtesy of the British Public Records Office.)

9 William Heirens

In some respects, William Heirens was the product of a decidedly dysfunctional upbringing. But does that explain what he did? He killed two women, assaulted several others, and kidnapped a six-year-old child from her bedroom, before killing her, engaging in necrophilia with the corpse, decapitating, and dismembering her.

Heirens was first arrested at age thirteen and was convicted eventually of crimes such as burglary and murder. When police searched his dorm room at the University of Chicago, they found surgical instruments, lingerie, Nazi memorabilia, and six suitcases full of stolen items. He had a criminal alter ego named George Murman, and an IQ that may have been in the genius range.

Human sexuality challenged Heirens beyond his ability to respond effectively. His was a complicated pathology of intertwined unfulfilled sexual fantasy, social and spiritual confusion, and psychological disease. Sexual release for Heirens came in the form of defecation and urination resulting from successful residential break-ins. He would leave these organic deposits at the crime scene and typically steal a woman's underpants.

His communication provided two separate clues that led police to their serial killer. A message scrawled on a victim's bedroom wall and a ransom note became investigative assets. But the real importance of this rhetoric was its value to the killer. Some of Heirens's messages were merely expressive and cathartic; other communications were cold and calculated.

THE FIRST KILLING

Josephine Alice Ross was Heirens's first known murder victim. She was found on June 3, 1945, in her North Kenmore Street fifth-floor apartment on Chicago's Gold Coast, close to Lake Michigan. She had been viciously murdered, stabbed numerous times on the face and neck. Her jugular vein had been cut deeply. According to A 2 Z of Serial Killers, "Attacking ruthlessly, he cut her throat and stabbed her several times"[1] Ross's daughter had been disturbed to find her mother's pit bull terrier hiding under a couch, whimpering and cowering. Searching through the apartment, the teenager found her mother's body in the bathroom.

After he killed her, the assailant did not immediately flee from the premises. The coroner estimated that bandages were placed on her body about an hour and a half after her death.[2] The killer had begun to burglarize the apartment before the murder, and he had plenty of time to continue to search for valuables after her death. One account suggests that Heirens was interrupted in the process of looting Ross's apartment. When she awoke, he murdered her. His net take from the crime was a paltry amount, "His haul amounted to a miserable $12."[3]

After inflicting the knife wounds, the killer bathed her and then placed the bandages on some of the cuts. He tied a nylon stocking and her red skirt around her neck. After her death, "He spent two hours at the scene, wandering aimlessly from room to room as he enjoyed multiple orgasms."[4]

THREE UNSUCCESSFUL ATTEMPTS

On October 1, 1945, Veronica Hudzinski heard a tapping sound coming from her window. When the nineteen-year-old opened the window of her North Winthrop Avenue room, two shots were fired. One bullet entered her shoulder. Investigators searched the outside of her home, and "Beneath Hudzinski's window police later found a revolver wrapped in a crude mask that had been made from a shower curtain."[5]

Three days later, on October 4, Evelyn Peterson encountered Heirens much as Ross had, but she lived to tell her story. Author Michael Newton noted that Peterson returned home while Heirens was burglarizing it, and "Heirens decked her and fled."[6] Authors Colin Wilson and Donald Seaman reported a slightly different version of events:

"Once inside an apartment, he was in such a state of intense excitement that any interruption would provoke an explosion of violence. That is why he knocked Evelyn Peterson unconscious with an iron bar when she stirred in her sleep." A third version of the attack was provided by the crime historian Gini Scott, who contended that "Peterson was knocked unconscious with a heavy metal bar when a prowler dropped down from a trap door in the ceiling of her sister's apartment on Drexel Avenue—near the South Side campus of the University of Chicago. When she awoke, her arms were bound with lamp cord."[7]

Marian Caldwell was the third nonfatal Heirens victim. Two months after the attack on Evelyn Peterson, a shot was fired at Caldwell as she sat in the kitchen of her Sherwin Avenue home. This December 5 incident turned out relatively well for Caldwell, who was slightly grazed by the bullet, which shattered a window and lodged in a baseboard. The police theorized that the shot was fired from a rooftop across the street.[8]

MORE KILLING

Frances Brown was found half-dressed, draped over her bathtub, five days later. Her pajama top was wrapped around her neck. Apparently, Brown had discovered Heirens in her apartment, going through her purse. When she screamed, he shot her twice. He then stabbed her with a kitchen knife from the victim's own kitchen. Crime scene investigators found the knife plunged into her neck so forcefully that it protruded from one side of her throat to the other.

Brown, a thirty-year-old former member of the Waves, the World War II women's naval auxiliary organization, was a secretary at A. B. Dick, the office machine store. Brown's maid found her dead in her apartment on December 10, 1945. Her killer had gained access to her apartment at about 4 A.M. by climbing an eight-foot iron fence, jumping onto the fire escape, and then onto the ledge. As in the Ross crime, he spent considerable time at the apartment, lingering at the scene for approximately two hours.

Brown's body was left lying on the rim of the bathtub, by then filled with bloody water. In an apparent attempt to wash away the blood, an unusual habit of the killer, Heirens had dragged his victim into her bathroom. There Brown was left. Although the victim was cleaned up, these efforts made a mess of the bathroom; towels soaked in blood remained on the floor.

MYSTERIOUS WALL WRITING

After shooting then stabbing Ms. Brown, Heirens used her lipstick to write a message on her bedroom wall. The partly printed, partly written message baffled investigators at the crime scene. The message read:

> For heaven's
> sake catch me
> before I kill more
> I cannot control myself.[9]

A contemporary description of the style and appearance of this wall writing, provided by Scott, can be considered. The top line of the message was six feet from the floor. The letters varied in size: some were three inches, while others were as large as six inches. A few of the letters were printed as capitals, while most others were in script.

Why did Heirens write this wall message? When police asked Heirens that question, he reportedly replied, "I wrote the message because I had an awful sick feeling and felt bad. I had a headache."[10] When doctors asked Heirens what his purpose was when he wrote the wall writing, he answered, "That was George and I could not help what I was doing, and he was myself."[11] "George" was Heirens's criminal alter ego, the actual culprit responsible for Heirens's misconduct—according to Heirens. Handwriting analyst Herbert J. Walker testified that Heirens had written the wall message.[12]

The content of this message can be summarized in several ways. There was a reference to "Heaven's sake," perhaps indicative of some spiritual/religious conflict. The writer wanted to be caught, the message claimed, because otherwise there would be more killing. Why? The wall writer/killer admitted that he could not control himself. The style of this brief wall message was marked by its composition in four balanced lines. There was no punctuation, and a combination of printing and writing was used. The emotional tone was one of panic and emotional intensity. The rhetorical theme conveyed desperation and threats.

The murder of six-year-old Suzanne Degnan was extraordinarily horrible. Heirens snatched the child from her bed in her parents' North Kenmore Avenue home on January 7, 1946. Suzanne had been excited about the resumption of classes at the Sacred Heart Convent School after the Christmas vacation. When James E. Degnan went into his daughter's bedroom that morning, he immediately noticed that her window was open and that she was not in her bed. The slightly chubby, blonde-haired little girl was gone.

Although he had already killed the little girl, Heirens left a ransom note at the scene. Newton explained the curious role of this note and Heirens's probable motive in writing it; he referred to Heirens's "leaving a written demand for $20,000 as a ruse, to baffle the police."[13] There is some confusion over the discovery of the note, specifically about who found it. Wilson and Seaman suggested that after Degnan discovered his daughter's absence, "He called the police, and it was a policeman who found the note on the child's chair." A very different account was reported by Scott: "In his frantic search to figure out what had occurred, Degnan discovered a piece of oil-stained paper on the floor."[14]

When Heirens initially accosted Suzanne in her bed, the sounds of the assault woke Suzanne's mother. She almost stumbled on the criminal's presence: "He broke into the child's room and subdued Suzanne in her bed. But he wasn't quiet about it. After hearing strange noises, the child's mother called out to see if she was all right, almost discovering the crime in progress."[15] Heirens forced Suzanne to tell her mother that she was fine, and Suzanne was killed soon afterward. Once again, Heirens spent a couple of hours in the victim's home. The coroner discovered that "Her blond hair had been washed after she was killed. This was the third victim whose body had been cleaned."[16]

The method of disposal of Suzanne's body used by Heirens was particularly unpleasant and horrifying. Suzanne's head was found under a manhole cover. Her left leg was found in a nearby sewer. The right leg was found in another sewer, and her torso in yet another. The arms were found in a different sewer, a few weeks later.

THE RANSOM NOTE

Another type of written crime-related document produced by Heirens was the ransom note left at the Degnan crime scene. As mentioned earlier, this note was probably intended to distract and delay the police by making them wait for contact from a kidnapper instead of initiating a murder investigation. This ransom note was described as "a crudely pencilled note," with instructions for James Degnan to prepare a total of $20,000 in five- and ten-dollar denominations, "& waite for word." The kidnapper had written a warning message on the other side of the paper, "Burn this for her safety."[17] The rhetorical theme of this ransom note was one of superiority and control.

A NOTE FROM AN ACCOMPLICE?

When apprehended, Heirens blamed his crimes on an alter ego named George, who used the names "George Murman, George M. S., and George LMFT."[18] He wrote letters to George and confessed that George was responsible for all of his criminal acts. When Heirens was caught, there was a letter from George to him in his wallet. The letter from George read:

May 17

Bill:

I haven't heard from you in a long time. I feel for you being in jail. Tough luck. You'll know better next time.

It seems that I'm caught up with and I'll have to make an exit if I want to enjoy life. Therefore I will entrust you with some of my belongings.

I will pick up most of my things in the future. Inside I enclose a key to the locker at the Randolph Street Station. Use the key as soon as possible.

Inside the locker you will find some papers and money. You can use some of the money. Please leave most of it alone so I can pick it up when I need some ready cash.

It's a good thing the police didn't search your place. I'd probably be the one in the coop now if they did. I remember once you told me that you wouldn't take the rap. I appreciate you taking those things off my hands when I was being followed.

I could have just as well dumped it but I can't see me losing all that jewelry. I'll give you a phone call before I come for the stuff.

I'm on my way to Milwaukee for a month and then El Paso. Jock has things fixed in that territory south of there. Tom, Sid, Pete and myself will start the road from there. Once the stuff is on the way it will be easy.

Howey, Johnny and Carl will be out of the Army soon with a few new ideas. I'll see you soon. If this doesn't pan out, the gang might be broken up. We aren't keeping any of our old plans, so burn what you have. We'll burn ours.

George M. S.[19]

Heirens explained the note away by claiming that it was part of an old school assignment.

Puzzled by this note, investigators considered that an accomplice might have written it. Thinking that another killer could still be on the loose, they aggressively interrogated Heirens for days, including the use of a spinal tap and an injection of sodium pentothal.

The content of this note included numerous salient facts. George told Heirens that he had not heard from him in a while, and commiserated for Heirens's time in jail. George informed Heirens that he had left town, and told him about a key and some money that was available to Heirens if needed. George confessed that he was responsible for the crimes being charged to Heirens. He mentioned planned trips to Milwaukee and El Paso, and he referred to seven other members of their gang. The gang might have to split up, George informed Heirens, in which case Heirens was advised to burn their plans.

The style of this lengthy note was basically informative. The tone was low key and calm, and the style seemed to be relatively informal. It certainly was detailed, providing plenty of exculpatory material for Heirens's defense.

The note found in Heirens's wallet, like the letters, was a rational and calculated part of his serial murder plans. If he was caught, he reasoned, the note would throw police off his track. He was correct, for a short time, until investigators and psychiatrists decided that George did not exist outside of Heirens's mind.

A LETTER TO GEORGE

During his incarceration awaiting trial, jailers discovered a letter in his cell. Heirens wrote the following letter to his criminal alter ego, George:

Dear George,

   You have got me into a lot of trouble now and you failed to help me get out of it. I realize that you are my friend, but I think it is not the right thing to let me take the blame for everything. If you have left I sure would like to have you back to straighten things out. Before you helped me out by getting me things I wanted and helped me pay my way through school. I appreciate that, but can't you help me now. If you can, please do.
Yours, Bill Heirens.[20]

Several content dimensions of this letter were notable. It began with the main point, George was the cause of Heirens's legal problems. George was not helping him, Heirens wrote, and that was not fair because George was his friend. It was not right that George allowed Heirens to take the blame for George's crimes, the letter maintained, while alluding to George's past kindnesses to Heirens. The style of this brief letter was whining and complaining. It was accusatory and surprisingly formal considering that it was a letter between two good friends. Were Heirens's letters to and from George evidence of severe psychological illness, or were they crafty attempts at avoiding criminal responsibility by feigning insanity? I have to agree with the psychiatrists: Heirens, while seriously sexually maladjusted, was not psychotic or schizophrenic. He knew that George was a figment of his imagination.

A FUTURE KILLER'S DIARY

Heirens kept a sort of dairy, or journal, which he termed his high school "scrap book." He began this self-expression exercise during his early adolescence. It revealed his ambivalence, his hormonally exacerbated highs and lows. Like all teenagers, his lows were quite low (errors have been retained in all quoted material):

> Just who am I? I begin to wonder after all I could be human as the rest are but to myself, I would laugh at such a thought. Oh these seem so much more superior. In plain words I think I'm a worm. It's fun being a worm though, I like it: insignificant and obsolete.... You god damned nincompoop. Why the hell do you live is all I can wonder.
>
> Your one of the most unworthy persons I've understood to be able to live. Your sure not following your golden rules for control. In fact, you've been standing still for the last two weeks.[21]

On the other hand, news of his acceptance into the University of Chicago provoked a far different display of affect. He wrote to himself:

> I'm now shaking with excitement. My hopes and prayers have been answered in one of my biggest chances in life. If I can only use my chance to my best advantage. The University of Chicago has accepted me into its enrollment. This is my first chance at showing how good I am to society and I intend to show even better signs. Tonight I feel as if the world were mine. All I have to do now is pray, giving thanks and vowing to do my best as humanly possible.[22]

Heirens also speculated about power, and how it is attained:

> I wonder why I can't run the world. It seems only great men have that choice. Its funny but I don't understand why I haven't the same equal

chance. I guess they probably just know where to start & I don't. Wouldn't it be great to have that much power. Men sacrifice their lives for it. There must be an easier and faster way to gain control. . . . Why am I thinking all these things. It's all nonsense. Probably never ever entered another mind.[23]

The content of this diary consisted largely of four kinds of topics. There was a great deal of self-criticism, and expressions of self-doubt. Events in Heirens's life were chronicled, as were his future plans. Finally, there was a good deal of philosophizing, especially for one so young. The style of the diary was emotional and immediate. It was lengthy, and very informal. Most of all, it was critical—of himself, of life, and of others. Self-reflection was the typical rhetorical theme.

"PLOTS"

Written crime plans were also part of Heirens's serial murder communication behavior. He called plans for individual crimes "Plots." Here is the text of Plot VII: "Considering my present college status, considering my inability to control society, considering that I am loosing my moral code slightly; I hereby intend to change my whole way of living. Since I have devoted more time to psychology it should be easy. My plan described in this plot should be carried out fully. I shall attack human nature to my fullest extent."[24]

Heirens explained to police the cathartic role sometimes played by his plans:

> I would just put my hand on the table, then the headache would get too strong and I thought if I could just get out it would help. I had to get into any old thing. When I got these urges I would take out plans and draw how to get into certain places. I would burn up the plans; sometimes that helped. I was playing a game with myself. I would draw up plans and burn them or tear them up. I must have drawn about 500 plans on how to enter a house or rob a train or things of that sort.[25]

The content of the crime plans fell into five categories. They included (1) casing and evaluating "jobs," (2) entry, (3) crime scene conduct, (4) escape, and (5) concealment. The style of these lengthy documents was detailed and informative. The tone was low key and calm, although there was an element of grandiosity present in most of the plans.

Despite the diversity in these plots, there are some common themes. One was the rationalization of his crimes. Another theme concerned his specific planned criminal tactics for future crimes. In addition, this rhetoric revealed a grandiose, unrealistic self-perception.

AN EAR IN THE MAIL

Before the apprehension of William Heirens in the brutal death of Suzanne Degnan, the *Chicago Tribune* had offered a $10,000 reward for the killer. The offer generated nothing but worthless tips for the Chicago Police Department. A few oddities did turn up, however, thanks to the reward offer: "One crank letter was written in lipstick, like the 'Catch Me' message, and another contained a human ear, but the handwriting on the accompanying letter did not match the ransom note Suzanne's killer had written."[26] A very different version of this story was recalled by Heirens's advocate Dolores Kennedy. She has written a detailed study of the case, sympathetic to Heirens. She recalled, "A human ear was mailed to [Mrs.] Suzanne Degnan, along with a threatening note."[27]

Did Heirens send the ear? We do not know if any of his victims was missing an ear, but since this assertion has never been mentioned in any published accounts of these crimes, it is unlikely. I doubt that this was a Heirens act. But it was a human ear. And it was removed from someone by someone else and mailed to the police or Mrs. Degnan by someone.

OTHER LETTERS

Two other letters bear mention, as they were taken very seriously at the time of these crimes. One letter was sent to Walter Storms, the Chief of Police in Chicago. It read:

> Why don't you catch me. If you don't ketch me soon, I will cummit suicide. There is a reward out for me. How much do I get if I give myself up. When do I get that 20,000 dollars they wanted from that Degnan girl at 5901 Kenmore Avenue.
>
> You may find me at the Club Tavern at 738 E. 63rd St. known as Charlie the Greeks. Or at Conway's Tavern at 6247 Cottage Grove Av.
>
> Please hurry now.[28]

The second letter was sent to Chicago Mayor Edward J. Kelly and appeared to cast the murder of Suzanne Degnan in a political light. The barely decipherable letter read: "This is to tell you how sorry I am I couldn't get ole Degnan instead of his girl. Roosevelt and OPA made their own laws. Why shouldn't I and a lot more?"[29] The rhetorical theme of the Storms letter was one of taunting. The letter mailed to Mayor Kelly shared a political and moral sarcasm theme.

THE CRIMINAL

It must be emphasized that Heirens's birth and infancy were unpleasant. The panel of medical and mental health experts appointed to evaluate his fitness to stand trial concluded that he suffered a series of accidents, many involving damage to his head. Undetected neurological damage may have occurred.[30]

There is contradictory information on the precise cause of Heirens's sexual pathology, but there is little doubt that his basic problems stemmed from his childhood. At approximately eleven years of age, he saw a couple making love and informed his mother. She told him, "All sex is dirty. If you touch anyone, you get a disease." Many years later, as a young man necking with a girlfriend, Heirens began to cry and vomited in the girl's presence.[31]

Whatever the precise genesis, Heirens became a sexually maladjusted person. His psychiatric evaluation declared, "When aged 9, the patient began to be interested in 'the feeling and color' and then 'the stealing' of women's underclothing. He began to take these, at first from clothes lines, then from basements, and later from strange houses, the doors of which he found open or ajar."[32] The same panel of psychiatrists noted Heirens's sexual-criminal progression: "When 12 or 13 years of age, he secured the desired garments by going into houses through windows. This furnished more excitement."[33] In a police interrogation session on July 26, 1946, he confessed that he began to steal when he was ten years old. He did not just take items from the homes, however. After he stole women's panties, he would urinate and defecate in the houses he had broken into.[34] Heirens described his compulsion to the police:

When I was about ten years of age ... at that early time the mere act of stealing carried with it sex satisfaction. At that age I was conscious of sex. About this time I saw a motion picture of Dr. Jekyll and Mr. Hyde, and to this day in some way or another the song "Rose O'Day" connects itself with this picture. In this picture I also remember quite vividly a hand, a body of a woman and blood. They are about the only things from this picture that I now carry in my mind. I never have been given to masturbation or other abnormal sex desires nor have I up to this time ever had sexual intercourse nor attempted to have any relations with any female.[35]

There is a probable explanation for Heirens' criminal behavior—pathological sexual deviancy from the norm—which appears to have been present in his life from as early as age nine. None of Heirens's victims was raped. For Heirens, sexual fulfillment resulted from the forbidden and dangerous nature of his acts, and the childish excitement of knowing he was breaking the law, not from sexual performance.

There is considerable evidence that the specific mix of mental maladies afflicting Heirens revealed a strong conflict between his psychosexual status and his self-esteem. He matured unusually early, experiencing his first nocturnal emission at nine years of age. Before long, he started stealing women's panties from their clotheslines and homes, and wearing them. He considered normal heterosexual stimulation to be disgusting. He began burgling apartments and experiencing sexual excitement, to a climax, when he did so. Author Donald T. Lunde reported that the only way Heirens could attain an erection was by breaking and entering.[36] When he tired of women's underwear, Heirens began to gratify himself by entering apartments through a window or door. He would then urinate and/or defecate on the floor in the dwelling he had entered. At about this time he also began lighting small fires.[37]

At the request of Heirens's attorneys and the state's attorney, the court ordered a psychiatric examination before trial. A three-person panel was selected: Dr. Harry R. Hoffman, "State Alienist" and Director of the Neuropsychiatric Institute; Dr. William H. Haines, Director of the Behavior Clinic of the Criminal Court of Cook County, and Dr. Foster Kennedy, past-president of the American Neurological Association and Director of Neurological Services at Bellevue Hospital. Their diagnosis of Heirens? "This patient, in our opinion, is not suffering from any psychosis, nor is he mentally retarded: he has average intelligence. He has a deep sexual perversion and is emotionally insensitive and unstable. He has sufficient intelligence to understand the nature and object of the proceedings against him. He rightly comprehends his own position in regards to these proceedings and had sufficient mind to conduct his defense in a rational and reasonable manner."[38]

Heirens had a lengthy juvenile rap sheet. Before he was even a teenager, he had acquired an unusually long record for burglary and arson. Serial killer sleuth Robert Keppel mentioned that besides brutally killed two women and a six-year-old girl, Heirens committed at least twenty-six other crimes including burglaries, robberies, and assaults.[39] His 1947 psychiatric evaluation documented his record. It described his arrests for burglary at the ages of thirteen and fifteen. In 1942, at thirteen years of age, Heirens was a suspect in nearly fifty burglaries. He brought a loaded gun to school that year; searching his home, police found three more pistols and a rifle hidden behind the refrigerator, and four more firearms on the roof. He was sent to a youth facility for three years and on his release, resumed his burglary career while attending the University of Chicago.

Much has been made of Heirens's intellect, but not all sources agree that he was brilliant. His psychiatric evaluation noted that when his intellect was tested, he had an intelligence quotient of 110, which is considered to be average. He attended the University of Chicago from September 1945 until his arrest during the summer quarter of 1946. His academic record there was characterized as average and below average, largely due to numerous absences from class.[40] Heirens had little difficulty with cognitive tasks. As a youth he was incarcerated in a Catholic semi-correctional residential youth institution. He was there only a year when he transferred to a Catholic academy, where he was considered to be a brilliant student. It is claimed that he was allowed to forgo his first-year classes at the University of Chicago, making him a seventeen-year-old sophomore at the relatively prestigious University of Chicago.

A central aspect of Heirens's defense was the alleged existence of George Murman, the person Heirens blamed for the crimes. The panel of court-appointed psychiatrists offered their diagnosis of George Murman's role in Heirens's criminal life: "These conversations regarding 'George,' in our opinion, reveal a power for hysterical fantasy to be expected in a hysterical individual passing through long sustained emotional conflict."[41]

The very name George Murman may have significance. Scott observed that the last name Murman, "which some have taken to be a version of Murder Man," might have been a telling subconscious choice. Newton confirmed Scott's suspicions about the hidden meaning of the name Murman: "In jail, the teenager blamed his crimes on an alter-ego, 'George Murman,'—short for Murder Man.''[42] Heirens claimed that he met Murman, who was five years older, at an Indiana reform school, then ran into him in Chicago again in 1943, after which they became frequent companions.[43]

Heirens was uncooperative when arrested. When asked for his name by the arresting police, Heirens told them he was ''Joe Blow.''[44] The 1947 psychiatric study of Heirens noted that he was held at the House of Correction in Chicago and treated at its medical facility for scalp wounds received while being arrested. Here, he refused to answer any questions, and he mocked his questioners.

Heirens recovered from the injuries sustained during his arrest at the city jail infirmary called the Bridewell. He claimed to have attempted suicide there on two occasions, trying ''too gouge my eyes out in the hope they wouldn't notice it till I was dead but that failed because they were watching me just like when I tried to reopen the wounds in my head to bleed to death.''[45] Heirens was just as uncooperative with his family. When his father attempted to see him, ''The boy acted as if he were comatose, gazing at the ceiling with a vacant stare and pretending that he could not hear the doctors or nurses.''[46]

During his postarrest interrogation sessions, Heirens was administered a polygraph examination. Although he lied repeatedly, blaming the nonexistent George Murman for his crimes, he passed the test designed to scientifically detect deception. How did Heirens ''beat'' the sodium pentathol–enhanced interrogation? Scott explained, ''The accuracy of the sessions is a matter of speculation, because Heirens had used doses of sodium pentathol at the university to get high. Therefore his injections did not affect him as fully as someone who had never been exposed to the drug.''[47] Heirens offered this explanation for his successful deception of the deception detection device, ''I was too nervous when they used the truth serum for it to have any effect but when they started to question me I decided to play along & so I wanted to aggravate them against me so I blamed George M. S. of whom I have a note concerning. That all worked very well but I think I should have told them I did it in the truth serum.''[48]

During the sodium pentathol–induced examination, and under police supervision in the prison hospital, Heirens was asked, ''Did you kill Suzanne Degnan?'' He replied, ''George cut her up.'' Initially he claimed that George was an actual, living, real person, a boy five years older than him and whom he had first met at school. He later admitted that George was his alter ego: ''He was just a realization of mine, but he seemed real to me.''[49]

TWO SERIAL KILLER COMMUNICATION CLUES

William Heirens left two different communication clues. Both his wall writing at one murder scene and his ransom note left at another would come back to haunt him. Originally, he was arrested for burglary. While Heirens was in custody, however, police were able use his communication to link him to murder.

Heirens's wall writing was the clue implicating him in Frances Brown's murder: "A break in the case came when Storms noticed that the 'e' in the note was written as it is on a typewriter—as it was in the 'Catch Me Before I Kill More' message in the Brown murder."[50]

Scientific examination of the ransom note also yielded clues, as Scott explained:

> Police let *Chicago Daily News* staff artist Frank van Hamel photograph the ransom message as part of a newspaper story. He excitedly told Storms that by carefully examining the paper under a magnifying glass, you could see faint impressions. Police studied the note again by using a bright light held at an angle and could tell that the paper was taken from a pad on which some words had been written on a sheet above it. Hamel helped several detectives decipher the markings. They discovered a few names and phone numbers, leading them to University of Chicago students and a popular restaurant near campus. But four letters kept turning up together had no evident meaning: eire.[51]

Of course, "eire" could just be part of his name: H*eire*ns.

WAS HEIRENS INNOCENT?

Some believe that Heirens did not receive a fair trial. They maintain that the press exerted pressure that resulted in a hasty conviction. Judge Luther Swygert, late of the U.S. Court of Appeals, noted in his dissent to the court's denial of Heirens's appeal, "The case presents a picture of a public prosecutor and defense counsel, if not indeed the trial judge, buckling under the pressure of a hysterical and sensation-seeking press bent upon obtaining retribution for a horrendous act."[52]

Newspaper interest in and coverage of the case was overwhelming. In one ten-week period, the story was headlined on at least 157 occasions in Chicago papers. Kennedy explained her criticism of the press in the Heirens case: "Little of what is 'known' about the Heirens story is based on fact. And those who remember the happenings of 1946 actually recall only what the newspapers told them was true."[53]

Serious misbehavior on the part of the press in this case has also been suggested. The role of *Chicago Tribune* writer George Wright in particular has been questioned. Kennedy contended that, "Sixteen days before the state's attorney felt there was sufficient evidence for murder indictments, George Wright of the *Chicago Tribune* invented and published a false confession story, which was unquestioningly picked up by the Associated Press and the remaining four Chicago papers." Kennedy claimed that when she tried to obtain files, "What we found was a massive cover-up of all actions and investigations leading to the conviction of Bill Heirens."[54]

CONCLUSION

William Heirens was a complicated person who was quite possibly a victim of his maternal upbringing. His mother convinced him at a very early age of the evil nature of human sexuality. This may have resulted in his sexual pathology. It seems to me that his aberrant sex drive and predilections were the root of his criminal behavior. Whether he was the genius some claim that he was or merely bright enough to be a sixteen-year-old freshman at the University of Chicago, Heirens was not lacking in intelligence. He simply directed his talent and energies in the wrong direction. Even in the midst of his illness, he realized, at times, that he was behaving incorrectly, but he was ultimately incapable of controlling himself. His communications revealed the polar tendencies he was fighting internally and the terrible self-conflict he was experiencing.

These messages were important. The wall writing clearly manifested Heirens's conflicted internal state. The letter from George, Heirens's alter ego, and the note found on Heirens when he was arrested, however, were different. They demonstrated the rational and calculated nature of Heirens's crimes, as he attempted to divert attention away from himself and onto another possible suspect. It is difficult to generalize about Heirens's crime-related communication. He was a diverse communicator; some messages seemed spontaneous and others reflected a degree of premeditation and planning. Ultimately, two of them provided useful clues for the police.

The infamous Heirens's lipstick wall writing.

10 The Black Dahlia Avenger

The case of the Black Dahlia was one of the first post–World War II murders to grip the nation's attention. Elizabeth (Beth) Short, better known by her famous film-inspired nickname, was the heroine of a truly tragic tale, which did not end with her horrible mutilation and death. It is ironic that she has received the fame and public attention she sought in life after her death; in fact, it was because of the manner of her death that she is known today. A study of the Black Dahlia case noted that Short was made famous in newspapers, books, and cinematic treatments in teleplays and feature films, and, accordingly, she now possesses a place in our folklore.[1]

This case featured communication. The killer made at least one phone call and sent a postcard, letters, and a package. He also carved a brief but relevant message into Short's body.

The remains of the Black Dahlia were displayed in a vacant lot in a residential neighborhood of Los Angeles on January 15, 1947. She had been cut in half at the waist. The two sections were placed carefully on the ground, a little more than a foot apart. The injuries and abuses to her body were frightful. Her face had been widely lacerated, giving her the appearance of a clown's leering smile. A piece of her left thigh had been cut out and inserted into her vagina, along with a clump of grass. She was forced to eat her own excrement. All the blood was drained from her body, which was washed. Although she had earned her nickname because of her lustrous black hair, her killer used henna to dye her hair red. That was a substance Short had not been known to use. The coroner estimated that she had been tortured for three days before death.

Her killer communicated with the authorities during and after the murder. He carved the initials ''BD'' into her thigh, made several phone calls to the police, and sent numerous letters to the police and the press. This chapter discusses the case of the Black Dahlia's murder and the killer, the self-named Black Dahlia Avenger, along with the previous and subsequent related crimes.

THE GEORGETTE BAUERDORF CASE: A CHILLING PRECURSOR

It is uncertain precisely how many persons the Black Dahlia Avenger killed. In addition to the murder and mutilation of Elizabeth Short, there was the string of copycat murders following the Dahlia crime. And, there was the murder of Georgette Bauerdorf, a Short acquaintance who was allegedly killed by the prime suspect in the Dahlia murder prior to the Dahlia's death.

"Georgie," as she was known to her many male friends, was a graduate of prestigious preparatory schools Westlake and Marlborough, lived in a lavish Mediterranean-style apartment near the Sunset Strip, and drove a green Oldsmobile sedan. In a rather unpleasant but telling characterization, she was described as a "free-wheeling, dusk-to-dawn, good-time girl," by a private investigator hired by her father.[2] She had served as an Official Junior Hostess at the Hollywood Canteen, welcoming American servicemen. More than one hundred sets of fingerprints from servicemen were identified in her apartment. Bauerdorf had dated a tall soldier, who walked with a limp, until she suddenly became afraid of him and refused to see him. According to the Crime Library, "Deputies were never able to locate the very tall soldier who had dated the attractive wealthy Georgette. She had been frightened by this man and had broken off her relationship with him."[3]

Georgette was found dead, floating face down in her bathtub on the morning of October 12, 1946, by her neighbor. An actress named Stella Adler noticed that Bauerdorf's apartment door was open. One account of the crime scene reported that she was strangled and then raped and dumped in the bathtub. A towel was jammed into her throat to stop her from screaming.[4]

Another neighbor, who remained anonymous, was an apparent earwitness to the murder. She described what she heard to the police: "I heard a female cry, 'Stop, stop, you're killing me!' The screams then went quiet and I thought it was a squabble and went back to sleep. It was about 2:30 in the morning."[5]

Bauerdorf's father, George Bauerdorf, had been a Wall Street magnate who was an oilman and gold mine owner. Based on some misleading preliminary crime scene conclusions and his own sense of the situation, he decided that his daughter's death had been an accident. He held a press conference in New York later that day, announcing his daughter's accidental drowning death. The autopsy quickly set facts straight. No evidence was found that she died by drowning, so it could not be an accidental death. She was killed before she was put in the tub. The Bauerdorf death was ruled a homicide by autopsy physician Dr. Frank R. Webb.[6]

Not only was it a homicide, there was evidence of premeditation and planning. Deputy A. L. Hutchison found that the killer had sought out the darkness to conceal his identity. The automatic light over her apartment entrance had been sabotaged. The bulb had been unscrewed, so the switch would not turn it on, Hutchison noted of the disablement of the eight-foot high light.[7]

Bauerdorf's killer left behind a considerable amount of valuables, but did take her car. It was recovered the next day, abandoned in the southeastern section of downtown Los Angeles. The green Olds was found on East 25th Street, near San Pedro, with the keys in the ignition and an empty gas tank. Fingerprints lifted from the vehicle matched those located on the lightbulb, and also some found in Bauerdorf's apartment.

Was the killer a necrophiliac? The autopsy physician, Dr. Webb, thought that she was raped during or after her death. Los Angeles County Sheriff's Captain Gordon Bowers was certain, however, that Bauerdorf was choked to death, in a matter of seconds, and then was raped.[8]

One more important fact must be recognized: as stated previously, Short and Bauerdorf were acquainted. Both spent considerable time at the Hollywood Canteen. One of their mutual friends, a man named Arthur Lake, suggested that the two actually resembled each other and acted in a similar manner.[9] The Crime Library observed that Bauerdorf most likely met Beth Short at the Hollywood Canteen, one of the hangouts where Short socialized with the wealthy socialite her own age.[10]

Aggie Underwood, a crime reporter for the *Herald-Express*, wanted the Los Angeles Police Department (LAPD) to look into Bauerdorf's murder. She believed that Bauerdorf's murder and the Black Dahlia crime were connected.[11] Bauerdorf's suspected killer was described as a tall, lean soldier with a limp, of whom she was afraid. His name was Jack Anderson Wilson. There was a political problem, however. The unsolved Bauerdorf case was in the sheriff's jurisdiction, and LAPD was investigating the Dahlia case. There were striking similarities in the two crimes, but personal and political pettiness kept the LAPD and sheriff from cooperating.

DISCOVERY OF THE BLACK DAHLIA

In the Black Dahlia murder case, the victim is as famous as the culprit is forgotten. A woman's body, drained of blood and cut in half at the waist, was discovered in a vacant lot in Los Angeles on January 15, 1947. Crime historian Gini G. Scott described the scene: "A housewife and her three-year-old daughter were on their way to a shoe-repair shop on the gray morning of January 15, 1947. The woman saw something in the weeds and discovered the horrible remains in a vacant lot at 39th and Norton."[12] In a different scenario, Hollywood historian Kenneth Anger contended that it was a "sunny Southern California morning," and that the mother was accompanying her daughter to school.[13] In both accounts, Betty Bersinger has been identified as the unlucky housewife involved in the discovery of this grim crime.

There has been disagreement as well over what time Bersinger called the police. The LAPD received the call at 10:35 A.M. However, Anger states that the call was received at 7:30 A.M., while former Los Angeles journalist Will Fowler claimed in his book, *Reporters,* that the call came in at 9:05 A.M.[14]

The murder of Elizabeth Short was one of the most savage recorded in Los Angeles up to that time. Maybe that is why "the discovery of her body set in motion the biggest LAPD crime hunt in the city's history."[15] According to the coroner's report, Short was kept alive and tortured for approximately seventy-two hours. Her face was so disfigured, "it was impossible to photograph her for identification."[16] She had also been beaten with a hammer. A team of pathologists conducted a postmortem examination of Elizabeth Short's body and arrived at a sobering conclusion: "The victim had been mutilated with a knife while she was hung by her ankles; the mutilations had been inflicted while she was still alive."[17]

Although the official autopsy report was sealed by court order, it has leaked out in various forms. Dr. Frederick Newbarr, Chief Surgeon, conducted the autopsy, assisted by Dr. Victor Cefalu and Webb. The cause of death was listed as "hemorrhage and shock due to the concussion of the brain and lacerations of the face."[18] Newbarr's report continued:

The body is that of a white female about 15 to 20 years of age, measuring 5'5" in height and weighing 115 lbs.

There are multiple lacerations to the midforehead, in the right forehead, and at the top of the head in the midline. There are multiple tiny abrasions, linear in shape, on the right face and forehead. There are two small lacerations, 1/4 in. each in length, on each side of the nose near the bridge. There is a deep laceration on the face 3" long which extends laterally from the right corner of the mouth. The surrounding tissues are ecchymotic and bluish purple in color. There is a deep laceration 2 1/2 inches long extending laterally from the left corner of the mouth. The surrounding tissues are bluish purple in color. There are five linear lacerations in the right upper lip which extend into the soft tissues for a distance of 1/8."

Upon reflecting the scalp there is ecchymosis in the right and upper frontal areas. There are localized areas of subarachnoid hemorrhage on the right side and small hemorraghic areas in the corpus callosum. No fracture of the skull is visible.

There is a depressed ridge on both sides and in the anterior portion of the neck, which is light brown in color. There is an abrasion, irregular in outline, in the skin of the neck in the anterior midline. There are two linear abrasions in the left anterior neck. There are two depressed ridges in the posterior neck, pale brown in color. The lower ridge has an abrasion in the skin at each extremity.

There is an irregular laceration with superficial tissue loss in the skin of the right breast. The tissue loss is more or less square in outline and measures 3 1/4" transversely and 2 1/2" longitudinally; extending toward the midline from this irregular laceration are several superficial lacerations of the skin. There is an elliptical opening in the skin located 1/4" to the left of the left nipple. The opening measures 2 3/4" in a transverse direction and 1 1/4" in a longitudinal direction in its midportion. The margins of these wounds show no appreciable discoloration. There are multiple superficial scratches in the skin of the left chest on the anterior wall.... There are four small superficial lacerations in the skin of the lower chest on the left side close to the midline. There is no discoloration at the margins. There are superficial linear abrasions in the skin of the upper left arm on its external aspect. There is a double ridge around the left wrist close to the hand.... There are superficial lacerations and scratches in the skin of the external surface of the right forearm. There is a double ridge depressed around the right wrist.

The trunk is completely severed by an incision, which is almost straight through the abdomen severing the intestine at the duodenum and through the soft tissue of the abdomen, passing through the inter-verterbral disk between the second and third lumbar vertebrae. There is very little ecchymosis along the tract of the incision. There is a gaping laceration 4 1/4″ wide which extends longitudinally from the umbilicus to the suprapubic region. On both sides of this laceration there are multiple superficial lacerations. There are multiple crisscross lacerations in the suprapubic area, which extend through the skin and soft tissues. No ecchymosis is seen.

There is a square pattern of superficial lacerations in the skin of the right hip. The organs of the abdomen are entirely exposed. There are lacerations of the intestine and both kidneys. The uterus is small and no pregnancy is apparent. The tubes, ovaries, and cul-de-sac are intact.... There is an abrasion which extends through the lower half of the labia minora and the margin shows some bluish discoloration. Within the vagina and higher up there is lying loose a piece of skin with fat and subcutaneous tissue attached. On this piece of loose skin there are several crisscrossing lacerations. Smears for spermatazoa have been taken.

The anal opening is markedly dilated and the opening measures 1 1/4″ in diameter. There are multiple abrasions, and a small amount of ecchy-mosis is seen at the margins. The laceration of the mucous membrane extends upward for a distance of 1/2″. At a point about 1″ up from the anal opening there is a tuft of brown curly hair lying loose on the anal canal. The hair corresponds in appearance to the pubic hair. Smear for spermatazoa has been taken.

There is an irregular opening in the skin on the anterior surface of the left thigh with tissue loss. The opening measures 3 1/2″ transversely at the base and 4″ from the base longitudinally to the upper back. The laceration extends into the subcutaneous soft tissue and muscle. No ecchymosis is seen. There is a ridge in the skin of the lower right thigh, anterior surface, located 5″ above the knee. There is a diagonal ridge in the skin of the upper third of the right leg which is light brown in color; extending down from this point there are three light brown depressed ridges. There is a circular ridge around the left lower leg and also a diagonal depression ridge just below this area. The skin of the plantar surface of the feet is stained brown.

The stomach is filled with greenish brown granular matter, mostly feces and other particles, which could not be identified. All smears for spermatozoa were negative.[19]

"Grass had reportedly been forced into her vagina, and she had reportedly been sodomized after death," noted Pamela Hazelton, an authority on the Black Dahlia crimes.[20] Bill Nash, a thirty-four-year-old captain with the Los Angeles Fire Department, happened on the dump site and called the police. He noticed a handful of grass sticking out of her vagina. Knowlton and Newton claim that Newbarr withheld mention of the vaginal grass insertion to accommodate police requests that this specific fact be withheld as a polygraph key.[21]

Although there was no mention of it in the sections of the autopsy released to date, the killer may have taken some of Short's internal body parts. LAPD Officer Frank Perkins, who was among the first to arrive at the dump site, described an opening in the body through which it looked as though internal organs had been removed.[22] It should be emphasized that the organ removal allegation was mentioned only once in the literature and was never reported in any official document or substantiated version.

A car was noted at the crime scene at the time of the discovery of the body. Unfortunately, as is often the case in serial murder investigations, the eyewitness accounts contradicted each other. Anger reported Bersinger's recollection of events: "The housewife who came upon the body reported seeing a light coupe cruising by, which sped off when she screamed at her grisly discovery. She could not describe the car in any detail."[23] However, a paper carrier taking a shortcut through the field where the body was found noticed a black car, possibly a late-model Ford sedan. The car, which was spattered with mud, was parked in the street adjacent to where the body would be found later that morning.[24]

A black suede shoe and a purse were found in a garbage dump at 1800 East 25th Street, on January 26. An acquaintance, Robert "Red" Manley, swore that they belonged to Short.[25]

WHO WAS THE BLACK DAHLIA?

Despite substantial research by several authors, little is known about Elizabeth Short. Her early life is fairly well documented, but once she arrived in California, her activities and associations are largely unknown. At seventeen, she left Massachusetts and traveled to California to pursue her dreams of becoming an actress in Hollywood. Unfortunately, according to one report, there is evidence that she had drifted into the sex market of Santa Barbara, Long Beach, San Diego, and Los Angeles for approximately five years.[26]

Elizabeth Short was born in Hyde Park, Massachusetts, a suburb of Boston, on July 29, 1924. She was one of five daughters born to

Cleo and Pheobe Short. Cleo Short faked his suicide and abandoned his family in 1922. When Elizabeth Short went to California, she first stayed with him, until arguments between them drove her out of his house.[27]

Kenneth Anger provided one description of Short. He noted that she was twenty-two years old at the time of her death, standing five feet, five inches tall, and weighing about 120 pounds. A Caucasian female with black hair and blue eyes, she had a rose tattoo on her left thigh.[28] Relatively similar information was recorded in the official memorandum on her death, written at the Hall of Justice at 2:45 P.M. on the day of the discovery of the body. The corpse weighed 115 pounds, and she was five feet, five inches in height. Her complexion was described as light; she had a small nose and round chin. Her eyebrows were brown, she had extremely bad teeth, and she had a relatively small build. Her eyes were gray-green in color, and her age was estimated at between fifteen and thirty.[29] Why was the medical examiner so uncertain about the victim's age? The major factor was the sexual underdevelopment of the body. There was very little pubic hair and an unusually shallow vaginal canal. According to Dr. Newbarr, "She did not have fully developed genitals. The area is shallow indicating that she did not have a completed vaginal canal."[30]

Beth Short was interred at Mountain View Cemetery in Oakland. Six family members were in attendance, outnumbered by police and media at a respectful distance. Her pink marble headstone read, DAUGHTER, ELIZABETH SHORT, and listed the dates of her life, July 29, 1924–January 15, 1947. She was laid to rest in Plot #66, Grave #913.

AN INITIAL COMMUNICATION

Short's murderer evidently was familiar with her nickname. This is apparent because "The one immediate clue was a pair of initials, 'BD,' sliced into one of the thighs, a grotesque parody of the sort of inscription a lovestruck boy might carve into the bark of a tree." Nickel confirmed Everitt's perception of the body carving on the Black Dahlia; the killer of Elizabeth Short carved "BD" into the inner thigh of Short's right leg. This gave investigators their first clue to the identity of the victim, when they discovered that the initials signified the Black Dahlia.[31] In light of the available evidence, which is very limited, I agree with Everitt and Nickel. The LAPD officer currently in charge of the case, Detective Brian Carr, could not confirm the BD carving: "All the rumors and the speculations about the murder—henna in Beth Short's hair, a tattoo, a 'BD' carving in her leg—can't be answered because these are issues in which the answers have been 'sealed' in the files since January 15, 1947." Similarly, Hazelton, who interviewed Detective Carr, decided that rumors of henna treatment to her hair and the initials BD carved into her leg remain unconfirmed.[32] Other information points in a different direction. A report archived by the College of Education at the University of Southern California flatly concluded, "She had been mutilated and cut in half. The killer had also carved the letters 'BD' into one thigh."[33]

We end this analysis of this body message by considering its content and style. The basic content element of the Black Dahlia body communication was the initials, "BD," but this was a highly context-dependant message. Therefore, to understand the message conveyed by the initials, you need to know Elizabeth's Short's nickname, the Black Dahlia. This fact casts this body message in a much different light. Now, the carving proves that the killer knew the victim well enough to know her nickname. This was, therefore, no random crime or chance encounter—it was a targeted murder and mutilation.

The style of this body message was brief, obviously, comprised as it was of two letters. Nevertheless, it was truly horrible and terrifying, despite its small size. The clear intent of the killer/mutilator was to cause fear and a sense of revulsion.

THE BLACK DAHLIA "COPYCAT" CRIMES

Some investigators believed there was a connection between the decapitation and dismemberment slayings in Cleveland and Pennsylvania during the late 1920s, 1930s, and early 1940s and similar crimes in Los Angeles in the 1940s. One of these Los Angeles murders was that of the Black Dahlia. There were several others with similar geographic, timing, degree of violence, and crime scene message characteristics.

After Short's murder, there were six copycat crimes in Los Angeles that same year. In one, there was body carving. Another of the Los Angeles slayings involved dismemberment, that of Mrs. Evelyn Winters on March 11, 1947. The forty-nine-year-old Vassar graduate was found clubbed to death where the Santa Fe railroad crossed Ducommun Street, although her underwear and shoes were found at the intersection of Commercial and Center streets, a block away.

Some detectives believed that the Mad Butcher (chapter 3) killed Elizabeth Short and the other Los Angeles victims of similar murders.

Cleveland detective Peter Meyerlo, for example, recognized some distinct similarities to the work of the Torso Murderer. The bisecting of the torso was a trait of Mad Butcher mutilation, one he had performed on at least six of his Cleveland victims. The Los Angeles coroner report stated that someone with surgical training and experience had skillfully executed the cutting. The Los Angeles victims had abrasions on their wrists and ankles, suggesting that they had been bound and held captive, just as Edward Andrassy and some of the Youngstown victims had been. That the bodies of the Los Angeles victims had been cleaned and drained of blood, constituted yet another remarkable similarity.

Other authorities have speculated about a link between the Cleveland Mad Butcher crimes and the Black Dahlia slaying. Former FBI agent John Douglas, for example, suggested, "Others thought they were dealing with a serial offender. In this vein, one suggested suspect was the 'Mad Butcher of Kingsbury Run,' who had killed, mutilated and dismembered a dozen people in Cleveland between 1935 and 1938."[34]

As with other well-publicized serial murder cases before it, Elizabeth Short's killing elicited a spate of copycat murders. Three days after Short's body was found, Mary Tate was strangled with a silk stocking. Within a month, Jeanne French was found mutilated. Obscenities had been scrawled all over her body in lipstick. Then a third woman was murdered and mutilated, followed by three more horrible deaths through beating and/or strangulation. Each of these crimes had some features that seemed to relate them to Short's death. Detectives probed hard to determine if there were any connections. Tate was savaged. Her hair was partly cut, and the left side of her face was gone from the lip to the ear. A breast was severely slashed, and there was some significant body writing. The killer had written "Fuck you—B.D. Killer" on the torso, in her lipstick. One report adds the word, "Cocksucker." The killer signed the message, too. Under the initials "B.D.," was "What appeared to be 'Tex,' and 'O'."[35]

It has been suggested repeatedly throughout the years that the Black Dahlia murder was part of a serial murder series. A grand jury was impanelled to hear evidence in the Black Dahlia case. It concluded, "The 1949 Grand Jury probed into the murder of Elizabeth Short, who is known as the 'Black Dahlia.' This is but one of a number of brutal unsolved murders which have taken place in Los Angeles in the last six or seven years."[36] LAPD Detective Brian Carr recently told an interviewer, "It's a lot different. It's got signs of serial murder all over it, but again they never found another [murder] linked to it."[37]

THE TELEPHONE CALL

On January 22, *Los Angeles Examiner* city desk editor James Richardson took a call from the Black Dahlia Avenger. After inquiring if Richardson was the city desk editor, and asking his name, the caller said, "Well, Mr. Richardson, I must congratulate you on what the *Examiner* has done in the Black Dahlia case." After being thanked, the caller added "You seem to have run out of material. Maybe I can be of some assistance." When Richardson acknowledged the value of such material, the response was, "I'll tell you what I'll do. I'll send you some of the things she had with her when she, shall we say, disappeared?" Richardson asked what kind of things. "Oh, say, her address book and her birth certificate and a few other things she had in her handbag," was the reply. When would the items be sent? He said, "Oh, within the next day or two. See how far you can get with them. And now I really must say goodbye. You may be trying to trace this call."[38] Two days later the package with Short's belongings was received. A rhetorical theme of superiority was clearly evident. In addition, the call was informative in nature.

THE BLACK DAHLIA AVENGER LETTERS

After the Black Dahlia was found in a Los Angeles field on January 15, 1947, her killer quickly communicated. Someone who identified himself as "The Black Dahlia Avenger" communicated via the mail at least four times. The first letter contained the previously mentioned authenticating items. The initial communication was a brief message, sent in anonymous package, with text assembled from letters and words cut out of a newspaper. It arrived at the *Los Angeles Herald-Examiner* on January 24. The message was, "Here is Dahlia's belongings. Letter to follow."[39] The timing of the arrival of the first letter was suspicious. When it appeared that the Black Dahlia case had fallen from page one, a mysterious package addressed *"To the Los Angeles Examiner and other Papers"* was found in a mailbox near the Biltmore Hotel.[40] In an alternate version of this story, a package wrapped in brown paper was intercepted by Los Angeles postal inspectors. This initial letter and the accompanying package have been called the most controversial aspect of the Dahlia case. One source close to the investigation told the *Orange County Register* that the mailed items were the personal effects of

Elizabeth Short, but it is thought that they were mailed by someone with no involvement in the killing, perhaps a friend or a former landlord of Short's.[41]

Although the origins of the letter were controversial, it was undeniable that the package contained some of Short's personal items. Here is one inventory of what the package contained:

> All sources mention Mark Hansen's address book.... Other items retrieved from the parcel, or not, as listed in various sometimes contradictory reports, included Short's birth certificate and Social Security card, an unspecified I.D. card, a comb and makeup, a membership card in the Hollywood Wolves Association, a Greyhound luggage claim check dated January 9, "a few" snapshots, a press clipping on Matt Gordon's marriage with the bride's name crossed out, plus "miscellaneous" cards and papers, scraps with names and numbers on them.[42]

The content of this brief letter included three noteworthy dimensions. Initially, it is important to understand that this letter, like many other serial killer letters, was essentially a letter of transmittal or cover letter for some of Short's belongings. In addition, the letter identified the owner of the mailed material and foretold the arrival of another letter from the killer.

This letter's style was characterized by extreme brevity and a relatively simple sentence structure. There were two sentences of about the same length, written in an informative style. The tone was low key and calm, but there was one extraordinary element of the style. Instead of being written or typed, the letter was made of letters and words cut out from newspapers and then reassembled to form the desired message. This letter's rhetorical theme was informative.

There were at least three other letters from the Black Dahlia Avenger. The first was actually a postcard mailed to the *Los Angeles Examiner* from downtown Los Angeles. Written in block letters in ink, the message declared, "Here it is. Turning in Wed., Jan. 29, 10 A.M. Had my fun at the police. Black Dahlia Avenger."[43]

The next day, a letter was received at the Los Angeles District Attorney's office. The envelope bore a typewritten return address, above which was written, "Sorry, Greenwich Village, not Cotton Club." This letter, like the first, was created from letters cut out of newspapers. The brief text stated, "Dahlia Killer cracking—wants terms."[44]

The last letter was received on January 29, the day set for the killer's surrender. It too was a newspaper cut-and-paste creation. It read,

"Have changed my mind. You would not give me a square deal. Dahlia killing was justified."[45]

What can we make of the content of these Black Dahlia Avenger letters? The phrase, "Have changed my mind," indicated two things. First, the letter writer had undergone a change of heart about turning himself in for the Black Dahlia murder. A previous message had claimed that the killer was about to surrender, but this last letter revealed an alternate decision. In addition, another part of this letter contained the killer's assertion that the killing was justified, so there would be no confession of guilt. The style of this partly released letter can best be described as brief and self-justifying. Rationalization was the dominant theme of this final letter.

THE CRIMINAL

We do not know who killed the Black Dahlia, although her killer gave himself the nickname, "The Black Dahlia Avenger." There were several "good" suspects, but on further examination, none panned out for one reason or another. One suspect, Jack Anderson Wilson, died before the case against him could be developed. Six suspects, including Wilson, are discussed in this chapter.

The initial suspect was probably Robert "Red" Manley, a salesman who met Short in San Diego on January 8, 1947. The married traveling salesman offered to give her a ride from San Diego to Los Angeles, which she accepted. Instead of driving to Los Angeles that evening, they stayed in a hotel overnight. There are different accounts of how they spent the time, with one story declaring that they went out to different nightspots, but all accounts agree on several things. He made a pass at her, she declined, and they slept separately that night.[46]

The next day they drove to Los Angeles, where Manley dropped her off at the Biltmore Hotel. Because he had been the last person to see her, Manley was the initial suspect in the killing. LAPD intensely interrogated him, administering two polygraph exams. After he was released he collapsed from exhaustion. Later, Manley was given shock treatments for depression. Although exonerated of complicity or responsibility for Short's murder, Manley nevertheless paid a steep price for his dalliance with the Dahlia. He was committed to Patton State Hospital as a psychiatric patient, and he died thirty-nine years to the day after he had dropped Short off at the Biltmore.[47]

A quartet of other men was suspected, albeit briefly. Joseph Dumais, Daniel Voorhees, John Audry, and Leslie Dillon all excited investigative interest for a time, until their interrogations cleared them. Army Corporal Joseph Dumais was in the brig at Ft. Dix on February 8, 1947, when he confessed to the Black Dahlia crimes. In custody for embezzlement, his confession reportedly convinced Captain William Florence, commander of the Ft. Dix facility. Jack Donohoe, one of the early LAPD Dahlia investigators, reportedly gave the Dumais confession serious attention. Dumais wrote a fifty-page confession, describing and detailing his deed. He wrote, "It is possible I could have committed the murder but to the best of my knowledge I am still not positive."[48] He had been bar-hopping with Short on January 9 or 10, then he "blacked out." The next thing he knew, he woke up outside of Pennsylvania Station in Manhattan. "It is possible I could have committed the murder. When I get drunk I get rough with women," Dumais reportedly admitted.[49] In another version of the Dumais story, another soldier turned Dumais in to military police after they had an argument about money. It was reported, "After returning from a 42-day furlough, Dumais was found with bloodstains on his clothing. He also had a slew of newspaper clippings about the murder."[50]

Suspect Daniel Voorhees was a thirty-three-year-old former restaurant worker, who telephoned the police and requested that they come bring him in for questioning. When they did, he initially mumbled, "I killed her," then decided not to talk. Pressed by detectives to continue talking, he replied, "Ah, I'm not going to talk to you. I want to see my attorney," and that ended his confession.[51]

John Audry was a pharmacist who reportedly "boasted about his ability to cut up bodies." After his arrest for involvement in Short's murder, he initially claimed responsibility. Then he changed his story; he said, "Well, I'm capable of doing it."[52] Finally, he decided that he was not involved at all.

Perhaps the strangest Black Dahlia Avenger suspect story belonged to Leslie Dillon, at the time a twenty-seven-year-old bellhop and an aspiring author who lived in Miami with his wife and baby daughter. After reading a magazine article about the Black Dahlia investigation, Dillon wrote to Paul de River, a police psychiatrist working on the case, who had been mentioned in the article. Dillon had a friend, Jeff Connors, who might know something about the murder, Dillon wrote. De River flew Dillon to Las Vegas. Once there, Dillon quickly found that de River considered him to be a suspect. Dillon claimed, "They kept me in a motel room until three or four other men arrived and then they began to question me. . . . But they wouldn't let me make any kind of calls. I couldn't talk to anybody, only the doctor and the detectives." Dillon claimed that he was then transported in handcuffs to San Francisco, where a day was spent unsuccessfully searching for Jeff Connors. Dillon was then taken to the Strand Hotel, on Figueroa Street in Los Angeles, where two additional trios of detectives took turns questioning him. While out at dinner, Dillon dropped a note on the street, requesting help. The note was addressed to a well-known Los Angeles defense attorney, Jerry Giesler, and it read, in part, "I am being held in room 219-21 Strand Hotel . . . in connection with the Black Dahlia murder, by Dr. Paul de River as far as I can tell. I would like legal counsel."[53]

Dillon was taken to LAPD the next morning, and interviewed by numerous detectives. The authorities seemed united in their assurance of his guilt. Chief Clarence Horrall declared, "There is no doubt in my mind that Dillon is the hottest suspect there has ever been in this case." Dr. de River asserted that Dillon "knew more about the Dahlia murder than the police, and more about abnormal sex psychopathia than most psychiatrists." A district attorney added, "I'm convinced and support the police assertion that Dillon is the hottest suspect ever." Dillon was booked on suspicion of murder, but Jeff Connors was located soon thereafter. His story supported Dillon's, except that Connors denied having told Dillon he knew about the murder.[54] Dillon was released, and Connors was arrested. He was quickly released.

An informant approached LAPD about a man who called himself "Arnold Smith," and who knew the Black Dahlia Avenger. It is believed that Smith was in fact Jack Anderson Wilson, and that he himself was the killer. Los Angeles County Sheriff's Detective Joel Lesnick identified "Arnold Smith" as one of the known aliases of Wilson. Later, an undercover officer named Louise Sheffield met Arnold Smith. She remarked, "The individual I had met was later identified as Jack Anderson Wilson."[55]

According to the LAPD informant, Smith claimed that a man named Al Morrison, a female impersonator, had killed Elizabeth Short. The informant brought a nine-minute tape to LAPD Detective Marvin Enquist of Smith describing Morrison's story. According to Smith, Morrison said he killed her in a house on 31st Street near San Pedro. Enquist took the tape to LAPD Detective John St. John, who had headed the Black Dahlia investigation for a year. St. John eventually accumulated eighty-eight pages of transcripts and a tape recording of Arnold Smith talking about the crime, a recording in which Smith lapses between first- and third-person accounts of the murder and mutilations. Using confidential police file material and information from a woman who had known Short, St. John verified many of the details about the life of Beth Short and her murder that Smith gave. A Los Angeles County Sheriff's Department document noted, "Jack Anderson Wilson is a plausible suspect for the Bauerdorf murder and the murder of Victim Short." The LAPD provided copies of the Arnold Smith transcripts and other pertinent information from the case files to Dr. John Money, of the Johns Hopkins University School of Medicine. He concluded, "I think it is very likely that 'Arnold Smith' himself is the murderer of Ms. Short."[56]

Before the informant could set up an interview for St. John with Arnold Smith, the *Los Angeles Herald-Examiner* ran a story about this new development in the case. Within days, Jack Anderson Wilson was dead from a fire that gutted his room at the Holland Hotel. Arnold Smith was identified as Jack Anderson Wilson by police informants, his knowledge of Wilson's crimes, and through law enforcement records. Besides, after the fire that killed Wilson, Arnold Smith was never heard from again. The Los Angeles District Attorney issued this conclusion: "The case cannot be officially closed due to the death of the individual considered a suspect...it is conceivable that Jack Wilson might have been charged as a suspect in the murder of Elizabeth Short."[57]

Were there other potential suspects? Although the Black Dahlia is reported to have had in her possession Mark Hansen's address book and a press clipping of Matt Gordon's wedding announcement (with the bride's name crossed out) it is not believed that either was considered a suspect by the LAPD. However, the records remain tightly sealed.

CONCLUSION

What are we to make of the mysterious mutilation/murder of Elizabeth Short? Were the seemingly similar cases copycat crimes, or was there a serial killer at work in Los Angeles in the years following World War II? I am inclined to believe that the Black Dahlia Avenger was not satisfied with only one murder, that of Elizabeth Short. To me, it is much more likely the same man killed Bauerdorf, Short, and several others. Was it the Mad Butcher of Cleveland, who dismembered and decapitated his victims? Probably not, as Short was not decapitated, and most of the other Los Angeles-area murders did not approach the level of violence inflicted on the Cleveland victims' bodies.

In any event, the Black Dahlia Avenger was never caught. There were a number of confessions, however. The School of Education at the University of Southern California noted, "Once the body of the Black Dahlia was identified there was a steady stream of false confessions, from both men and women."[58] One study reported that there have been at least thirty-five false confessions.[59] LAPD Detective Brian Carr estimated that "there have been more than fifty 'confessing sams' who say they killed Beth Short, but all have been ruled out."[60] According to Knowlton and Newton, there have been approximately five hundred confessions in the years since the murder of Elizabeth Short.[61]

Although the identity of the Black Dahlia Avenger is unknown, there are conclusions that can be reached based on evidence. For example, the expert opinions of those who witnessed the mutilations and dismemberment firsthand indicate that it is likely the Black Dahlia Avenger had medical training. One account observed, "The dismemberment indicated medical knowledge and training."[62] LAPD Detective Carr arrived at a similar conclusion: "Its likely the killer had some sort of medical-type knowledge, in respect to the way the victim was cut in half."[63] Harry Hansen told a reporter, "I suppose I allow myself to lean slightly toward the theory of a male murderer, someone with medical training. I based that merely on the physical elements of the case."[64]

One more conclusion can be advanced. There is reason to believe that Beth Short knew her killer. Detective Carr told an interviewer in 1999 that "The killer probably knew Beth Short."[65] It is unknown whether the killer was merely an acquaintance or someone close to her.

Doctor or not, acquaintance or close friend, the Black Dahlia Avenger was a communicator. In initials carved on a body, taunting telephone comments, and self-justifying letters, the killer showed a concern for explaining his acts to others. He was certainly rhetorically motivated. It is certainly fair to say that this individual had decided communicative tendencies. We know these messages were from the killer, because the phone call and package authenticated each other, and the same person was involved in both. Similarly, there is little doubt about the legitimacy of the body carving. It is reasonable to conclude that these rhetorical acts were important to the killer, since he communicated repeatedly and in a variety of ways.

Conclusion

For many serial killers, it is apparently not enough to murder a number of innocent persons. For a large number of offenders, there is a need to communicate during and after the homicidal acts. Ten serial murderers have been examined to ascertain the role played by rhetoric in their crimes. In each case, crime-related communication was a critical and common component of the serial slayings. Sometimes it was deliberately left as a clue. This serial killer communication must be considered noteworthy and deserving of close study. It is quite important to the serial murderers, and it is potentially invaluable to the police.

This final chapter attempts to wrap things up and offers some conclusions about this diverse and consistent criminal communicative conduct. I offer three main points in this conclusion for your consideration. They are: (1) a central finding, (2) serial killer communication findings, and (3) the significance of serial killer communication.

A CENTRAL FINDING

The most basic conclusion emerging from this analysis of serial killers is the primacy and importance of communication. Each of these repeat murderers felt the necessity to share parts of their homicidal experience with someone, in some fashion, during, and/or after the fact. This consistent compulsion to communicate characterizes these serial killers.

These communicative urges were satisfied in a variety of ways. Some serialists wrote on walls using their victims' blood, while others sent taunting postmurder missives to the authorities. Most communicated more than once, and they seemed to derive some psychic or psychological benefit from the interaction. In some cases, the serial murderer combined communication modes within a single communication act, for example, by calling someone to tell them to look for a note in a particular place.

SERIAL KILLER COMMUNICATION FINDINGS

It is the central finding of this book that communication is an integral part of many serial killers' crime scene and subsequent crime-related behavior. In fact, one can suppose a rhetorical motive for many serial killings, and certainly for much of what serial killers do. These killers communicated more often than they killed, and they murdered a considerable number of people.

The ten serial killers discussed in this book vary tremendously from each other. Their criminal careers ranged from 1888 to 2002, and they killed in different ways, for different reasons, at different places. Despite this diversity, it is possible to arrive at some generalizations concerning their crime-related communication practices.

Seven conclusions can be made about the communication of the serial killers studied in this book:

1. A significant number of serial killers engaged in communication with law enforcement, the media, and/or victims' families.
2. This communication was deliberate, intentional, and purposive.
3. In several cases, this purpose of this communication seemed to be to deliberately leave clues.
4. There were several modes of serial killer communication. These included notes left at the crime scene, messages left on the bodies, wall writing, phone calls, letters, notes found on killers, e-mail, crime plans, crime records and diaries.
5. Despite the diversity of serial killer communication, there were certain common content themes. These included:
   a. Taunts and insults aimed at law enforcement. These were typical serial murderer messages. Serial killers enjoy ridiculing their pursuers, and they frequently did so. The Unabomber, The BTK Strangler, the Zodiac, and Jack the Ripper all took pleasure in harassing and taunting law enforcement.
   b. Reinjury to victim's loved ones. This was commonplace, as the killer called or wrote family members or friends to share details about the torture they inflicted on the victim prior to

an equally painful and terrifying death. The Zodiac, The BTK Strangler, and the Unabomber especially seemed to enjoy causing emotional pain.

    c. Threats of future murders. These were quite common, as killers bragged and boasted about their planned murders. Jack the Ripper, the Zodiac, the DC Sniper and The BTK Strangler all threatened to commit further murders.

    d. Clues to the killer's identity. Kaczynski was caught when someone, his brother, recognized his communication.

    e. Issuance of demands. Although not quite as common as the previous themes, serial killers did sometimes try to extort things from someone. The DC Sniper tried to cash in on the sniper killings by requesting $10 million to stop. The Zodiac and the Unabomber successfully demanded free, unedited media placement of their communications.

    f. Explanations. Some killers, such as the Mad Butcher, have explained the cessation of their crimes. Others, including the Black Dahlia Avenger, have tried to justify their killings through their explanations. John Robinson tried to convince people that his victims were still alive.

6. Diversity characterized the communication style of every serial killer studied. They made telephone calls, left notes or other writing at crime scenes, mailed letters, and/or kept dairies and records of their serial escapades.

7. The incidence of serial killer communication was probably understated. Quite likely, numerous cases of such communication escaped my attention.

THE SIGNIFICANCE OF SERIAL KILLER COMMUNICATION

In the introduction to this book, I briefly mentioned the significance of serial killer rhetorical behavior. We need to appreciate fully the importance of serial killer rhetoric, because these messages motivated some of these killers and facilitated other killers' related crime plans. I now return to that topic and conclude this book with a few additional things to consider.

Law enforcement must understand the importance of serial killer communication. There is much to learn about serial killers by studying their messages. Perhaps more important, from the law enforcement perspective, serial killer communication frequently leads to an apprehension.

The relative role and importance of communication to serial killers probably varies individually, and perhaps even situationally. In the DC Sniper and Unabomber cases, this communication was an intrinsic part of the crimes. The Mad Butcher and The BTK Strangler were comparatively reticent, although still very communicative; their messages were not part of an apparent overall plan, but served other purposes.

Serial killers had different motives for their communication. Some had a philosophy to advocate; others vented against those who had wronged them. Some seemed to want to leave clues for the police.

Taken collectively, these messages are very important for the following three reasons.

Symbolic Extension of Killings

There have been two notable examples of this tendency in Western culture: Jack the Ripper and the Zodiac. In both cases, the murders largely or completely ceased prior to the initiation of an extensive letter-writing campaign. The letters kept the public in fear, however, as they promised more murders. "What the Zodiac had effectively done was create the illusion he was still active whether he truly was killing people or not. As long as he wrote to claim credit, the lore surrounding him would continue," Douglas and Olshaker suggested.[1] The Zodiac communication, in fact, outlasted the killings by more than a decade.

Way to Understand Serial Killers

It makes sense: to understand someone, learn to understand his rhetoric. Joel Norris, one of the first serial murder authorities, suggested that the way to understand serial killers is to consider their communication. This direct use of serial killer communication is often possible. Serial killer narratives place their lives within a frame of reality, but it is *what* they disclose about themselves that reveals a greater reality, Norris noted.[2] He concluded, "To understand the implications of serial murder one has to hear about it in the killer's own words."[3]

Key to Apprehension

Some serial killers have been tripped up as a result of their communication. According to a psychiatric perspective, "Evidence of symbolism within the spatial or temporal organization of the crime scene could provide clues regarding the identity of the killer."[4] This happened in the case of William Heirens. When he was in custody, a policeman observed that Heirens's signature had a conspicuous curve flourish, which was identical to the handwriting on the ransom note and the crime scene message written in lipstick.[5]

The Unabomber was apprehended due to his messages. Mike Rustigan was a criminology professor at San Francisco State University when Kaczynski was arrested. He noted, "The Unabomber would have been bombing into old age but his mistake was demanding that his manifesto be published."[6]

The final example is the most recent, the case of the DC Sniper. The *Washington Post* reported that the letter and accompanying telephone conversations with the sniper gave them clues that resulted in the arrests of John Allen Muhammad and John Lee Malvo.[7] Similarly, the stolen laptop computer found in their possession allegedly contained incriminating information.

Guillen emphasized the potential investigative value of publicizing serial killer messages. Because serial killer communication contains clues that might tie murders to a specific suspect, the police should publicize them, and there have been numerous cases where the police apprehended the offender through public-provided information.[8] Chances are good that a person close to the serial murderer will recognize the communication and contact authorities, leading to a quicker apprehension of the offender. "Law enforcement agencies on the local and federal level should study this area to develop the best strategy to entice the killers to keep communicating. The more these killers communicate, the more chances investigators may have to identify him-her or get fingerprints or other evidence that can lead to solving a case or obtaining a conviction once there is an arrest," Guillen noted.[9]

It must be acknowledged that the serial murder problem is a serious one, and likely to remain so far into the future. Given this situation, it behooves us as rational citizens and policymakers to enhance our understanding of serial murderers. By adding the communication dimension of serial murder to our psychological and sociological insight, it might be possible to combat more effectively this source of social stress and sorrow.

The specifics of serial killer communication differ somewhat from killer to killer. Some of this communication was instrumental in the killer's crime plans. In other cases, the murderer's messages seemed purely expressive and perhaps cathartic—letting off steam, so to speak. There was evidence of premeditation and planning in some of this interaction, while other incidents seemed spontaneous and spur-of-the-moment.

But one thing unifies each case. And that is the purposeful communication concerning the serial murders by the murderer. These killers called and wrote the media, police, and victims' loved ones. Their motives and specific messages varied, but each one engaged repeatedly in a variety of modes of serial killer communication. Why is that important?

Law enforcement can use serial killer communication to better understand these criminals, and in numerous cases this communication has resulted in the detection of the offender. If serial killer communication were better understood, it might be possible to use this aspect of the crimes to understand, identify, and apprehend more of these repeat murderers—and sooner.

FUTURE RELATED RESEARCH

There remain valuable future related research opportunities. Analysis of a large sample of serial killers might support or reassess the research into the ten killers' rhetoric presented here. In-depth case studies can yield rich qualitative insight. Because of the importance that serial killer communication has played in the apprehension of some of society's greatest threats, it is an area deserving of further investigation.

Notes

INTRODUCTION

1. James Alan Fox and Jack Levin, *Mass murder & serial killing exposed* (New York: Plenum Press, 1994), pp. 19, 41.

2. David Everitt, *Human monsters: An illustrated encyclopedia of the world's most vicious murderers* (Chicago: Contemporary Books, 1993), p. ix.

3. Donald Sears, *To kill again: The motivation and development of serial murder* (Wilmington, Del.: Scholarly Resources, 1991), p. x.

4. Ronald M. Holmes and Steven T. Holmes, *Murder in America* (Thousand Oaks, Calif.: Sage Publications, 2001), p. 22. According to another estimate, "At any given time in the country, roughly 5,000 serial killers were actively pursing their prey," claimed a Missouri law enforcement officer familiar with serial murder investigations. See Dan Mitrione, *Suddenly gone* (New York: St. Martin's, 1995), pp. 141–42.

5. Joel Norris, *Serial killers* (New York: Anchor Books, 1988), p. 15.

6. Robert Ressler, Anne W. Burgess, John E. Douglas, Carol R. Hartman, and Ralph B. D'Agostino (1986, September), "Serial killers and their victims: Identifying patterns through crime scene analysis," *Journal of Interpersonal Violence* 1:3, p. 22. Prentky et al. added, "Of even greater concern is that the frequency of these random, seemingly motiveless, murders appears to be increasing"; see Robert A. Prentky, Anne W. Burgess, Frances Rokous, Lee Austin, Carol Hartman, Robert Ressler, and John Douglas, "The presumptive role of fantasy in serial homicide," *American Journal of Psychiatry* 146, July 1989, p. 887.

Wilson and Seaman perceived an increase of a serial killer each month; see Colin Wilson and Donald Seaman, *The serial killer: A study in the psychology of violence* (New York: Carol Publishing Group, 1992), p. 2. According to Lane, "The leading experts are probably right to note that they have sharply increased since the middle 1970s"; see Roger Lane, *Murder in contemporary America: A history* (Columbus: Ohio State University Press, 1997), p. 320. Caputi noted "a new phenomenon—the rapidly rising number of serial sex killings. FBI statistics show serial murders to have increased drastically in the last twenty years"; see Jane Caputi, *The age of sex crime* (Bowling Green, Ohio: Bowling Green State University Press, 1987), p. 1.

Hickey referred to "a ten-fold increase in the number of cases during the past 20 years in comparison to the previous 174 years"; see Eric Hickey, *Serial murderers and their victims* (Pacific Grove, Calif.: Brooks/Cole, 1991), p. 75. Jenkins provided this conclusion:

> In summary, between 1949 and 1964 a serial murder case was recorded every 10 months or so on average, and an "extreme" case every 43 months. Between 1971 and 1990, a serial case could be expected to emerge in the media every 39 days, and an extreme case every 77 days. By this coarse measure, serial murder cases overall can be seen to be 8 times as likely in the later period as in the earlier, and extreme cases were reported more than 16 times as frequently. The conclusion seems inescapable: Serial murder has become more frequent in recent years, and offenders tend to kill larger numbers of victims. (Philip Jenkins, "Myth & murder: The serial murder panic of 1983–5," *Criminal Justice Research Bulletin,* 1988, 3:11, p. 183)

7. Mark Seltzer, *Serial killers: Death and life in America's wound culture* (New York: Routledge, 1998), p. 9. According to "Serial Killer Communications," such communication is not unusual, "The serial snipers around Washington, D.C. is the latest in a line of serial killers who feel compelled to communicate with their pursuers." See "Serial killer communications," http://abclocal.go.com, October 23, 2002, p. 1.

8. "Communicating with a killer," abcNEWS.com., http://more.abcnews.go.com, October 23, 2002, p. 1. Former FBI profiler Roy Hazelwood emphasized the importance of serial killer communication, which he called a common occurrence: "He may keep diaries, write manuscripts, logs or journals. Calendars help him plan and remember dates. He may draw maps, invent codes, take photographs, or record audiotapes and videotapes. I have read countless pages from offenders' notebooks. I have reviewed thousands of still photographs they've taken of their victims"; see Roy Hazelwood and Stephen G. Michaud, *Dark dreams* (New York: St. Martin's Press, 2001), p. 67.

Law enforcement agents agree with Hazelwood: "The content can expose a killer's thinking, too. Police can study handwriting, prose style, spelling and word choice to build a likely profile, according to Robert Fitzpatrick, a Boston-based profiling consultant who worked on the Ted Bundy murders as an FBI agent"; see "Serial killer communications," 2002, p. 1. According to a clinical psychologist, "It's not unusual at all for serial killers to inject themselves into the investigation. The public looks at this kind of behavior, and wonders why would they do that if their goal was to remain out of sight? Why would you place a phone call? Why would you write a letter?"; see Don Oldenburg, "A killer begging to be caught? Criminal experts reject the idea," http://www.washingtonpost.com, October 25, 2002, p. C1.

9. E. L. Boyer, *Scholarship reconsidered: Priorities of the professoriate* (Princeton, N.J.: Carnegie Foundation for the Advancement of Teaching, 1990), pp. 19, 21.

CHAPTER 1: THE SON OF SAM

1. David Everitt, *Human monsters: An illustrated encyclopedia of the world's most vicious murderers* (Chicago: Contemporary Books, 1993), p. 212.

2. Elliott Leyton, *Hunting humans: Inside the minds of mass murderers* (New York: Simon & Schuster, 1988), p. 155.

3. Ibid.

4. Ibid., pp. 155–56.

5. Ibid., p. 156.

6. Ibid.

7. Everitt, *Human monsters*, p. 210.

8. Brian Lane and Wilfred Gregg, *The encyclopedia of serial killers* (New York: Berkeley Books, 1995), p. 46.

9. Leyton, *Inside the minds*, pp. 156–57.

10. Ibid., p. 157.

11. Robert K. Ressler and Tim Schactman, *Whoever fights monsters* (New York: St. Martin's Press, 1992), p. 69.

12. George Capozi, *Son of Sam: .44 caliber killer* (New York: Manor Books, Inc., 1977), p. 73.

13. Leyton, *Inside the minds*, pp. 157–58.

14. Ibid., p. 158.

15. Ibid.

16. Capozi, *.44 caliber killer*, p. 10.

17. Leyton, *Inside the minds*, p. 157.

18. Ibid., p. 159.

19. Ibid., p. 160.

20. Ibid.; Lane and Gregg, *The encyclopedia*, p. 46.

21. Michael Newton, *Hunting humans: The encyclopedia of serial killers* (Port Townsend, Wash.: Loompanics Unlimited, 1990), p. 311.

22. Leyton, *Inside the minds*, p. 161.

23. Jack Levin and James Alan Fox, *Mass murder: America's growing menace* (New York: Plenum Press, 1985), p. 43.

24. Laura Foreman (Ed.), *True crime: Serial killers* (Alexandria, Va.: Time-Life Books, 1992), p. 144.

25. Ibid., p. 168.

26. Ibid., p. 167.

27. Brian King (Ed.), *Lustmord: Writings and artifacts of murderers* (Berkeley, Calif.: Bloat, 1996), p. 14.

28. Lane and Gregg, *The encyclopedia*, p. 48.

29. Leyton, *Inside the minds*, p. 161.

30. Ibid.

31. Ibid.

32. Ibid., p. 162; Newton, *Hunting humans*, p. 311.

33. Leyton, *Inside the minds*, p. 162.

34. Everitt, *Human monsters*, p. 212. Hickey added, "Police found a sub-machine gun and a note to authorities lying on the seat of his car." See Eric W. Hickey, *Serial murderers and their victims* (New York: Wadsworth Publishing Company, 1997), p. 177.

35. Leyton, *Inside the minds*, p. 162.

36. "Killers of the Innocent," The History Channel.

37. Lawrence D. Klausner, *Son of Sam: Based on the authorized transcription of the tapes, official documents, and diaries of David Berkowitz* (New York: McGraw-Hill, 1981), pp. 313–16.

38. Newton, *Hunting humans*, p. 313.

39. Leyton, *Inside the minds*, p. 155.

40. A 2 Z of Serial Killers, "David Berkowitz," http://www.a2zofserialkillers. com, 2000 (accessed September 10, 2002).

41. Klausner, *Son of Sam*, pp. 265–71.

42. King, *Lustmord*, p. 18.

43. Brian Lane, *Forces from beyond* (New York: Avon Books, 1995), p. 39.

44. Leyton, *Inside the minds*, pp. 155, 191. Another wall writing declared, "As Long As/Craig Glassman/IS IN the WORld/there will never/ be any PEACE/ But they'll [*sic*] be/Plenty OF/MURders." See Foreman, *True crime*, p. 174. Next to the hole in the wall, there was another message, "My neighbors/ I have no respect/For and I treat them/Like shit./Sincerely, 'Williams'." See Capozi, *.44 caliber killer*, p. 296.

45. Ressler and Schactman, *Whoever fights monsters*, p. 69.

46. Joseph C. Fisher, *Killer among us: Public reactions to serial murder* (Westport, Conn.: Praeger, 1997), p. 91.

47. Ibid.

48. A 2 Z of Serial Killers, "David Berkowitz."

49. Leyton, *Inside the minds*, p. 177.

50. Newton, *Hunting humans*, p. 312.

51. Lane, *Forces*, p. 39.

52. Leyton, *Inside the minds*, p. 175.

53. A 2 Z of Serial Killers, "David Berkowitz."

54. Newton, *Hunting humans*, p. 312.

55. Leyton, *Inside the minds*, p. 178.

56. Ibid., pp. 180, 188.

57. Hickey, *Serial murderers*, p. 176.

58. Foreman, *True crime*, p. 156.

59. Hickey, *Serial murderers*, p. 176.

60. Foreman, *True crime*, p. 153.

CHAPTER 2: THE DC SNIPER

1. Angie Cannon, *23 Days of terror* (New York: Pocket Books, 2003), pp. 8–10.

2. Ibid., pp. 11–14.

3. Ibid., pp. 11, 12.

4. Ibid., pp. 15–16.

5. Ibid., pp. 21–23.

6. Ibid., pp. 29–30.

7. Ibid., pp. 66–67.

8. Ibid., pp. 78–79.

9. Associated Press, "D.C. sniper leaves card; 'I am God'," *Guardian Unlimited*, http://www.guardian.co.uk, October 9, 2002, p. A6.

10. Del Quintin Wilber, Stephen Kiehl, and Alec MacGillis, "Police to sniper: 'Call us back.' Garbled call fallows [*sic*] threatening letter seeking money; Chief pleads, 'so we can clearly understand;' Ashland case is linked," *Baltimore Sun*, October 22, 2002, p. 2.

11. Cannon, *23 Days*, p. 81.

12. Ibid., pp. 106–7.

13. Ibid., pp. 110–12.

14. Ibid., pp. 131–32.

15. Ibid., pp. 154–55.

16. Ibid., pp. 155–56.

17. Ibid., pp. 196–97. The limitations of telephone hotlines were clearly displayed in the DC Sniper case. On October 22, 2002, officials said that a 30-second phone call that was received at police headquarters was so garbled that police couldn't understand it. It was assumed that the voice was a tape recording. See Wilbur, Kiehl and MacGillis, "Police to sniper," 1.

18. Ibid., pp. 190, 193.

19. Ibid., p. 193.

20. Serge F. Kovaleski and Sari Horwitz, "In letter, killer makes demands and threats," *Washington Post*, October 26, 2002, p. A14.

21. Ibid.

22. Ibid.

23. Ibid.

24. Gail Gibson and Stephen Kiehl, "Appeal issued to sniper. Shooter apparently left message, phone number after Saturday attack; Police see first hope of contact; Bullet is recovered from victim during surgery last night," *Baltimore Sun*, http://www.sunspot.net, October 21, 2002, p. 1.

25. Cannon, *23 Days*, pp. 208–9.

26. Ibid., pp. 216–17.

27. Bob Woodruff, Beverly Lumpkin, Pierre Thomas and Ellen Davis, "Catalog of deaths: Sniper suspects allegedly kept record of attacks; both appear in court," abcNEWS.com, http://www.abcnews.com, November 8, 2002, p. 1.

28. Cannon, *23 Days*, pp. 218–19.

29. Jayson Blair and Eric Lichtblau, "Computer 'diary' cited in sniper case," nytimes.com., http://www.nytimes.com, November 8, 2002, p. 1.

30. Cannon, *23 Days*, p. 88.

31. Blair and Lichtblau, "Computer 'diary'," p. 1.

32. Maria Glod and Allen Lengel, "Fairfax indicts suspects in sniper killing: Prosecutors cite anti-terror law, seeks death penalty trial," *Washington Post*, November 7, 2002, p. 2.

33. Blair and Lichtblau, "Computer 'diary'," p. 1.

34. Craig Whitlock, Sari Horwitz and Manuel Roig-Franzia, "Three key calls and a fingerprint," *Washington Post*, http://www.washingtonpost.com, October 25, 2002.

35. Andrew Jacobs, "Witness recalls days spent with the sniper defendants," nytimes.com, http://www.nytimes.com, November 15, 2002, p. 1.

36. Gilbert M. Gaul and Scott Higham, "Teenager's past remains a mystery," *Washington Post*, October 25, 2002, p. 3.

37. Jacobs, "Witness recalls," p. 2.

38. Gaul and Higham, "Teenager's past," p. 3.

39. Cannon, *23 Days*, p. 164.

40. Matthew Barakat, "Sniper suspect evaluation rejected," Associated Press/*Albuquerque Journal*, November 20, 2002, p. A4.

41. Adam Liptak, "Prosecutors in sniper case deny rights were violated," nytimes.com, http://www.nytimes.com, April 30, 2003, p. 1.

42. "Malvo confession admissible," *Albuquerque Journal*, May 7, 2003, p. A3.

43. "Sniper case defense," p. 1.

44. Associated Press, "Sniper suspect brags to officials: 18-year-old said he'd do it again," *Albuquerque Journal*, April 6, 2003, p. A1.

45. Ibid. Malvo told a prison guard that the motive behind the shooting of the schoolboy was to elicit an emotional reaction from police chief Charles Moose. Joseph Stracke, a guard at Baltimore's federal prison, said that when he asked Malvo why the boy was shot, he replied, "To make Chief Moose upset, to make him emotional so he wouldn't think straight, and it worked." See Associated Press, "Sniper suspect told of motive, guard testifies," nytimes. com, http://www.nytimes.com, July 25, 2003, p. 1.

46. Associated Press, "Young suspect found snipings laughable, prosecutors say," nytimes.com, http://www.nytimes.com, April 22, 2003, p. 1.

47. Associated Press, "Detective says Malvo joked about shootings," *Albuquerque Journal*, April 29, 2003, p. A5.

48. Matthew Barakat, "Sniper suspect: Mattress too thin, light too bright," Associated Press/*Albuquerque Journal*, November 16, 2002, p. A3.

49. April Witt and Justin Blum, "Muhammad failed at home and work," *Washington Post*, October 25, 2002, p. 2.

50. Marcia Slacum Greene, "In his scope: John Muhammad's ex-wife believes the sniper suspect concocted 'an elaborate plan' to kill her," *Washington Post*, November 9, 2002, p. F4.

51. Ibid.

52. Ibid.

53. Cannon, *23 Days,* p. 52.

CHAPTER 3: THE MAD BUTCHER

1. Michael Newton, *Hunting humans: An illustrated encyclopedia of modern serial killers* (Port Townsend, Wash.: Loompanics Unlimited, 1990), p. 112.

2. John J. Badal, *In the wake of the butcher: Cleveland's torso murders* (Kent, Ohio: Kent State University Press, 2001), pp. 154, 175.

3. Steven Nickel, *Torso: The story of Eliot Ness and the search for a psychopathic killer* (Winston-Salem, N.C.: John F. Blair Publisher, 1989), p. 219.

4. Ibid., p. 173.

5. Badal, *In the wake*, pp. 22–23.

6. Ibid., p. 23.

7. Nickel, *Torso,* p. 15.

8. Badal, *In the wake*, p. 30.

9. Ibid., p. 37.

10. Ibid., p. 50.

11. Ibid., pp. 51–54.

12. Nickel, *Torso*, p. 52.

13. Badal, *In the wake*, pp. 50–51.

14. Ibid., pp. 60, 62–63.

15. Nickel, *Torso*, p. 67.

16. Badal, *In the wake*, p. 69.

17. Nickel, *Torso*, p. 73.

18. Ibid., pp. 72, 76; Badal, *In the wake*, p. 75.

19. Nickel, *Torso*, p. 77. Badal spells the name ''Pearce,'' while Nickel and others spell it ''Pearse.''

20. Badal, *In the wake*, p. 77.

21. Nickel, *Torso*, p. 98.

22. Badal, *In the wake*, p. 103.

23. Ibid., p. 104.

24. Nickel, *Torso*, p. 107.

25. Badal, *In the wake*, p. 113.

26. Nickel, *Torso*, p. 110.

27. Badal, *In the wake*, pp. 117–18.

28. Nickel, *Torso*, p. 124.

29. Badal, *In the wake*, pp. 121, 129.

30. Torso Murder Files, Cleveland Police Department. The letter, postmarked in Los Angeles, arrived at Cleveland's Central Police Station the day after Christmas, 1938, and, according to Nickel, ''The typing, like the spelling, was crude, perhaps deliberately.'' See Nickel, *Torso,* p. 147.

31. Ibid., p. 152.

32. Ibid., p. 173.

33. Ibid.

34. Newton, *Hunting humans,* p. 226.

35. Badal, *In the wake,* p. 158.

36. Ibid., p. 159.

37. Ibid., pp. 95–96.

38. Ibid.

39. Nickel, *Torso,* p. 171.

40. Newton, *Hunting humans,* p. 226.

41. Ibid., p. 212.

42. Ibid.

43. Frank R. Sweeney, Personal communication, February 14, 1954. Western Reserve Historical Society.

44. Badal, *In the wake,* p. 168.

45. Nickel, *Torso,* p. 78.

46. Badal, *In the wake,* p. 63.

47. Nickel, *Torso,* pp. 83–85.

48. Ibid., pp. 207–9.

49. Ibid., p. 101.

50. Badal, *In the wake,* p. 119.

51. Ibid., p. 79.

52. Ian Brady, *The gates of Janus: Serial killing & its analysis* (Los Angeles: Feral House, 2001), p. 186.

53. Badal, *In the wake,* p. 129.

54. Nickel, *Torso,* p. 217.

55. Badal, *In the wake,* p. 169.

56. Ibid., p. 9.

57. Nickel, *Torso,* pp. 24, 47, 89, 96.

58. Ibid., p. 69.

59. Brady, *The gates,* p. 184.

60. Badal, *In the wake,* pp. 182–201; Nickel, *Torso,* pp. 155–68.

61. Badal, *In the wake,* pp. 177–81, 215–28; Nickel, *Torso,* pp. 202–3.

62. Nickel, *Torso,* p. 4.

63. Brady, *The gates,* p. 178.

64. Nickel, *Torso,* p. 215.

CHAPTER 4: THE UNABOMBER

1. Nancy Gibbs, Richard Lacayo, Lance Morrow, Jill Smolowe, and David Van Biema, *Mad genius: The odyssey, pursuit and capture of a Unabomber suspect* (New York: Warner Books, 1996), p. 71; Alston Chase, *Harvard and the Unabomber* (New York: W. W. Norton & Company, 2003), p. 53.

2. John C. Douglas and Mark Olshaker, *Unabomber* (New York: Lisa Drew, 1996), p. 164.

3. Ibid., p. 165.

4. Chase, *Harvard*, p. 57.

5. Gibbs et al., *Mad genius*, p. 78.

6. Ibid., p. 80.

7. Chase, *Harvard*, p. 65.

8. Ibid.; Douglas and Olshaker, *Unabomber*, p. 169.

9. Chase, *Harvard*, p. 66.

10. Douglas and Olshaker, *Unabomber*, p. 171.

11. Chase, *Harvard*, p. 69.

12. Ibid., p. 71.

13. Gibbs et al., *Mad genius*, p. 87.

14. Ibid.

15. Ibid., pp. 88–89.

16. Robert Graysmith, *Unabomber: A desire to kill* (New York: Berkeley Books, 1998), pp. 214–15.

17. Chase, *Harvard*, p. 73.

18. Gibbs, *Mad genius*, pp. 99–100.

19. Ibid., p. 100.

20. John C. Douglas and Mark Olshaker, *Anatomy of motive* (New York: Scribners, 1999), p. 281.

21. Gibbs et al., *Mad genius*, p. 97.

22. Chase, *Harvard*, p. 78.

23. Declassified Federal Bureau of Investigation Document, File # K-1131-60411039-D-UI.

24. Ibid.

25. Chase, *Harvard*, pp. 79–80.

26. Gibbs et al., *Mad genius*, p. 111.

27. Graysmith, *Unabomber*, p. 291.

28. Declassified Federal Bureau of Investigation Document, File # K-1131-60411039-D-UI.

29. Graysmith, *Unabomber*, p. 273.

30. Declassified Federal Bureau of Investigation Document, File # K-1131-60411039-D-UI.

31. Chase, *Harvard*, p. 53.

32. Ibid., p. 55.

33. Ibid., pp. 58–59.

34. Ibid., p. 41.

35. Gibbs et al., *Mad genius*, p. 20.

36. Ibid.

37. A 2 Z of Serial Killers, "The Unabomber," http://www.a2zofserialkillers.com (accessed September 10, 2002).

38. Ibid., pp. 52–53.

39. Ibid., p. 53.

40. "Serial killer communications," http://abclocal.go.com, October 23, 2002, p. 1.

41. Douglas and Olshaker, *Anatomy of,* p. 293.

42. Roger Lane, *Murder in contemporary America: A history* (Columbus: Ohio State University Press, 1997), 314–15.

43. Chris Waits and Dave Shore, *Unabomber: The secret life of Ted Kaczynski* (Helena, Mont.: Helena Independent Record, 1999), pp. 7–8, 178.

CHAPTER 5: THE ZODIAC

1. One Zodiac letter claimed that he had killed thirty-seven people, but there were in fact only seven confirmed Zodiac murder victims, according to A 2 Z of Serial Killers. This estimate excluded Cheri Jo Bates, placing her in a category of possible Zodiac victims. This group also included Kathleen Johns and Donna Lass. See A 2 Z of Serial Killers, "Zodiac," http://www.a2zofserialkillers.com (accessed September 10, 2002).

2. Ibid.

3. Brian King, *Lustmord: The writings and artifacts of murderers* (Berkeley, Calif.: Bloat Publishing, 1996), pp. 287–88.

4. John C. Douglas and Mark Olshaker, *The cases that haunt us* (New York: Scribners, 2000), p. 191.

5. King, *Lustmord,* p. 289.

6. Jake Wark, "Vallejo," http://www.crimelibrary.com, 2003, p. 1.

7. "Definite Zodiac victims: David Faraday and Betty Lou Jensen," Zodiackiller.com, http://www.zodiackiller.com, n.d., p. 1.

8. Wark, "Vallejo," p. 2.

9. "Definite Zodiac victims: Darlene Ferrin and Mike Mageau," Zodiackiller.com, http://www.zodiackiller.com, n.d., p. 1.

10. Ibid.

11. Wark, "Vallejo," p. 4.

12. "Definite . . . Darlene Ferrin," p. 1.

13. Robert Graysmith, *Zodiac* (New York: Berkeley Books, 1986), pp. 32–33, 40–41, 291.

14. Courtesy of the *San Francisco Chronicle.* King, *Lustmord,* pp. 289–90.

15. Ibid., pp. 290–1.

16. Graysmith, *Zodiac,* pp. 50–51.

17. Reprinted with permission of the *Times-Herald.* King, *Lustmord,* pp. 291–92.

18. Graysmith, *Zodiac,* p. 68.

19. "Definite Zodiac victims: Cecilia Shepard and Bryan Hartnell," Zodiackiller.com, http://www.zodiackiller.com, n.d., p. 1.

20. Ibid.

21. Graysmith, *Zodiac*, p. 75.

22. Michael Newton, *Hunting humans: The encyclopedia of serial killers* (Port Townsend, Wash.: Loompanics Unlimited, 1990), p. 369.

23. State of California, Department of Justice. Bureau of Criminal Identification and Investigation. Report Number 1-15-311-F9-5861. October 3, 1969, p. 1.

24. "Definite Zodiac victim: Paul Stine," Zodiackiller.com. http://www.zodiackiller.com, n.d., p. 1.

25. Ibid.

26. Courtesy of the *San Francisco Chronicle*. King, *Lustmord*, pp. 292–93.

27. Douglas and Olshaker, *The cases,* p. 219.

28. Brian Lane, *Forces from beyond* (New York: Avon Books, 1995), p. 262.

29. Douglas and Olshaker, *The cases,* p. 220.

30. Graysmith, *Zodiac*, p. 108.

31. Ibid., p. 187.

32. Ibid., p. 234.

33. Ibid., p. 269.

34. Ibid., pp. 150–51.

35. Ibid., pp. 183–84.

36. Davina Willett, "Famous cold cases: The Zodiac killer," COURTTV ONLINE, http://www.news.findlaw.com, November 26, 2002, p. 1.

37. FBI Memorandum, From {Redacted}, To Special Agent in Charge, San Francisco FBI Field Office (252B SF 9447), March 23, 1992, p. 1. Declassified FBI Document.

38. "Possible . . . Cheri Jo Bates," p. 1.

39. Jake Wark, "Riverside," http://www.crimelibrary.com, 2003, p. 1.

40. "Definite . . . Cecilia Shepard," p. 1.

CHAPTER 6: THE BTK STRANGLER

1. Sarah Weinman, "The cases that haunt me," Bookbyte, http://www.booksnbytes.com, November 3, 2002, p. 2.

2. Tomas Guillen, "Serial killer communiqués: Helpful or hurtful?" *Journal of Criminal Justice & Popular Culture* 9:2, 2002, p. 59; Michael Newton, *Hunting humans: An encyclopedia of modern serial killers* (Port Townsend, Wash.: Loompanics Unlimited, 1990). p. 56.

3. Brian Lane and Wilfred Gregg, *The encyclopedia of serial killers* (New York: Berkeley Books, 1990), p. 73.

4. According to Lane and Gregg, the killer wrote an anonymous letter to a local television station that had given him his pseudonym. Admitting responsibility for the deaths of the Otero family, Shirley Vian, and Nancy Jo Fox, "The killer signed himself 'BTK' for 'Blind [*sic*], Torture, Kill'." See Lane and Gregg, *The encyclopedia*, p. 73.

5. Stan Finger, "A new look at the BTK murders. A Canadian detective will use the Wichita serial killings to explain how 'geographic profiling' works," *Wichita Eagle*, May 7, 1998, p. 14A.

6. Weinman, "The cases," p. 3.

7. Guillen, "Serial killer communiqués," p. 59.

8. Newton, *Hunting humans*, p. 56.

9. Weinman, "The cases," p. 3.

10. Guillen, "Serial killer communiqués," p. 59.

11. Laura Parker, "Elusive sniper makes a few names for self," *USA Today*.com, http://www.usatoday.com, October 15, 2002, p. 1.

12. Newton, *Hunting humans*, p. 57.

13. Guillen, "Serial killer communiqués," p. 59.

14. David Lohr, "BTK: Bind-Torture-Kill. Vanishing act," http://www.crimelibrary.com, 2000, pp. 1–2.

15. Ibid., p. 1.

16. Ibid., p. 2. According to retired Wichita Police Department officer Bernie Drowatzky, KAKE-TV also received a letter containing a few of the intended victim's scarves.

17. Lohr, "BTK: Bind-Torture-Kill. The next step," http://www.crimelibrary.com, 2000, p. 1.

18. John Jenks, "Autopsies show cause of 3 deaths," *Wichita Eagle*, January 2, 1988, pp. 1A, 2A.

19. Ibid.

20. David Lohr, "BTK: Bind-Torture-Kill: Cold case squad," http://www.crimelibrary.com, 2002, p. 1.

21. Lohr, "The next step," p. 1.

22. Greta Van Sustern, FOXNews, March 26, 2004.

23. David Lohr, "BTK: Bind-Torture-Kill: A chilling discovery," http://www.crimelibrary.com, 2002, p. 2.

24. Guillen, "Serial killer communiqués," p. 58; Bill Hirschman, "20 years after first inspiring fear, BTK Strangler inspires frustration," *Wichita Eagle*, January 15, 1994, p. 1A.

25. Lohr, "Cold case squad," p. 2.

26. Newton, *Hunting humans*, p. 57.

27. Lohr, "Cold case squad," p. 2.

28. Debra Schurman-Kauflin, Violent Crimes Institute, "Psychological Profile of the BTK Strangler," 2000.

29. Ibid.

30. Ibid.

31. Ibid.

32. Lori Lessner, "Man who coined term 'serial killer' to speak at WSU. Former FBI veteran Robert Ressler helped develop a profile on Wichita's most notorious murderer," *Wichita Eagle*, March 10, 1997, p. 11A.

33. Lohr, "Cold case squad," p. 1.

34. Lohr, "BTK: Bind-Torture-Kill: Ghostbusters," http://www.crimelibrary .com, 2000, p. 2.

35. Weinman, "The cases," p. 2.

36. Evan Sycamnias, "Evaluating a psychological profile of a serial killer," http://www.uplink.com.au, n.d., p. 2.

37. Weinman, "The cases," p. 3.

38. Lohr, "Next step," p. 1.

39. Lohr, "Vanishing act," p. 1.

40. Weinman, "The cases," p. 2.

41. Lohr, "Cold case squad," p. 2.

42. Finger, "A new look," p. 14A.

43. Hirschman, "20 years after," p. 1A.

44. Lohr, "Ghost busters," p. 1.

45. Guillen, "Serial killer communiqués," p. 60.

46. Jon Yates, "Serial killer's letters puts Midwestern city on edge. Fear has gripped many Wichita residents on news that the BTK Strangler has resurfaced," *Chicago Tribune*. Reprinted in the *Albuquerque Journal,* March 28, 2004, p. A-1.

CHAPTER 7: JOHN ROBINSON SR.

1. Sue Miller Wiltz, "Kansas v. Robinson: Internet 'Slavemaster' murder trial," COURT-TV.com., http://www.courttv.com, August 10, 2003, p. 4. How did Robinson produce signed typed letters or handwritten notes after his victims were already dead? The police found the answer while searching Robinson's locker. In the locker investigators found several dozen blank sheets of paper, signed by both Trouten and Lewicka, and with envelopes addressed to various family members and friends. Celia Crosby, who almost married Robinson, backed out of the marriage when he made some unusual requests. She became suspicious when he asked her to write letters to her family, which would be dispatched later as they traveled overseas. When Crosby asked why, Robinson responded that she would be too busy to write later. See John Glatt, *Internet slavemaster* (New York: St. Martin's Press, 2001); pp. 201, 232.

2. John Milburn, "Trial set for murder suspect accused of stashing victim's bodies in barrels," The Associated Press, *Athens Banner-Herald,* http://www.onlineathens.com, September 16, 2002, p. 1.

3. Glatt, *Internet slavemaster,* pp. 47–48.

4. Ibid., p. 48. Robinson claimed to have received a letter from Paula, too. His letter stated that she was really sorry about stealing his money and car. See Glatt, *Internet slavemaster,* pp. 48–49.

5. Ibid., p. 63.

6. "Lisa Stasi" letter to Betty Stasi, January 10, 1985, Overland Park Police Department, Overland Park, Kan.

7. "Lisa Stasi" letter to Cathy Stackpole, January 11, 1985, Overland Park Police Department, Overland Park, Kan.

8. abcNEWS.com, "Investigating the 'Slavemaster'," p. 1; Wiltz, "Kansas v. Robinson," p. 4.

9. Glatt, *Internet slavemaster,* pp 114–15; Milburn, "Trial set," p. 2.

10. Wiltz, "Kansas v. Robinson," p. 5.

11. abcNEWS.com, "Investigating the 'Slavemaster'," p. 2.

12. Wiltz, "Kansas v. Robinson," p. 6.

13. Ibid.

14. abcNEWS.com, "Investigating the 'Slavemaster'," p. 2.

15. Ibid.

16. Glatt, *Internet slavemaster*, p. 198.

17. Ibid., p. 228.

18. Ibid., pp. 175–76.

19. Ibid., p. 167.

20. Ibid., pp. 168–69.

21. Ibid., pp. 169–70.

22. Ibid., p. 180.

23. Ibid., p. 181.

24. Ibid.

25. Ibid., pp. 182–83.

26. International Council of Masters; Glatt, *Internet slavemaster,* p. 128.

27. Antonio Mendoza, *Killers on the loose* (London: Virgin Publications Ltd., 2001), pp. 248–49.

28. International Council of Masters, p. 32.

29. "Bistate task force thinks it has USA's first Internet serial killer," *Law Enforcement News* 26:536, http://www.lib.jjay.cuny.edu, June 30, 2000, p. 5.

30. Ibid.

31. Wiltz, "Kansas v. Robinson," p. 3.

32. Ibid.

33. Gary Tuchman, "One of 2 bodies found in barrels on Kansas farm may be missing Polish immigrant, prosecutor says. Police fear there may be 9 victims," CNN.com, http://www.cnn.com, June 8, 2000, p. 2.

CHAPTER 8: JACK THE RIPPER

1. William Beadle, *Jack the Ripper: Anatomy of a myth* (Brighton, U.K.: WAT TYLER BOOKS, 1995), p. 79.

2. Francis E. Camps, *The investigation of murder* (London: Michael Joseph, 1966), p. 17.

3. Martin Howells and Keith Skinner, *The Ripper legacy: The life and death of Jack the Ripper* (London: Sphere Books Ltd., 1987), p. 20.

4. Martin Fido, *The crimes, detection and death of Jack the Ripper* (New York: Barnes & Noble, 1993), p. 35.

5. Colin Wilson and Robin O'Dell, *Jack the Ripper: Summing up & verdict* (London: Bantam, 1987), p. 126.

6. Scott Palmer, *Jack the Ripper: A reference guide* (Lanham, MD: The Scarecrow Press, Inc., 1995), p. 107.

7. David Abrahamson, *Murder & madness: The secret life of Jack the Ripper* (New York: David Fine, 1992), p. 18.

8. Richard Wallace, *Jack the Ripper: Light-hearted friend* (Melrose, Mass.: Gemini Press, 1996), pp. 147–48.

9. Tom Cullen, *When London walked in terror* (Boston: Houghton Mifflin Company, 1966), p. 226.

10. Phillip Sugden, *The life and times of Jack the Ripper* (London: Siena, 1996), p. 46.

11. Steven Knight, *Jack the Ripper: The final solution* (Chicago: Academy Press, 1986), p. 185.

12. Wilson and O'Dell, *Jack the Ripper,* p. 137.

13. *Illustrated Police News,* August 18, 1888, p. 1.

14. Paul Begg and Keith Skinner, *The Scotland Yard files: 100 years of the CID* (London: Headline Book Publishing Company, 1992), p. 125.

15. "Summary of news-domestic," *Manchester Guardian,* September 1, 1888, p. 1.

16. John Spratling, Report to Police Superintendent Thomas Arnold, August 31, 1888, p. 2.

17. "The Whitechapel murder. Funeral of the victim," *The Eastern Post & City Chronicle,* September 8, 1888, p. 1.

18. Donald Swanson, Report to the Home Office, October 19, 1888, p. 3.

19. "The Whitechapel horrors. Scenes at the inquest. Funeral of the victim. Latest particulars. Work of the police," *East London Advertiser,* September 15, 1888, p. 1.

20. "Inquest: Mary Ann 'Polly' Nichols," *The Daily Telegraph,* September 3, 1888, p. 4.

21. Swanson, "Report to Home Office," pp. 1–2.

22. "The East-End murders," *London Times,* October 6, 1888, p. 3.

23. "The East-End murders," *London Times,* October 4, 1888, p. 1.

24. "Inquest on body found in the city," *Pall Mall Gazette,* October 4, 1888, p. 1.

25. "Murder in the city," *City Press,* October 3, 1888, p. 1.

26. "The Whitechapel fiend," *British Daily Whig,* October 1, 1888, p. 1.

27. "The East-End murders," *London Times,* October 5, 1888, p. 3.

28. "The East End murders. Intended employment of bloodhounds. A mysterious telegram," *Pall Mall Gazette,* October 6, 1888, p. 2.

29. "Inquest," *Daily Telegraph,* October 4, 1888, p. 3.

30. Donald McCormick, *The identity of Jack the Ripper* (London: Pan Books Ltd., 1959), p. 75.

31. Paul Begg, *Jack the Ripper: The uncensored facts* (London: Robson Books, 1988), p. 126.

32. "Strange writing at the East End," *London Times,* October 18, 1888, p. 3.

33. Donald Swanson, Report to the Home Office, November 6, 1888.

34. Stewart P. Evans and Keith Skinner, *The ultimate Jack the Ripper companion: An illustrated encyclopedia* (New York: Carroll & Graf, 2000), p. 213.

35. Alfred Long, Police Report, September 30, 1888, p. 1.

36. "Eddowes Inquest," Corporation of London Records Office.

37. Melvyn Fairclough, *The Ripper and the royals* (London: Duckworth Publishing House, 1991), p. 39.

38. Beadle, *Jack the Ripper,* p. 63.

39. Fairclough, *The Ripper,* p. 40.

40. Terence Sharkey, *Jack the Ripper: 100 years of investigation* (New York: Dorset Press, 1987), p. 48.

41. Cullen, *When London,* pp. 162–63.

42. Palmer, *Jack the Ripper,* p. 112.

43. *City Press,* October 20, 1888, p. 1.

44. *London Times,* October 20, 1888, p. 1.

45. *East London Observer,* October 20, 1888, p. 1.

46. "The Whitechapel horrors. Latest details," *East London Observer,* November 17, 1888, p. 1.

47. "Another Whitechapel horror. More revolting mutilation than ever," *Illustrated Police News,* November 17, 1888, p. 1.

48. "Another horrible murder in Whitechapel," *Eastern Post & City Chronicle,* November 10, 1888, p. 1.

49. "The Whitechapel horrors. Another horrible tragedy. The head cut off. Frightful mutilations. The bloodhounds at work. Latest details," *East London Observer,* November 10, 1888, p. 1.

50. "Another Whitechapel horror," *Illustrated Police News,* p. 1.

51. "The Whitechapel murder," *London Times,* November 12, 1888, p. 1.

52. Ibid.

53. "The Whitechapel atrocities. Funeral of the latest victim," *East London Advertiser,* November 24, 1888, p. 1.

54. Thomas Bond, Report to the Home Office, August 1889, p. 3.

55. Evans and Gainey, *Jack the Ripper,* p. 153.

56. "Another Whitechapel murder. 'Jack the Ripper' again. The inquest," *East London Advertiser,* July 20, 1889, p. 1.

57. Thomas Arnold, Report to the Home Office, July 17, 1889, p. 1.

58. Ibid.

59. "Inquest," *London Times,* July 17, 1889, p. 1.

60. "The Whitechapel murder. The inquest on the latest victim is finished, but the jury returns an open verdict, and the coroner describes East London," *East London Observer,* August 17, 1889, p. 1.

61. "Inquest," *London Times,* p. 4.

62. Dirk C. Gibson, "The Whitechapel crimes as public relations," *Public Relations Quarterly,* Winter 2002, pp. 22–33.

CHAPTER 9: WILLIAM HEIRENS

1. A 2 Z of Serial Killers, "William Heirens," http://www.a2zofserialkillers. com (accessed September 10, 2002).

2. Gini G. Scott, *Homicide: 100 years of murder in America* (Los Angeles: Lowell House, 1998), p. 117.

3. Brian Lane and Wilfred Gregg, *The encyclopedia of serial killers* (New York: Berkeley Books, 1992), p. 207. Scott agreed, claiming that, "Only $12 was taken from Mrs. Ross' purse." See Scott, *Homicide: 100 years,* p. 117.

4. Michael Newton, *Hunting humans: An encyclopedia of modern serial killers* (Port Townsend, Wash.: Loompanics Unlimited, 1990), p. 166.

5. Scott, *Homicide: 100 years,* p. 118.

6. Newton, *Hunting humans,* p. 166.

7. Colin Wilson and Donald Seaman, *The serial killers: A study in the psychology of violence* (New York: Carol Publishing Group, 1992), p. 181; Scott, *Homicide: 100 years,* p. 118.

8. Ibid.

9. Brian King (Ed.), *Lustmord: The writings and artifacts of murderers* (Berkeley, Calif.: Bloat Publishing, 1996), p. 102.

10. Scott, *Homicide: 100 years,* p. 120.

11. Foster Kennedy, Harry R. Hoffman, and William H. Haines, "A study of William Heirens," *American Journal of Psychiatry* 104, August 1947, p. 119.

12. Dolores Kennedy, *William Heirens: His day in court* (Chicago: Bonus Books, Inc., 1991), p. 88.

13. Newton, *Hunting humans,* p. 166.

14. Wilson and Seaman, *Serial killers,* p. 179; Scott, *Homicide: 100 years,* p. 121. Keppel and Birnes agreed with Scott, noting that, "A ransom note which was found by the child's father was the only trace left by her abductor." See Robert Keppel and William J. Birnes, *Signature killers: Interpreting the calling cards of the serial murderer* (New York: Simon & Schuster, 1997), p. 39.

15. Keppel and Birnes, *Signature killers,* p. 39.

16. Scott, *Homicide: 100 years,* p. 122.

17. Ibid.

18. King, *Lustmord,* p. 99.

19. Ibid., pp. 103–4.

20. King, *Lustmord,* p. 107.

21. Ibid., p. 101.

22. Ibid.

23. Ibid.

24. Ibid.

25. Kennedy et al., "A study," p. 118.

26. Scott, *Homicide: 100 years,* p. 123.

27. Kennedy, *William Heirens,* p. 51.

28. Ibid.
29. Ibid., p. 50.
30. Kennedy et al., "A study," p. 115.
31. Newton, *Hunting humans,* p. 165.
32. Kennedy et al., "A study," p. 117. In contemporary psychological parlance, Heirens's interest in women's underwear would be termed a fetish. Newton added a political element to Heirens's sexual behavior, "His adolescent frustration began to find other outlets, with Heirens dressing in women's garments, achieving climax as he leafed through a scrapbook filled with photos of Hitler and other ranking Nazis." See Newton, *Hunting humans,* p. 166.
33. Ibid.
34. King, *Lustmord,* p. 100; Keppel and Birnes, *Signature killers,* p. 39.
35. King, *Lustmord,* p. 100.
36. Donald T. Lunde, *Murder & Madness* (San Francisco: San Francisco Book Company Inc., 1976), p. 58.
37. Wilson and Seaman, *Serial killers,* p. 181.
38. Kennedy et al., "A study," pp. 113–14.
39. Keppel and Birnes, *Signature killers,* p. 39.
40. Kennedy et al., "A study," p. 1164; Lane and Gregg, *The encyclopedia,* p. 207. Heirens's I.Q. was 129, according to one source. See Keppel and Birnes, *Signature killers,* p. 39.
41. See Kennedy et al., "A study," p. 119.
42. Newton, *Hunting humans,* p. 166.
43. Scott, *Homicide: 100 years,* p. 127.
44. King, *Lustmord,* p. 99.
45. Ibid., p. 105.
46. Scott, *Homicide: 100 years,* p. 126.
47. Ibid., p. 180.
48. King, *Lustmord,* p. 105.
49. Kennedy et al., "A study," pp. 118–19.
50. Scott, *Homicide: 100 years,* p. 122.
51. Ibid.
52. Kennedy, *William Heirens,* p. xv.
53. Ibid., pp. vii, xi.
54. Ibid., pp. x–xi, xiv.

CHAPTER 10: THE BLACK DAHLIA AVENGER

1. Janice Knowlton and Michael Newton, *Daddy was the Black Dahlia killer* (New York: Simon & Schuster, 1995), p. xiv.
2. John Gilmore, *Severed: The true story of the Black Dahlia murder* (Los Angeles: Zanja Press, 1994), p. 53.
3. Crime Library, "The investigation," http://www.crimelibrary.com, 2003, p. 3.

4. Ibid.

5. Gilmore, *Severed*, p. 49.

6. Ibid.

7. Ibid., pp. 50–51.

8. Ibid., p. 51.

9. Ibid., p. 45.

10. Crime Library, "The Black Dahlia," http://www.crimelibrary.com, 2003, p. 1.

11. Crime Library, "The investigation," p. 3; Gilmore concurred, adding that an employee in the sheriff's office also had connected the Bauerdorf murder to the Dahlia case. See Gilmore, *Severed;* pp 170, 174–75.

12. Gini G. Scott, *Homicide: 100 years of murder in America* (Los Angeles: Lowell House, 1998), p. 130.

13. Kenneth Anger, *Hollywood Babylon II* (New York: Dutton Publishing Company, 1984), p. 127.

14. Knowlton and Newton, *Daddy was*, pp. 10, 163, 350.

15. Anger, *Hollywood Babylon II*, p. 132.

16. Scott, *Homicide: 100 years*, p. 130.

17. David Everitt, *Human monsters: An illustrated encyclopedia of the world's most vicious murderers* (Chicago: Contemporary Books, 1993), p. 132.

18. Crime Library, "Broken doll," http://www.crimelibrary.com, 2.

19. Office of the Coroner, County of Los Angeles, "Coroner Report on Elizabeth Short," January, 1947.

20. "The Black Dahlia murder," http://www.bethshort.com, June 13, 1999, p. 1.

21. Knowlton and Newton, *Daddy was*, p. 22.

22. Gilmore, *Severed*, p. 13.

23. Anger, *Hollywood Babylon II*, p. 130.

24. Gilmore, *Severed*, p. 9.

25. Knowlton and Newton, *Daddy was*, p. 30.

26. Steven J. Nickel, *Torso* (Winston-Salem, N.C.: John F. Blair Publisher, 1989), p. 189. Others have investigated whether or not Beth Short worked as a prostitute. One study, by Hollywood historian Kenneth Anger, found that before long she resorted to prostitution. See Anger, *Hollywood Babylon II*, p. 130. Another account referred to her "hard-drinking, sexually active life." See Everitt, *Human monsters*, p. 133. Los Angeles newspapers compiled a list of fourteen taverns in the Hollywood and Vine area where she was a regular. Cleo Short called her "boy-crazy," and said she would write letters to as many as twelve men a night. Harry Hansen referred to her as "a bum and a tease." See Knowlton and Newton, *Daddy was*, pp. 176–79.

Others disagree. One account admitted that Short loved the night life, but in spite of rumors to the contrary, she was definitely not promiscuous. The Crime Library referred to a persistent rumor that Short sometimes prostituted herself, which it referred to as not likely. The reason? The Dahlia was not physically equipped for that conduct, nor was she that kind of girl. See Crime Library, "The Black Dahlia," http://www.crimelibrary.com, 2003, pp. 2–3.

27. For an extended account of this period of Beth Short's life, see Gilmore, *Severed,* pp. 24–47.

28. Anger, *Hollywood Babylon II,* p. 130.

29. Gilmore, *Severed,* p. 21.

30. Crime Library, "Broken doll," p. 1.

31. Everitt, *Human monsters,* p. 132. Knowlton and Newton, on the other hand, reject the body-carving story as untrue. They flatly declared that "No words or cryptic letters had been carved into her flesh." See Knowlton and Newton, *Daddy was,* p. 22; Nickel, *Torso,* p. 188.

32. Hazelton, "The LAPD," p. 1.

33. "The Black Dahlia murder, 1947," http://www.usc.edu, n.d., p. 1.

34. John C. Douglas and Mark Olshaker, *The cases that haunt us* (New York: Scribners, 2000), p. 239. Los Angeles investigators made an official request to Cleveland authorities for assistance. Between 1991 and 1992, the Cleveland Police Chief, Edward Kovacic, was requested by the Los Angeles police to investigate any link between Cleveland's Mad Butcher killings and the brutal murder and dismemberment of Elizabeth Short and others in 1947. See James J. Badal, *In the wake of the butcher: Cleveland's torso murders* (Kent, Ohio: Kent State University Press, 2001), p. 215.

35. Knowlton and Newton, *Daddy was,* pp. 208–9.

36. Gilmore, *Severed,* p. 187.

37. Pam Hazelton, "The LAPD interview with Detective Brian Carr," http://www.bethshort.com, June 28, 1999, p. 1.

38. Knowlton and Newton, *Daddy was,* p. 28.

39. Everitt, *Human monsters,* p. 134. There is a very different description of how the parcel came into the hands of law enforcement. A Los Angeles Postal Inspector called the *Los Angeles Herald-Examiner's* night editor and LAPD detectives, and they met him at the Federal Building to open the package, ostensibly because it was partially open at one end. See Gilmore, *Severed,* pp. 162–63.

40. Gilmore, *Severed,* p. 162.

41. Knowlton and Newton, *Daddy was,* p. 193.

42. Ibid., p. 194.

43. Ibid., pp. 30–31.

44. Ibid., p. 31.

45. Ibid.

46. Crime Library, "The investigation," http://www.crimelibrary.com, 2003, p. 1.

47. Douglas and Olshaker, *The cases that haunt us* (New York: Scribners, 2000), p. 238.

48. Knowlton and Newton, *Daddy was,* p. 192.

49. "The Black Dahlia murder," p. 2.

50. Ibid.

51. Ibid., p. 192.

52. Ibid.

53. Gilmore, *Severed,* pp. 181–83.

54. Ibid., pp. 185–86.

55. Ibid., p. 225.

56. Ibid., p. 228.

57. Ibid., pp. 236–37. In what might be a mere coincidence, it is nevertheless worth mentioning that one of the Cleveland Mad Butcher suspects was named Jack Wilson. A workhouse inmate named Helen O'Leary reportedly identified Jack Wilson as the murderer of Flo Polillo. See Badal, *In the wake,* p. 58.

58. "The Black Dahlia murder," p. 1.

59. Nickel, *Torso,* p. 190.

60. Hazelton, "The LAPD," p. 3.

61. Knowlton and Newton, *Daddy was,* p. 191.

62. Douglas and Olshaker, *The cases,* p. 239.

63. Hazelton, "The LAPD," p. 2.

64. Knowlton and Newton, *Daddy was,* p. 299.

65. Hazelton, "The LAPD," p. 3.

CONCLUSION

1. John C. Douglas and Mark Olshaker, *The cases that haunt us* (New York: Scribners, 2000), p. 221.

2. Joel Norris, *Serial killers* (New York: Avon Books, 1988), p. 108.

3. Ibid. Hazelwood added, "This material, together with the crime scene itself, is what we call the ritualistic offender's 'work product.' It is by far the richest and most reliable source of information not only about him as a criminal, but about his personality as well." See Roy Hazelwood and Stephen G. Michaud, *Dark dreams* (New York: St. Martin's Press, 2001), p. 67.

4. John Liebert, "Contributions of psychiatric consultation in the investigation of serial murder," *International Journal of Offender Therapy and Comparative Criminology* 28, 1985, p. 189. Douglas described the application of this technique to serial murder probes. In behavioral science terms, some of this is accomplished using psycholinguistic analysis, which involves using the subject's chosen words and phrases to assess his personality, degree of sophistication, amount of intrinsic motivation, and his criminal capability. See John C. Douglas and Mark Olshaker, *Anatomy of motive* (New York: Scribners, 1999), p. 122.

5. Robert Keppel and William Birnes, *Signature killers: Interpreting the calling cards of the serial murderer* (New York: Simon & Schuster, 1997), p. 41. Heirens's writing incriminated him, as Scott recalled, "A break in the case came when Storms noticed that the 'e' in the note was written as it is on a typewriter—as it was in the 'Catch Me Before I Kill More' message in the Brown murder." See Gini G. Scott, *Homicide: 100 years of murder in America* (Los Angeles: Lowell House, 1998), p. 122.

6. Darlene Superville, "Killers often undone by own mistakes," http://news. findlaw.com, October 11, 2002, p. 1. Others have confirmed Superville's opinion: "The clues in a killer's message can jog someone's memory and ultimately identify him, as in the published manifesto recognized by the brother of Unabomber Theodore Kaczynski." See "Serial killer communications," p. 1.

7. See Craig Whitlock, Sari Horwitz and Manuel Roig-Franzia, "Three key calls and a fingerprint," *Washington Post*, http://www.washingtonpost.com, October 25, 2002, p. 1.

8. Tomas Guillen, "Serial killer communiqués: Helpful or hurtful?," *Journal of Criminal Justice & Popular Culture* 9:2, 2002, p. 59; Michael Newton, *Hunting humans: The encyclopedia of serial killers* (Port Townsend, Wash.: Loompanics Unlimited, 1990), p. 64.

9. Ibid.

Selected Bibliography

BOOKS

Badal, John J. *In the wake of the butcher: Cleveland's torso murders*. Kent, Ohio: Kent State University Press, 2001.

Cannon, Angie. *23 days of terror: The compelling true story of the hunt and capture of the Beltway Snipers*. New York: Pocket Books, 2003.

Chase, Alston. *Harvard and the Unabomber: The education of an American terrorist*. New York: W. W. Norton & Company, 2003.

Douglas, John C., and Olshaker, Mark. *Anatomy of motive*. New York: Scribners, 1999.

———. *The cases that haunt us*. New York: Scribners, 2000.

———. *Unabomber*. New York: Lisa Drew, 1996.

Evans, Stewart, and Skinner, Keith. *The ultimate Jack the Ripper companion: An illustrated encyclopedia*. New York: Carroll & Graf, 2000.

Everitt, David. *Human monsters: An illustrated encyclopedia of the world's most vicious murderers*. Chicago: Contemporary Press, 1993.

Fisher, Joseph C. *Killer among us: Public reaction to serial murder*. Westport, Conn.: Praeger, 1997.

Fox, James A., and Levin, Jack. *Overkill: Mass murder & serial killing exposed*. New York: Plenum Press, 1994.

———. *The will to kill: Making sense of senseless murder*. Boston: Allyn & Bacon, 2001.

Gibbs, Nancy, Lacayo, Richard, Morrow, Lance, Smolowe, Jill, and Van Biema, David. *Mad genius: The odyssey, pursuit and capture of a Unabomber suspect*. New York: Warner Books, 1996.

Gilmore, John. *Severed: The true story of the Black Dahlia murder*. Los Angeles: Zanja Press, 1994.

Glatt, John. *Internet slavemaster*. New York: St. Martin's Press, 2001.

Graysmith, Robert. *Zodiac*. New York: Berkeley Books, 1986.

———. *Unabomber: A desire to kill*. New York: Berkeley Books, 1997.

King, Brian, ed. *Lustmord: Writings and artifacts of murderers*. Berkeley, Calif.: Bloat, 1996.

Knowlton, Janice, and Newton, Michael. *Daddy was the Black Dahlia killer.* New York: Simon & Schuster, 1995.

Lane, Brian, and Gregg, Wilfred. *The encyclopedia of serial killers.* New York: Berkeley Books, 1992.

Levin, Jack, and Fox, James A. *Mass murder: America's growing menace.* New York: Plenum Press, 1985.

Newton, Michael. *Hunting humans: An illustrated encyclopedia of modern serial killers.* Port Townsend, Wash.: Loompanics Unlimited, 1990.

Nickel, Steven. *Torso: The story of Eliot Ness and the search for a psychopathic killer.* Winston-Salem, N.C.: John F. Blair Publisher, 1989.

Sugden, Philip. *The complete history of Jack the Ripper.* New York: Carroll & Graf, 1994.

Waits, Chris, and Shors, David. *Unabomber: The secret life of Ted Kaczynski.* Helena, Mont.: Helena Independent Record/Montana Magazine.

PERIODICALS

Gibson, Dirk C. "The Whitechapel crimes as public relations," *Public Relations Quarterly*, 47, no. 4 (Winter 2002).

Guillen, Tomas. "Serial killer communiqués: Helpful or hurtful?" *Journal of Criminal Justice & Popular Culture*, 9, no. 2 (Winter 2002).

Kennedy, Foster, Hoffman, Harry R., and Haines, William H. "A study of William Heirens." *American Journal of Psychiatry*, 104 (August 1947).

Kovaleski, Serge F., and Horwitz, Sari. "In letter, Killer makes demands and threats." *Washington Post*, October 26, 2002.

"Police messages to suspected sniper." *Baltimore Sun.* October 24, 2002.

INTERNET RESOURCES

Associated Press. "Letter from sniper demanded $10 million, 'Unlimited withdrawal' by a stolen credit card sought in Ashland note." http://www.sunspot.net. October 26, 2002.

"The Black Dahlia murder." http://www.bethshort.com. June 13, 1999.

"The Black Dahlia murder, 1947." http://www.usc.edu. n.d.

Crime Library. "The Black Dahlia." http://www.crimelibrary.com. 2003.

———. "Broken doll." http://www.crimelibrary.com. 2003.

———."The investigation." http://www.crimelibrary.com. 2003.

Gibson, Gail, and Kiehl, Stephen. "Appeal issued to sniper. Shooter apparently left message, phone number after Saturday attack; Police see first hope of contact; Bullet is recovered from victim during surgery last night." http://www.sunspot.net. October 21, 2002.

Hazelton, Pam. "The LAPD interview with Detective Brian Carr." http://www.bethshort.com. June 28, 1999.

Lohr, David. "BTK: Bind-Torture-Kill: A chilling discovery." http://www. crimelibrary.com. 2000.

———. "BTK: Bind-Torture-Kill: Aftermath." http://www.crimelibrary.com. 2000.

———. "BTK: Bind-Torture-Kill: A vanishing act." http://www.crimelibrary. com. 2000.

———. "BTK: Bind-Torture-Kill: Bind them, torture them, kill them." http:// www.crimelibrary.com. 2000.

———. "BTK: Bind-Torture-Kill: Cold case squad." http://www.crimelibrary. com. 2000.

———. "BTK: Bind-Torture-Kill: Different worlds collide." http://www. crimelibrary.com. 2000.

———. "BTK: Bind-Torture-Kill: Ghostbusters." http://www.crimelibrary. com. 2000.

———. "BTK: Bind-Torture-Kill: Profile." http://www.crimelibrary.com. 2000.

———. "BTK: Bind-Torture-Kill: The next step." http://www.crimelibrary. com. 2000.

McCaffrey, Shannon, Borenstein, Seth, and Pugh, Tony. "DC Sniper: 'Your children are not safe.' Threat and $10 million demand reported after latest Maryland killing." *Detroit Free Press*. http://www.freep.com. October 23, 2002.

Woodruff, Bob, Lumpkin, Beverly, Thomas, Pierre, and Davis, Ellen. "Catalog of deaths? Sniper suspects allegedly kept record of attacks; both appear in court." abcNEWS.com. http://www.abcnews.com. November 8, 2002.

GOVERNMENT DOCUMENTS

Bond, Dr. Thomas. "Medical report to the Home Office on the Whitechapel Murders." November 10, 1888.

British Public Records Office. "Jack the Ripper documents."

MEPO 3/3153	Ripper case files
MEPO 3/3157	Openshaw letter
MEPO 3/142	Jack the Ripper letters

This material in the Public Records Office is the copyright of the Metropolitan Police and is reproduced by permission of the Commissioner of Police of the Metropolis.

Swanson, Donald. "Report to the Home Office." November 6, 1888.

Warren, Sir Charles. "Report to the Home Office on the Goulston Street graffiti." November 6, 1888.

Index

About the Author

DIRK C. GIBSON is Associate Professor of Communication and Journalism at the University of New Mexico. He has published numerous articles on a variety of topics in such journals as *Public Relations Quarterly, Public Relations Review,* and *Southern Communication Journal.* He has also contributed several chapters to edited books, and is the author of *The Role of Communication in the Practice of Law* (1991).